Mauro Mendez
1896–1966

MAURO MENDEZ
From Journalism to Diplomacy

MAURO MENDEZ
From Journalism to Diplomacy

Sylvia Mendez Ventura

Foreword by Carlos P. Romulo

UNIVERSITY OF THE PHILIPPINES PRESS
QUEZON CITY, PHILIPPINES
1978

Copyright 1978 by Sylvia Mendez Ventura

ISBN 0-8248-0651-4

Distributed outside the Philippines
by the University Press of Hawaii

Printed in the Philippines
by the University of the Philippines Press

To my mother
and to
Manuel, Ben, Lisa, Mickey, and Popsy

FOREWORD

It was my great privilege to work with Mauro Mendez—first in journalism and subsequently in the diplomatic service of our country—and in all those years of association I knew him to be not only a highly competent and dedicated worker, putting his best into every task that he performed and invariably excelling in his endeavors, but also a true friend and a valuable and trusted ally. He was selfless and unmatched in his loyalty; he was sincere and deeply trusting and humble. He valued the human worth of his comrades as much as his own high regard for them. And he had no peer in his genius for friendship.

Thus, I have unhesitatingly offered to write the foreword to the book recounting the life and important works of Mauro Mendez—a sincere effort, as I see it, to present a true picture of the man and the role he played in influencing the course of many important and historic events in his country, and to give him his deserved place of distinction during an era in our national history that was replete with eventful and crucial happenings.

As a colleague in newspaper work, I knew Mauro Mendez to regard honor as much as the integrity of language and truth. He was unflinching in his regard for honorable conduct as well as the elegance of syntax. He was in journalism with me and he made newspaper work a pleasure, meaningful and challenging, in a large and benign way. He was one of the significant voices in the democratic dispensation of the Commonwealth, and his writings constitute a part of that important body of literature and letters that was to shape Filipino eloquence in the new idiom.

Mauro Mendez wrote with intelligence and objectivity, ever wary of his own prejudices, and thus helped in creating a canon for Philippine journalism: the utterance of opinions without ulterior motives. He helped professionalize our journalism, demanding of it a strict code of honesty and elegance, expressing through it the native wit and excellence of Filipino culture.

As a public official, Mauro Mendez served the national interest as well as universal causes competently in the United Nations. As his country's ambassador to Japan, he undertook the task of continuing a difficult job: that of effacing the vestiges of historical incidents that distract nations from cooperating and planning for a better world. He interpreted the national viewpoint well, adumbrating to a culture endemically Asian the sophistication and the Oriental aspect of our own.

As Secretary of Foreign Affairs, he was to serve without pomposity, bringing back to its conduct and affairs its traditional quiet dignity. He knew the treachery of being pompous, that it could be a guise for intellectual and moral bankruptcy. In any case, he conveyed very precisely, in his official acts as well as in his personal dealings, that the greediness of pomposity was not part of himself, and that, being sincere, he therefore had no use for beguiling people, and, having substantial merit, he did not have to keep a dazzling façade. He performed his duties well and quietly; his important acts anonymously; and the dictates of official commitments and service with honesty, conviction, and courage.

The present work includes an account of the life and times of Mauro Mendez by his daughter Sylvia Mendez Ventura, and an anthology of selected editorials, essays, poems, and other writings. This volume will, no doubt, enable the reader to appreciate better the true worth and merit of the man's performance, both as a writer and journalist and as a high government official. More than anything, the life of Mauro Mendez teaches the lesson that the ideal public servant need not remain an ideal. He can be an actuality.

Carlos P. Romulo

"Secretary Mendez was one of our gifted men who blazed the trail for others in journalism, in liberal thought, and in international diplomacy." —President Ferdinand E. Marcos, Jan. 2, 1966.

"He had a most distinguished career of which his posterity and our people will always be proud." —Former President Diosdado Macapagal, Jan. 3, 1966.

"His lifetime of devoted service to the Philippines, his statesmanship, and his wise counsel stand as inspiring examples to those who will follow him." —U.S. President Lyndon B. Johnson, Jan. 2, 1966.

"A dedicated statesman and patriot who leaves an inspiring record in the service of freedom." —U.S. Secretary of State Dean Rusk, Jan. 2, 1966.

"His most enduring legacy to his country is his devotion and selflessness, his courageous and steadfast defense of what he thought was right, his sacrifice of bodily comfort and health, his obedience to the call of duty, an obedience even unto death." —Secretary of Foreign Affairs Narciso Ramos, Jan. 1, 1966.

"He left an indelible imprint on the life of the nation. Indeed, his was a truly colourful government career which is not easy to match, let alone surpass." —Jesus Vargas, Secretary General, SEATO, Jan. 2, 1966.

"His unblemished record of loyal and efficient service to the country stands out as an inspiring model to all our government officials. His was a patriotism of the highest order." —Fr. Jesus Diaz, O.P., Rector Magnificus, University of Santo Tomas, Jan. 2, 1966.

"He was a master of the English language, but he was a greater master in editorially analyzing the day-to-day problems of the nation." —Norberto de Ramos, Registrar, University of Santo Tomas, Jan. 15, 1966.

"The Fourth Estate remembers him lovingly as one of its own, a journalist whose professional stature stands before our present crop of newsmen as a height to be coveted and attained." —EVENING NEWS, Jan. 3, 1966.

"A former newspaperman and editor who adhered rigorously to the norms of his profession, Mendez was one of the most valuable contributions of the Philippine press to the public service." —Manuel Abad Gaerlan, PHILIPPINES HERALD, Jan. 5, 1966.

"He was a newspaperman of the highest quality." —Jose C. Balein, MANILA CHRONICLE, Jan. 3, 1966.

"He never lost his sense of humor and his curiosity for passing events." —Teodoro F. Valencia, MANILA TIMES, Jan. 6, 1966.

"Mr. Mendez fought assiduously to preserve the nation's interests and security as journalist, diplomat, and faithful public servant." —Oscar Villadolid, MANILA DAILY BULLETIN, Jan. 3, 1966.

"He kept pace uncomplainingly with the fast tempo of diplomatic activities. Where his body was unwilling, his spirit of dedication was unflagging." —Nestor Mata, PHILIPPINES HERALD, Jan. 9, 1966.

"Mendez was an exemplary public servant . . . a man of outstanding honesty and propriety." —Luis D. Beltran, EVENING NEWS, Jan. 3, 1966.

"Secretary Mendez was among the cream of a respected generation of newspapermen who not only reported the news but also helped their countrymen in the patriotic struggle for the Philippines to regain *her independence."* —Feliciano Magno, Manila Daily Bulletin, Feb. 3, 1965.

"His distinguished and outstanding association with the United Nations is warmly remembered by us all." —Jose Rolz-Bennet, Acting Chief de Cabinet, United Nations, Jan. 2, 1966.

"I recall with fond admiration his sincere devotion to the cause of strengthening friendly ties between Japan and the Philippines." —Nobushe Kishi, Prime Minister of Japan, Jan. 1, 1966.

"His devotion and his contribution for the cause of peace and security in this region will be long remembered by us all." —Korean Ambassador Yangsoo Yoo, Jan. 1, 1966.

"Mendez did much to restore the traditional goodwill and friendship between the two countries although he served at a time when Malaysia and the Philippines had no formal diplomatic relations." —External Affairs Ministry, Kuala Lumpur, Jan. 2, 1966.

ACKNOWLEDGMENTS

It gives me honor to acknowledge the help of the following very important people (listed in alphabetical order) who helped me, in one way or another, in the preparation of this labor of love:

Professor Hernando J. Abaya, Antonio Arizabal, Sr., Professor Paulina Bautista, Celso G. Cabrera, Dr. Clemencia Joven Colayco, Jose Q. Dacanay, U.P. Librarian Marina Dayrit and her staff in the Filipiniana and Microfilm Divisions, Manuel Abad Gaerlan, Dr. Salvador P. Lopez, the late Dr. Leoncio Lopez-Rizal, former President Diosdado Macapagal, Professor Armando J. Malay, Federico Mangahas, Professor Esteban de Ocampo, Dr. Pedro Orata, Professor Vicente Albano Pacis, former Foreign Affairs Secretary Narciso Ramos, Ernesto Rodriguez, Jr., General Carlos P. Romulo, Cecilia V. Tiongson, Teodoro F. Valencia, and Oscar Villadolid.

In nonalphabetical order, a special acknowledgment goes to Professor Pacifico N. Aprieto, who, as director of the U.P. Press in 1975, suggested the theme of this work: "a critical evaluation of the life and works of Mauro Mendez, particularly his contribution to our national life as journalist and diplomat."

Also on my thank-you list are members of my own family: my sisters, Eloisa Mendez Arizabal and Nina Mendez Aquino, and my aunts, Natividad Policarpio Go and Angelina Mendez Sakdalan, for helping me piece the odds and ends of my recollections; my brother Ruben, my niece Cecilia Mendez Wallace, and my nephew Raymond Mendez, for their suggestions on how to improve my manuscript.

My greatest gratitude goes, of course, to my mother, Paz Policarpio Mendez, who had long dreamed of seeing this biography and anthology in print. This production would have been impossible without her encouragement and advice, her remembrance of things long past, and most valuable of all, her scholarly and wifely devotion in having collected most of Mauro Mendez's works from the time she realized that he was her type of man.

SYLVIA MENDEZ VENTURA
May 1, 1977

CONTENTS

Foreword by Carlos P. Romulo — vii

PART ONE

I THE POET — 1
The Manila High School. Piping Down the Valleys Wild. Enter the Filipino Spirit. Antipolo Vs. Michigan.

II THE RETURN OF THE NATIVE — 9
The Globe-Trotter. The *Philippines Herald*. The *Tribune*. Dolores Chit-Chats.

III THE EDITORIAL AS LITERATURE — 17
Life's Little Tragedies. "Arthur Brisbane of the Philippines."

IV EDUCATION AND POLITICS — 25
The *Philippine High School Readers*. Defending the Imperial Tongue. The Public-School System. U.P. Beloved. Ye Olde Student Power.

V ON WITH THE DANCE! — 33
The Hare-Hawes-Cutting Brouhaha. D-M-H-M and H-H-C. The Tydings-McDuffie Law. Woman Suffrage.

VI CONSTITUTION AND COALITION — 45
The Ideal Democracy. A Unilateral Peace Pact. Tilting at Windmills. Murder in the Independent Church. Pilots of the Ship of State.

VII THE COMMUNIST BEAR HUG — 56
Detente in '33. Glad Tidings for Labor. The Sovietization of Labor. Crusade against Communism. Cooling the Hotbeds of Discontent.

CONTENTS

VIII	SAKDALISM AND SOCIAL JUSTICE	65

The Sakdalistas. The Forgotten Village. Senseless Combustion of Energy. Quezon Attacks Poverty. Games Filipinos Play.

IX	THE COMMON TOUCH	75

Mga Balitang Pangbayan. "Apostle of Malacañang." Ang Wikang Pambansa. A Case of Abduction. Preview of an Air Raid.

X	ON THE WARPATH	85

The Japanese Tidal Wave. The Fighting Spirit. Yellow Interlude. The Puppet Press.

XI	LET FREEDOM RING	94

The Information Explosion. The Os-Rox Split. The *Morning Sun.* "Sun Beams." Drawing the Amnesty Line. Huks to the Left. Newspaper Blues.

XII	HANDS ACROSS THE SEA	110

Awakening in Delhi. To New York, with Love. The Philippine Mission to the U.N. La Vie Parisienne. Rizaliana in Wilhelmsfeld. "Monkey Business in Laos." Cherry-Blossom Country. China-Watching in Tokyo.

XIII	THE PREMIER POST	128

The Maphilindo Summit. Little Brown Americans Vs. Little Bung Karnos. Peeking into Peking. The Futility of Neutralism. An Indonesian Affair. Death in Crow Valley. Bombshell from Blair. The Mendez-Blair Agreement. "No Twisting, Please." The Changing of the Guard.

XIV	THE LAST DEADLINE	154
	POSTMORTEM ON THE MENDEZ-BLAIR AGREEMENT	158

PART TWO

SELECTED ESSAYS, ARTICLES, EDITORIALS, AND POEMS

The Philippines and Great Filipinos
   Rizal in the Nation's Library   165

CONTENTS

The Lesson of Balintawak	169
The Prince of Tagalog Letters	170
Mr. Average Man	173
The Redemption of Labor	178
Our National Defense	180
Recto to the Bench	184
Jose Abad Santos	185
Welcome to Romulo	187
The Torch of Liberty	187

World History and International Relations
Spain's Holiday	189
Bastille Day	190
Hands across the Sea	192
The Fiction of Red Propaganda	194
The Warning of Democracy	197
History and Democracy	200
The Price of Man's Frivolity	203
Interview with Nehru	207

Obituaries
Our Own Abelardo	211
A Great Man Passes	211
The King and the Poet	212

The Language Question
The Language Opportunity	214
Tagalog as the National Language	218
The Spanish Language	223

Education, Science, and the Humanities
Freedom for Our University	224
The Cause of Our Scientists	225
In the Masters' Magic Circle	228

The Press
The Share of the Press	230
When the Press Loses	231
Stalwarts of the Fourth Estate	232

CONTENTS

POEMS

Ode to a Song Sparrow	236
Evening in a Grave-Yard	238
In the Shadows	239
Booker T. Washington	240
Before Rizal's Monument	242
Antipolo	243
That Magic Day	244
To the Great Plebeian	245
A Christmas Poem	247
NOTES	249
INDEX	259

PART ONE

I

THE POET

In the 1916 *Annual* of the Manila High School, edited by Carlos P. Romulo, the following statement expresses the ambition of a graduating student named Mauro Mendez: "He cherishes the hope of laboring in the fields of Philippine journalism."

Whatever "fields" of journalism there were, he was destined to make his mark in all of them, and to excel in other fields as well. He was a pioneer-writer of Filipino poetry in English; a newspaperman of many parts; an editorial essayist with a national following; the government's first public information officer; a professor of English, journalism, and law; a distinguished diplomat; and the most colorful, if controversial, Foreign Secretary of the 1960s.

The dominant theme of his career as a writer and as a public servant was his belief that the Filipino people should be educated, democratic, and proud of their place in the commonwealth of free nations.

Mauro Mendez was born on November 30, 1896, a day which he often referred to as "Andres Bonifacio's birthday, not mine." The district of Trozo, where he was born, was formerly an island-barrio separated from the rest of old Manila by the esteros of Magdalena, San Lazaro, and Meisic. Originally accessible only by banca, it was the scene in 1892 of secret meetings between Bonifacio and his crew of Katipuneros in the making. A few months before Mendez's birth, the Spanish Volunteers invaded Trozo and found much incriminating evidence against the Katipunan.

By the turn of the century Trozo had settled down into a quiet neighborhood, with only the aura of recent events to mark it as a historic spot. Young Mauro lived on Benavides Street and learned to swim in the surrounding esteros, beside the flotsam that drifted from the kitchens and outhouses along the banks of the waterways.

Mauro was the second of five children of Esteban Mendez and Concepcion del Barrio. His father was a writer in Spanish and a regular contributor to *The Independent,* a bilingual weekly journal with a national circulation. Father and son spoke to each other in Spanish. The elder Mendez, a rigid disciplinarian, saw to it that Mauro's grammar was flawless and that he rolled his r's in true Castilian fashion. With his mother, Mauro spoke in Tagalog, pronouncing it "Tacaloc" like Manileños of those days. He learned English at the public schools in Meisic and Tondo, and mastered it at the Manila High School in Intramuros.

As a teenager, Mendez had a long face crowned by a mass of straight black hair that later softened into deep waves without benefit of a permanent. His pensive eyes seemed to speak his favorite adage, quoted beneath his picture in the high-school yearbook: "A man is never himself but in solitude." His melancholy expression belied a droll disposition. The "Twinkles of Humor" department, which he edited for the *Annual,* exhorted the reader to "Hang Those Worries!"

He began writing poetry in his teens and first broke into print in *The Independent.* For a while his family thought he would follow the footsteps of Cecilio Apostol, the famous Filipino poet in Spanish. Apostol was Mauro's cousin and godfather, and lived with the Mendezes for some time. Perhaps the only thing that prevented Mauro from writing poetry in Spanish was the American public-school system in which he was educated.

The Manila High School

During the first two decades of the American occupation, Manila High School (formerly the Escuela Municipal de Manila) was the dream alma mater of every *provinciano* in the Islands. When Mendez first enrolled on June 10, 1912, about 260 freshmen thronged the corridors, but of this number only 132 reached their senior year. Many students dropped out either because of the high academic standards or because of the prohibitive tuition fee of ₱80 per semester.

The class of 1916 was one of the most illustrious classes to graduate from Manila High. At that time the school had already produced many potentially outstanding Filipinos, among them Guillermo

Tolentino, Jose P. Laurel, Elpidio Quirino, Jose Yulo, Manuel A. Roxas, Ricardo Paras, Ricardo Nepomuceno, Jesus Barrera, and Pilar Hidalgo (the future Mrs. Vicente Lim).[1]

Manila High was reputed to be the first public school in the Philippines to recognize the value of extracurricular organizations. All students were members of one or more clubs—intellectual, musical, and athletic. A Girls' Literary Society was organized in 1914 to encourage the girls to speak English. Their motto was "Success crowns worthy efforts." The motto of the Mabini Literary Society (for both sexes) was "Literary men are a perpetual priesthood."

The luminaries of 1916, determined to live up to the class slogan, "Victory or Death," were victorious in many intramural competitions. In the fiction-writing contest, the first prize went to Jose S. Reyes, who was to become Executive Secretary to President Sergio Osmeña 29 years later. Carlos P. Romulo received the trophy for oratory in his senior year. The theme of his prize-winning oration was: "Let us take the plow and the hoe and with them erase the brand now stamped on the foreheads of all Filipinos those words, 'So much to do, so little done.'" Romulo's ambition, said the *Annual,* was to be a farmer.

At the Royal Theatre, the Cryptia and Rizal Debating Clubs argued the pros and cons of capital punishment. The Rizalians, headed by Jose Leido,[2] Julio Nalundasan,[3] and club secretary Mauro Mendez, defended the electric chair triumphantly against the Cryptians headed by Romulo.

Mendez was chosen class poet by virtue of his prize-winning poem, *Booker T. Washington,* probably the only Filipino ode ever written in honor of a black man. Its theme:

> ...'twas thou who didst proclaim
> Unto the blinded world that Man is Man
> According to his heart—not to his race!

Mendez belonged to that early generation of Filipinos who, according to Dr. Salvador P. Lopez, learned English through a system of "forced feeding" and ended up "infatuated" with the language.[4] It must have warmed the hearts of Mrs. Mildred G. Booth, Miss Anna H. Carter, and Miss Mary Klinefelter—English teachers all—to see their brown students at the Manila High School taking to the imperial tongue with enthusiasm. The best literary creations of the student body, all in fluent English, found their way into the glossy pages of the yearbook.

Piping Down the Valleys Wild

Mendez wrote more poetry than any of his contemporaries at Manila High, to judge from the number of selections that he contributed to the *Annual* and *The Independent*. One of the poems that won him the admiration of teachers and students alike was his melodious eleven-stanza *Ode to a Song Sparrow,* which was first published in the *Annual* of 1915.

Jose H. Hernandez, in a survey of Filipino writing in English, labels the period from 1900 to 1920 "an era of imitation and early experimentation" and cites Mendez's *Ode to a Song Sparrow* as an example of "pioneer poetry in English by Filipinos." Hernandez attaches great significance to this experimental stage in the evolution of Filipino literature in English:

> It is pleasant to record that the writers of this period were not only literary artists but benevolent teachers. At their feet we, of a later day, have worshipped and have gained inspiration and guidance. Thus, Paz Marquez de Benitez has tutored many a short story writer, Mendez and Maramag have inspired poets, and Romulo has been the model par excellence of all Filipino orators and lecturers since his professorial days.[5]

N.V.M. Gonzalez, short-story writer and novelist, also notes the importance of this early period:

> It is difficult to think of the stature that the Philippine press has attained to date without giving credit to such men as, say, Fernando Maramag and Mauro Mendez, whose interest in poetry preceded their professional commitment to the well-phrased headline and the concise yet thoughtful editorial.[6]

Mendez had so internalized the English poets that he unconsciously borrowed their images. In these two stanzas from *Ode to a Song Sparrow,* Mendez's Sparrow sounds like a first cousin of Shelley's Skylark:

> How sweet, in fresh and museful June
> You trill your wild, melodious tune,
>   Till Nature all seems mute;
> Methinks some cherub, mad with love,

> Has left the glorious worlds above,
>   And charmed some Lydian lute.
>
> Transcendant minstrel, ever meek,
> In vain my heart would learn to seek
>   The secrets that you know.
> O for a while to fly away,
> Amid the dying pomps of day
>   In twilight's purple glow!

Like the English Romantic poets, Mendez was most inspired by nature's evanescent aspects and twilight moods. A typical example is his *Evening in a Grave-yard,* which suggests an English countryside rather than La Loma Cemetery:

> Soft fades the lingering April day
> Behind the hills...fades like a scene
> Of some delightful golden dream
> Of Paradise; a mystic breeze
> Sweet with the dying bliss of calm
> Indistinct woodlands, stirs the trees...

Here 18-year-old Mauro grieves musically over a beloved relative, his recently deceased "uncle in Eden." Unfortunately, toward the end, the elegy degenerates into the bathos of Shelley's *Indian Serenade:*

> My bosom bursts! I gasp with pains
> I don't deserve! I die! I fail!

Enter the Filipino Spirit

Although the students of the post-Bagumbayan period had no formal lessons in Philippine history, they learned about the Revolution from the newspapers and from their elders, to whom Jose Rizal was a living memory. Students made an annual ritual of visiting Rizal's monument on December 30, thereby deriving inspiration for literary effusions of a patriotic nature.

Mendez's favorite poem on the national hero was Cecilio Apostol's *A Rizal,* written in 1898 on the second anniversary of Rizal's execution. Mendez loved to recite the famous passage beginning with "No llores de la tumba en el misterio..." He may have had this line in his subconscious when he wrote *Before Rizal's Monument,* an elegy which, incidentally, discloses the size of the Philippine population circa 1916:

> Weep not within the silence of your tomb,
> The land you loved from anguish now departs;
> The seeds you scattered on your way have bloomed
> Deep in the chambers of nine million hearts!

In 1918, when Mendez was studying at the University of the Philippines, his friend, Cornelio Balmaceda (a future Secretary of Commerce), showed him an oration that he had written on the subject of the Filipino flag. Balmaceda, then a student at the College of Law, was planning to join the annual oratorical contest at the U.P. Upon reading the oration, Mendez was inspired to write this apostrophe to the flag:

> Thou art no creature of the dust, oh morning
>   star of liberty!
> Fierce storms may rend the skies apart,
> Capitals may crumble, nations sink in war,
> Yet still thou shalt be ours, immortal as
>   thou art,
> And still in heaven's winds thy glorious folds
>   shall wave
> Transcendent in thy warning for the mighty's rod;
> A beacon light to deeds of manhood ever brave,
> A symbol of our union in the law of God.

He gave the poem to Balmaceda with the suggestion that he recite it at the conclusion of his oration. Balmaceda remembers having been "moved by its fervor and its intrinsic beauty." He has kept it among his papers ever since.[7]

As Mendez read deeper into Philippine history, he reached the conclusion that Andres Bonifacio was no less a hero than Rizal. In November 1928, the *Sunday Tribune Magazine* featured his ode, *To the Great Plebeian,* in which he hailed the warrior

> ...who stirred the blood
> Of brothers to the action of the strife
>   And made the despots quail!
> Defiant Proletaire, whose spirit rose
> Undaunted from our past colonial woe;
> Servant and Guardian of the native Cause,
> O Bonifacio, Great Plebeian, hail!

Antipolo vs. Michigan

Poetry flowed intermittently from Mendez's pen through the years; he had no intention of making a starving career out of it. To him the writing of poetry was a relaxing pastime, a euphonic outlet for his thoughts and feelings when nature moved him, when the fragrance of sampaguitas was in the air, when he was ecstatic and miserable by turns over a young lady. He never graduated to the esoteric realms of Jose Garcia Villa and his disciples; neither did he write poetry for social reform, with the exception of *Who Are The Usurers?*, an adolescent attack on "Shylocks vile," "the greedy vampire of the poor."

Despite the lack of total commitment to his art, Mendez evolved a style that was more original, more concise, and richer in the warmth of local color than his youthful style. The only foreigner whom he poeticized, after Booker T. Washington, was Jesus Christ. Not even the shadow of Santa Claus hovers over his *Christmas Poem,* with its images of "pealing bells" breaking "the hush of early morns," "flick'ring lights" in "fantastic lanterns red," and elderly hands receiving the "kiss of veneration" from the young.

The popular *Antipolo* is, without a doubt, his most successful creation. For the first time Mendez introduced a Tagalog word, *batis* (stream), and a Spanish word, *Virgen,* by then a part of the vernacular, into poetry that had hitherto been totally English. Thus:

>Here where the *batis* whispers sweet
>>Its secrets to the air,
>I find but traces of your feet
>>And perfumes of your hair.
>
>I know that where the *Virgen* treads
>>Your spirit must repose,
>As limpid as the dew that sheds
>>Its soul upon the rose.

Like the rippling *batis,* the lyric flows smoothly to its concluding sentiment, an ethereal surprise:

>And more than all I know how near
>>Your spirit is to mine;
>You might have been the beauty, dear,
>>In Antipolo's shrine.

The "beauty" he had in mind was Paz T. Policarpio, a *summa cum laude* from the University of the Philippines. When *Antipolo* first appeared in the *Sunday Tribune Magazine,* Mendez was informed that the readers were "in love" with it. The U.P. Woman's Club posted it on the bulletin board without knowing who had inspired it.

Pacita was then on the verge of leaving for the University of Michigan as a Barbour scholar and U.P. Fellow. Such an honor was not bestowed on many in the 1920s. Mendez was in a state of almost frantic despair, especially when Pacita received a letter postmarked Michigan, welcoming her into the residence hall which was to be her home while she worked for her Ph.D.

When he was resigned at last to her departure, he reverted to his favorite theme of fleeting moments in another *Tribune* poem, *That Magic Day:*

> Yesterday, I watched the day languish from the
>   world,
> As I watch you vanish from my sight sometimes,—
> A silken vision, a joy aerial, delicate,
> Exquisite. I saw the gold of the dying day
> Spread over the world like wine—
> Red, bubbling wine—spilled from the Cup
> Of God's eternal life...

In the futility of holding back the sunset, Mendez saw the hopelessness of keeping Miss Policarpio from boarding her ship:

> I watched the day melt away, but could not hold
> Back the marvel of its joy, nor make
> The substance of its beauty stay,
> And now, in the sweet flavor
> Of its inconstant picture, I am wondering, Dear,
> If you, too, Child of Fate, must disappear from me
> Forevermore...Just like that day. That magic day.

Pacita disappeared indeed, into the arms of her poet, and became Mrs. Mauro Mendez. It was "a Romance that Set the University Dove-Cote a-Flutter," gushed the *Philippines Free Press.* Manila society, in love with America, was outraged, and chastised her in public. She was truly a fickle thing, fickle to the U.P., fickle to Michigan U. But she vanquished her critics with a classic retort: "The affairs of my heart are mine." [8]

II

THE RETURN OF THE NATIVE

After Mendez's graduation from Manila High School, he enrolled at the U.P. as an English major. He also edited *The Rising Philippines,* the first weekly periodical to be put out exclusively by Filipinos educated in the American school system. The contents and quality of the paper, announced the *Manila Times,* "reflect high credit on those who are in direct charge of the publication." Mauro Mendez, editor, and Eliseo Quirino, business manager, were assisted by a "corps of young writers whose experience and attainments give assurance of the turning out of a paper worthwhile reading." [1]

The Rising Philippines came tumbling down three years later. "The weekly had the support of the English-speaking Filipinos," says Carson Taylor, one-time publisher of the *Manila Daily Bulletin,* "but after three years of a rather stormy existence burdened with good articles and numerous debts, it passed to the Great Beyond." [2]

The Globe-Trotter

After finishing the two-year A.B. course, Mendez joined the staff of the *Philippine Review* and contributed articles to the *Philippines Free Press* and the *Philippine-Chinese Advocate.* He also enrolled at the U.P. College of Law but dropped out after a few semesters to earn a living full time. He took the civil service examination and joined the Bureau of Commerce as assistant chief clerk.

He had no desire to be promoted to chief clerk. Against his father's wishes, he went to the United States in 1920 to join the staff of the Philippine Commercial Agency. Meanwhile, he fulfilled his high-school ambition by studying at the Pulitzer School of Journalism, Columbia University.

Mendez was the first Filipino to receive a diploma from the prestigious Pulitzer School. After graduation in 1922, he became a member of the Sigma Delta Chi, a national fraternity of journalists, which was to evolve later into a professional society of journalists with members from around the world.

He stayed on in the United States for two more years, a period that he was to remember fondly for the rest of his life. It was the Jazz Age of F. Scott Fitzgerald, and New York City was *This Side of Paradise* for Filipino students.

Mendez lived in a dismal apartment that swarmed with bedbugs in the summer. To save on ironing bills, he pressed his pants by laying them out under his pillow and sleeping on them. Occasionally he would splurge on a theatre ticket. America was then singing "Look for the Silver Lining," the hit tune from the Broadway musical *Sally*. "When Marilyn Miller sang the lyric, she had the audience at her feet," Mendez was to recall later. "It's the old, old lyric of life. Somewhere behind the clouds the sun must be. Everything dies except the silver lining of humanity's ever-surging hope." [3]

To augment his meager income, he worked as an apple picker until he could no longer endure the scent of apples. In an adventurous mood, he next found employment as a deck hand, menu typer, and busboy on ships that commuted between the United States and various European seaports. News of his father's death ended his peripatetic existence, and he decided to return to Manila for good.

Early in 1925 he sailed into the Philippine archipelago on a German ship that left him stranded and penniless in Pulupandan, Negros. Carlos P. Romulo, then assistant editor of the *Philippines Herald*, came to the rescue and sent him a ticket to Manila. As soon as he landed, Romulo took him in as city editor. C.P.R., incidentally, had earned a master's degree at Columbia and was an English professor at the U.P. He had given up his plans for the plow and the hoe; there was too much to do in other fields, as history has shown since.

The *Philippines Herald*

The *Herald* was founded in 1920 by a group of wealthy Quezon followers whose purpose was to help the Senate President counteract the anti-Filipino slant in the foreign-owned press. Charter members of the staff had previously worked for the *Bulletin,* the *Manila Times,* and the *Cablenews American,* but had gone on strike rather than continue being the white man's burden. Quezon helped the strikers survive for a few days by putting them on his payroll. In the evening of August 8, they all met at La Campana restaurant to discuss the layout of a new periodical. Quezon himself baptized it the *Philippines Herald.* Conrado Benitez was the first editor, and his staff included Narciso Ramos, Antonio Escoda, Bernardo Garcia, and Jose P. Bautista.[4]

Politically, the *Herald* opposed the supercilious policies of Governor-General Leonard Wood. As Mendez was to narrate many years later, Wood "was bent on tearing down the magnificent edifice that his predecessor, the liberal Francis Burton Harrison, had erected as an answer to their prayers of the past twenty years. That edifice was none other than Filipinization. . . . That was the day of the *Philippines Herald*. It became the mouthpiece of the outraged Filipinos. Resolving to swim or sink with them, it took up the quarrel with the foe."[5]

When Mendez joined the *Herald* in 1925, it was a medium-sized paper with an average of ten pages per issue. Large illustrated ads for the latest gleaming motor cars, like the Cadillac and the Willys Knight, often graced the front pages.

The paper carried two editorials—one in English and its translation in Spanish—as well as editorial quotations from the "American Press" and the "Filipino Press." Occasional business news appeared in the "Waterfront Gossip" of "Bill the Bo'Sun."[6] Godofredo Rivera wrote a small column, "Believe It Or Not," and Fernando Maramag wrote feature articles. The Sunday issue included a page devoted to "Woman's Clubs and Their Activities," edited by Trinidad Fernandez (the future Mrs. Benito Legarda).

The *Tribune*

Despite its well-heeled backing, the *Herald* was a financial loss. American businessmen saw no reason why their Cadillacs and their Willys Knights should continue supporting a nationalistic sheet. As Mendez put it, "Having thus avowed itself a political organ, although with the best of patriotic intentions, the *Herald* began to totter in its business knees and was soon going into receivership. Alejandro Roces, Sr. was the receiver." [7]

To save the *Herald* for Quezon, Vicente Madrigal bought it outright and kept the presses running, with Arsenio N. Luz at the helm. The Romulo-Quezon relationship had cooled in the meantime, and Romulo moved to the Roces camp to open another paper.

The news of the day on March 30, 1925, was that some young men were about to launch a five-centavo morning daily to be known as the *Manila Tribune.* The incorporators were Ramon Roces, Alejandro Roces, Jr., Carlos P. Romulo, Dr. Basilio Valdes, and Jose G. Sanvictores. Added to the Tagalog *Taliba* and the Spanish-language *La Vanguardia* (edited by Manuel Villa-Real), the *Tribune* completed the T-V-T chain of powerful Roces papers.

Not surprisingly, the *Tribune* staff was singing "That Old Gang of Mine," for they were all ex-*Herald* boys. Romulo was the first editor; Fernando Maramag and Mauro Mendez were associate editor and city editor, respectively. The principal staff members were Francisco Tonogbanua, Francisco Astilla, Crispin Gonzalez, Recaredo de la Rosa, Ceferino Montejo, Cornelio de los Reyes, Bill the Bo'Sun, Jose P. Bautista, and Anacleto Benavides. The last two, Mendez's closest friends next to Romulo, were to become editors of the postwar *Manila Times* and the *Manila Chronicle* respectively.

Others who joined the *Tribune* and who also became institutions in the Fourth Estate were Vicente Navarro, Cipriano Cid, Abelardo Valencia, Roberto Anselmo, Benito Sakdalan (Mendez's brother-in-law), Vicente Albano Pacis, Celso Cabrera (Romulo's first cousin), and Vicente del Fierro.

Twenty-two years later, del Fierro was to recall the unveiling of the *Tribune* on April 1, 1925:

> It was a big event in Philippine journalism, and the whole city was plastered with posters heralding the event.
> Selling for ₱.05 a copy for eight big, standard-size pages, the paper's first issue was a sell-out.[8]

Aside from working at the *Tribune,* Mendez taught English at the U.P. to supplement his income. As the volume of work increased at the *Tribune,* his employers offered to give him more than the equivalent of his U.P. paycheck if he would devote all his time to the insomniac job of shaping the fledgling newspaper. He was, by turns, copy editor, sports writer, feature writer, and even, at one time, society editor.

At 3:00 o'clock one Friday morning in July 1925, while Mendez was still at work, he dashed off this typewritten note to the lady he was then courting:

> Although only a humble B. Lit., and an obscure city ed, plus the aggravating circumstance of pertaining to the despised ranks of the proletaire, I am not altogether lacking in the satisfactions of the common man. For instance, tonight Mr. Edward Price Bell sent word, through our reporter, that he has found sufficient reason to communicate with the director of the Pulitzer School of Journalism to tell him that the former student of that institution who responds to the name of M.M. is "making good" on this side of the Pacific.
>
> I have not had the pleasure, Pacita, of meeting Mr. Bell, and only know that as the European correspondent of the Chicago Daily News he stands in the front rank of international scribes. However, I have handled his stories in my own humble way, and in his opinion I have done him full justice. Let alone, he says, the very progressive tone of the Tribune's headlines, yours [truly] has been able to extract just the very essence of his stories which he wants to be played up. And that is that.

The *Tribune* was the most informative and most entertaining Philippine periodical of the 1920s, with an editorial page that could have taken at least an hour to digest. Its news coverage in pictures from all over the globe was the widest in the Manila press.[9] The "Public Pulse" beat with edifying letters to the editor from readers on the threshold of their careers in public life, like Camilo Osias, Carlos P. Garcia, and Elpidio Quirino.

One of Mendez's innovations was the *Tribune Magazine,* the first weekly supplement to accompany the Sunday issue of a Philippine daily. A magazine for the whole family, it was responsible for launching the careers of many of the country's foremost fiction writers and poets. For the maiden issue Mendez wrote his reminiscences of Hamburg in an article entitled "A Thousand and One Nights."

For the success of the *Tribune* and of the T-V-T newspapers as a whole, Mendez gave credit to Alejandro Roces, Sr., known as the William Randolph Hearst of the Philippines:[10]

His grasp of reader psychology and his keen commercial calculations were his greatest assets. When he founded the Tribune, he figured on losing for five years, unlike some adventurers into the business who quit if they can't pile up a fortune in six months. It was exactly as Roces had calculated: after five years the profits began to roll in.

The TVT, with its modern rotary presses and printing machinery, represented the true beginning of organized newspaper business in the Philippines. It ushered in the era of newspaper publishing as a legitimate business and not merely as an effort to give expression to human grievances and human ideals. The spirit of mercantilism had come, America was in the Philippines. That meant big business, and big business meant advertising.[11]

Dolores Chit-Chats

One of Mendez's little-known contributions to the *Tribune* and to Filipino literature in English was a column called "Daily Chit-Chats." Under this title was a subtitle, "Dolores Says—", and a drawing of a female face. Only the *Tribune* staff and a handful of mutual friends knew that "Dolores" was Mauro Mendez in a wig and that his daily thoughts were addressed to Paz Policarpio.

Featured on the Society Page, "Daily Chit-Chats" was a forerunner of similar cozy columns that have enlivened the local press ever since. Jesus Valenzuela, in his *History of Journalism in the Philippine Islands,* cites "Dolores" as one of the main attractions of the the early Tribune.[12] The "Chit-Chats" were light essays covering a spectrum of topics, from stormy days and yellowing acacia leaves, to Latin-American poetry and Russian fiction. Dolores was a complex creature—alternately romantic, intellectual, sentimental, humorous, audacious, whimsical, and maddeningly mysterious. She was essentially an observer of Nature and of human nature, and inevitably, of course, a poet.

Dolores received piles of fan mail. Some readers accused her of being a flirt; others noted "the fluctuations of hope and fear" in her love affairs. "Don't think it impertinent of me, dear Dolores, if I ask how old you are."

In a note to Miss Policarpio, Mendez expressed his satisfaction at having aroused so much curiosity:

The Chats remain the subject of speculation. There was betting at the Ayuntamiento yesterday that the author is a man. Others think it's Mrs. Romulo. The latest guess is Nati Marquez. At any rate it is whispered about that the Chats will be included in the Phil. Classics soon to be published, so I am told. I'm fully satisfied. After all, to be able to intrigue the public is a premier pastime.

A masculine mind behind the "Chats" was suspected when Dolores revealed a more than casual acquaintance with manly sports, or when she injected intimate political trivia into her column. Once, after listening to an after-dinner speech delivered by Speaker Manuel Roxas, who was then reputed to be Quezon's protégé, Dolores observed "that the Mogul of the lower house is now a near-Quezon in his oratorical mannerisms, and the audience at the banquet was one in the verdict that here indeed is the perfect understudy of the Highest of them all!" [13]

For the student of Philippine culture, one value of the "Chit-Chats" lies in its depiction of rural folkways, such as the preparations for a typical town fiesta:

> For the past fifteen days Mang Emong, who wields the baton over our little world of music, has been brandishing his musical swords to a razor edge for the gala performance, the concierto de conciertos.... his band's instruments hold the major sway in the town's noises, only lapsing into minority with the hut-hut of the demon car so familiar to the dust of centuries that lies on the neighboring carretela....
> In the "batalan" of the houses a slaughter of innocents is going on. Ay de mi! even my best chicken has been sacrificed at the altar of culinary art and nothing is left but the feathers and the memory of the cackle I loved to hear. ... And my pig? Ah! that, too, has gone by the boards at the kitchen.[14]

In the summer of 1925, the "Chit-Chats" drifted back to the scenes that first inspired the composition of the poem *Antipolo*. Most picturesque of the reminiscences is Mendez's account of the journey to Antipolo via a man-carried hammock, for in his boyhood no carretela could negotiate the mountain trail to the summer "Mecca" of the Philippines.

> Our "duyan" had reached the last seven mountains on an evening in May. We were descending, softly, gently to the low-

lands and the town. Behind us we had left the solitude of the mountain trails and before us flickered the lights of gay Antipolo. And over the town a big yellow moon hung low, inundating our "duyan" with its splendor. How I remember that moon, that pretty laughing moon, and the joys that it stole away from life! When I visit Antipolo again I know there will be nothing left for me but the ghost of that moon.[15]

III

THE EDITORIAL AS LITERATURE

Mendez was news editor of the *Tribune* from 1925 to 1927, and managing editor from 1927 to 1933. Those years saw the expansion of the newspaper, improvements in content and layout, and the growth of professionalism in the Philippine press.

The nearest thing to a press club was the famous Tom's Dixie Kitchen on Carriedo. Membership was open to anyone who cared to sit at the Round Table with loquacious newspapermen and partake of coffee and conversation. According to David Boguslav, whose name was a byword in the newspaper world, "Those were the days when a cub reporter was accepted without question and could sit down beside his glamorous elders in the craft. Three months' apprenticeship at the Round Table was better than a course in journalism—was, in fact, a course in journalism that could not be obtained in the best universities."[1]

The average inexperienced cub reporter of the 1920s received a streetcar allowance instead of a pay envelope. After several weeks he graduated into a full-fledged reporter at a starting salary of ₱25 a month. The multi-faceted Vicente del Fierro earned ₱40 monthly, plus six streetcar tickets a day. Federico Mangahas, then a junior at the U.P., could hardly believe his ears when Romulo appointed him feature writer at ₱70 a month. With his first pay envelope, Mangahas ordered a sharkskin suit and a tie, bypassed the Meralco *tranvia*, and hailed the nearest taxi.[2]

Editors were paid according to their efficiency and their executive ability. If an editor drew ₱200 a month, he could afford a car. When Mendez bought a second-hand Ford at ₱800, some of his colleagues concluded that he was a one-man credit union.

Life's Little Tragedies

Although Mendez was the quintessence of the hard-boiled editor, everyone knew he was a soft touch. His wife often lectured to him on his incurable moneylending habit. Once upon a time he made the mistake (and not his last) of guaranteeing a loan of ₱160 for a *Tribune* newsman who promptly forgot to liquidate the debt. At the end of the month, Mendez's pay envelope was ₱160 thinner.

To top it all, the delinquent reporter played a prank that embarrassed the *Tribune*. He had been asked to solicit a New Year greeting from the Governor-General, one that would adorn the front page of the newspaper. The ingenious fellow, however, composed his own greeting and affixed the Governor-General's signature to it. Obtaining a copy of the signature was no trouble, for it could be found on many documents. When the fraud was exposed, the culprit had to flee to Hong Kong to escape the wrath of Mendez and Romulo.

It happened that at about the same time, Mrs. Mendez was teaching English at the U.P. and noticed in one of her classes an impoverished but brilliant student named Diosdado Macapagal. A physical checkup at the U.P. infirmary indicated that he was suffering from undernourishment. Mrs. Mendez asked her husband if he could please give the frail boy a job at the *Tribune*.

The rest of the story comes from former President Macapagal himself. He remembers how he went to the *Tribune* office one day and stood in line to see Mr. Mendez, who was then busy copyreading beneath his green eyeshade. The man in line before Macapagal was the money borrower and repentant forger of the Governor-General's greeting, newly returned from Hong Kong.

"I have come to pay my respects," said the man meekly.

"Pay your debts first," retorted Mendez without looking at him.

Overhearing this dialogue, poor Macapagal began to quake in his shoes. However, his interview was successful and gave him his first job as cub reporter.

"Arthur Brisbane of the Philippines"

Going over yellowing copies of the prewar *Tribune* would make one wonder if anything new had ever happened under the Philippine sun. Manilans were grumbling over the same chronic headaches that still plague the city: traffic jams, rampaging floods, gangsterism, pollution, prostitution, and mischief in high places. The main difference was that traffic nightmares in those days were usually blamed on "King Cochero."

On one occasion the stench of uncollected garbage was aired in front-page *Tribune* editorials two days in a row. Even the extortion tactics of watch-your-car boys merited several editorials and drove the police to wipe out the racket after some car owners found their tires punctured one night. To the credit of persistent criticism from the *Tribune,* the watch-your-car profession went into hibernation for two decades, reappearing again only in the 1950s.

Mendez once remarked that "the TVT was run upon the infallible basis of business figures."[3] Undoubtedly, he contributed in no small way to the multiplication of those figures. The profit motive, however, meant little to him in a personal way. In the words of Salvador P. Lopez, Mendez was "the prototype of the professional journalist."[4] He plunged into editorial writing with the idealism of a crusader, the vision of a historian, and the sensibility of a poet.

In 1932 the *Tribune* thought of a new way to boost its circulation while fulfilling its mission of serving the public interest. This was the use of the editorial essay originated by Arthur Brisbane, whose brash headlines and atrocity stories were credited for the phenomenal circulation of the *New York Journal*. The highest-paid editor of his time, he wrote an editorial column, "Today," which was syndicated in newspapers throughout the world.

The *Tribune*'s full-page editorial, Brisbane style, came out once a week, with the motif, "So the People May Know." At the top of the page or in the center was an eye-catching illustration drawn by Pablo Amorsolo, brother of the famous painter. The editorial itself filled the rest of the page with variations in typography—in capitals and italics, boldface and light. The effect of the whole was aesthetic, dramatic, and moving. It outdid Brisbane himself.

Mendez introduced the first doublespread editorial on June 24, 1932, with an attack on the misuse of government funds through extravagance, wasteful practices, and bureaucracy. His title, "Our Balete-Strangled Government," was based on the metaphor of a tree being overpowered by the creeping plant known as the balete.

The essay was an instant success. On July 6 the *Tribune* was pleased to publish on its front page a letter from Walter J. Robb, one-time star reporter of the *Manila Daily Bulletin* and editor of the *American Chamber of Commerce Journal*. Robb paid the editor this compliment:

> I read the Tribune's illustrated full-page editorial titled "Our Balete-Strangled Government" with the pleasure I had anticipated from the announcements of it which had been made. Its force is emphatic. It is additional evidence, and the best of evidence, of the rapid advancement of a high order of journalism in the Philippines; ten years hence it will be one of the traditions of the journalism of which it constitutes now one of the foundation stones—a journalism of the present generation, liberal, independent, and forthright, setting its own standards.

The prewar Philippine dailies were distinguished by their strong editorial pages. It was not unusual for Mendez to write four editorials of varying lengths for one issue, as well as one long Brisbane-type essay for the same day. As Arsenio N. Luz once remarked, "During that expansive period of the early twentieth century, the Philippine press was dominated by... great editors and personalities. It was the second golden age of personal journalism in the Philippines."[5]

Jesus Valenzuela, who wrote his *History of Journalism* in 1930, stressed the value of the daily newspaper to the Filipinos of that generation:

> To the Filipino, his newspaper is more than a mere purveyor of news, just as he is more than a mere reader of news. It is his *vade mecum* [handbook], the cherished companion of his leisure, the text-book of his family, the subject of fiery discussion in street corners and public squares, and his encyclopedia of local information.[6]

Public opinion in those days was waiting and willing to be molded by the press. With hardly any competition from local columnists, and none at all from broadcast media, editorial writers had the field to themselves. Before the onset of the knowledge explosion, when television was but a dream and news coverage via satellite was only for science fiction, readers had the leisure to savor the content and style of editorial essays. According to newsman Isidro Retizos, "The double-spreads of Mendez were always eagerly awaited and avidly read, the embodiment of provocative ideas written in brilliant English. His neat phrases were copied and committed to memory by college students."[7]

Although Mendez has never been cited among Filipino essayists in English, hundreds of his editorials are actually self-contained expository essays. The scope of his topics was almost encyclopedic. Even when he handled current issues, he invested them with the timeless and universal qualities found in essays worthy of the name *literature*. Imbued with a sense of the past, he traced the history of ideas and events in order to derive lessons for the present and the future. His purpose was not only to comment on the passing scene but also to educate, to stimulate thought, to reform, and, most of all, to uplift.

Objecting to the newspapers' glorification of criminals through sensationalism, Mendez once wrote:

> We are known as the Fourth Estate. We wield a tremendous power over public opinion which is ours many times to manipulate to suit our special ends.... This is the time to...prove that the press of this country is not out to make money by appealing to the base passions of man, but to carry out its aim of informing and guiding public opinion in its most decent way.
>
> The Press of this country...must be temperate, rather than wild; uplifting rather than degrading. It must sweep public opinion not downwards to the depth of shame, but upwards to the heights of enlightened thought.[8]

It was in this spirit that he filled his editorials with examples of Filipino greatness. "Rizal in the Nation's Library," an essay that provides the common reader with lucid insights into the *Noli* and the *Fili*, and "The Prince of Tagalog Letters," an eloquent tribute to Francisco Baltazar (Balagtas), are but two examples of his desire to inspire the reader with love of country and love of national literature.

Paying honor even to unknown but deserving Filipinos, Mendez once wrote a full-page editorial epitaph, "In Line of Duty," for a Philippine Constabulary officer and his detachment of nine, all of whom were killed by Moro outlaws on the outskirts of Jolo in October 1932. Lt. Vicente G. Alagar and his men had journeyed to the bushy district of Bud Panamao on a conciliation mission, only to be treacherously massacred while asleep in their tents.

In the light of the present government's peacemaking efforts in Mindanao, this editorial becomes particularly relevant:

> The story of our government's campaign for peace in Moroland is glorious with the heroism of Constabulary soldiers. The place has never mattered to these fighters of the force. Whether in the city or in the thick gloom of primeval forests...they have followed duty as only tried and true soldiers know how to follow duty.

The P.C. had been "maligned and vilified" for its blunders, noted Mendez, while its heroic achievements had been overlooked. Appealing for appreciation of the P.C.'s sacrifices, he concluded:

> And when the people come to realize that the Constabulary man who today marches in the flamboyant panoply of martial parade, and tomorrow seems unduly harsh in the enforcement of a quarantine order, may on the third day die in their defense, his breast pierced by an outlaw's spear, or his skull cloven by a bandit's bolo—then and only then will the country as a whole appreciate the force for what it is: a body of men who live in service, and die in line of duty.[9]

In the same uplifting spirit, Mendez sought to boost the morale of a people in the grip of a global depression. His Christmas-day editorial of 1932 began by reciting a catalogue of woes that beset a world whose economy was "out of joint." There was a "protracted standstill in the mills of human industry," and breadlines in many countries were lengthening by the day. Aggravating the general misfortune were the "tremendous exactions of a militaristic philosophy in the councils of Europe."

The Philippines, in the meantime, was grappling with its first economic problem of national consequence—the tariff. Furthermore, the organization of the insular government had forced drastic cuts in the public budget, resulting in reduced salaries and incalculable distress to thousands of Filipino families.

Under such gloomy circumstances, how was the *Tribune* editor to wish his readers a Merry Christmas and a Happy New Year? *Look for the silver lining,* Mendez must have thought to himself as he concluded his editorial with this message:

> Such is the picture before our eyes as the carols of this Christmas Day proclaim the advent of the Child Redeemer.

And because the picture is so somber, the benign sunlight of this hour shines with a peculiar beauty upon the length and breadth of Christendom.

In the evocation of that happy event in ancient Judea, Mankind entunes a song of praise today. Rich and poor, wise and ignorant, will break bread in a common tribute to the Man God who came to earth that the sins of this life might be washed away and peace might reign forever in the councils of men.

Across the page of the world's recent affairs, the message of this Christmas Day is written large. It is the message of peace for humanity's inquietudes, of good-will for the nation's recurrent feuds, of charity for the selfish forces striving to make this life more miserable.

It is the message to soften the human heart, to purify the mortal spirit, and to redeem a humanity from the mire of the sordid struggles into which it has been sunk by the force of uncontrollable circumstances.[10]

Mendez was so widely read that lawmakers even dissected his editorials in the halls of the legislature. The first *Tribune* editorial to be inserted in the records of the House of Representatives was "The Salariat."[11] Mendez wrote this essay when the legislature was planning to abolish the positions of about 2,000 government employees in order to save money. He felt it would be a mistake to include the low-salaried employees—the salariat—in the drastic cost-cutting program.

The editorial is an excellent example of how Mendez tried to educate his readers by tracing the evolution of word meanings. In distinguishing the salariat from the proletariat, the essay traces the original *proletarius* to the alleys of ancient Rome, where he was regarded as "the lowest and meanest of the destitute, whose fault lay not in his destitution...but in the remarkable preference he showed for the squalor and vice that are the concomitants of poverty, and in his flat refusal to...raise himself out of his environment."

In its original sense, therefore, the term *proletarius* cannot apply with justice to the modern laborer who has always wanted to free his family from the misery of their daily existence. However, with the evolution of modern libertarian thought, the word *proletariat* has come to apply to the laboring class, "its back bowed under the burden of the whole structure of humanity," "the class of the poor whom, the scriptures say, we shall always have with us."

The class of the salariat, on the other hand, stands for the "government salary-slave," bearing on his shoulders the massive structure that forms the complex government found in every country in the world. In the following paragraph Mendez simultaneously defines, describes, and defends the salariat by means of a repetitive pattern for emphasis:

> It is the class, as long as it remains a class, that stands for order and stability. It is the class that sticks most closely to the traditions of family, of a decent respect for the forms of life, for the edicts of the law. It is the class that is distinguished for its unfailing loyalty to constituted authority. It is the class least likely to be affected by subversive doctrines spread by irresponsible, self-seeking demagogues. It is the class on the loyalty of which the government, as at present constituted, can always depend.

Such a class, once destroyed by the government it looks up to, may not be rebuilt for many generations to come: in fact, it might even form the nucleus of movements which may have far-reaching and dangerous effects. Mendez cites the Nazi movement in Germany, which was not a movement of the proletariat but the "embodied protest of a middle class, once strong in its support of a government which stood by it—now equally strong in its determination to get its rights."

This was the kind of editorial writing that led another writer, the late Sol Gwekoh, to claim that even as a newspaperman, Mendez was "a public figure by reason of his reputation not only as a pioneer but also as a peerless journalist." Gwekoh mentioned the following among the reasons for giving Mendez a place in his "Hall of Fame":

> His courage and steadfast stand in upholding what was right, his high regard for honorable conduct, and his continuous and grinding editorial work constituted a career and an example worthy of emulation.
>
> A master of the English language, Mendez wrote brilliant and weighty editorials that were directly concerned with the people's welfare. His doublespread-page editorials which analyzed intelligently and objectively the day-by-day political, economic, educational and social problems of the nation not only made him one of the country's greatest editorial writers but also earned for him the title of "Arthur Brisbane of the Philippines."[12]

IV

EDUCATION AND POLITICS

The education of the Filipinos was a recurrent theme in Mendez's writings. For instance, in the early part of 1931, there were indications that Governor-General Davis was planning to appoint more Americans than Filipinos to the new textbook board. This drew from Mendez an editorial reminding the Governor-General that the public schools should be the repository of Filipino culture, and that nobody could appreciate and perpetuate that culture better than the Filipinos themselves. In fairness to the people, there should be more Filipinos than Americans on the textbook board, if the aim was "not to stifle but to keep alive the Filipino soul in our children."

The editorial also called Davis' attention to the following section of the "McKinley Instructions" to the colonial administration:

> ...the government...is designed not to our (American) satisfaction or for the expression of our (American) theoretical views, but for the happiness, peace, and prosperity of the people of the Philippines, and the measures should be made to conform to their customs, their habits, and even their prejudices, to the fullest extent consistent with the accomplishment of the indispensable requisites of just and efficient government.[1]

A week later, three Filipinos and two Americans were appointed to the textbook board.

The *Philippine High School Readers*

The Filipinization of textbooks began with Camilo Osias' series of *Philippine Readers* for elementary grades, and, as early as 1924,

Maria Valdez Ventura's *Philippine Primary Geography*. The Mendez contribution was the *Philippine High School Readers*, Books I and II, better known to many students by the names of the authors, Mendez, Mendez, Potts. The prescribed texts of previous years had been Irving's *The Alhambra,* Longfellow's *Song of Hiawatha* and *Evangeline,* and Arnold's *Sohrab and Rustum.* Every high-school freshman could declaim from memory the famous lines from *Evangeline,* beginning with "This is the forest primeval, the murmuring pines and the hemlocks..."

Publication of the *Readers* in 1932 was additional evidence of what friends of the couple called a "marriage of true minds." Mendez and Mendez did the bulk of the work together, while Merrill S. Potts, their co-author, lent prestige to the title page, for he was chief of the Publications Division of the Bureau of Education.

When the Mendezes began working on the *Readers*, they were handicapped by a dearth of Filipino material in English suitable for high-school students. Most of the works they had selected, including the poem *Antipolo,* were transferred by the Bureau of Education to its own publication, *Philippine Prose and Poetry.* As a result, the anthologies became less Filipino than they had been meant to be.

Book II contained more Filipino authors than Book I and encouraged local tourism with descriptive and historical sketches of Manila's churches, the walls of Intramuros, and scenic spots around the Islands. "See the Philippines First" was the theme of the first chapter, and to practice what they preached, Mr. and Mrs. Mendez braved the primitive trail to the Ifugao rice terraces, shot the rapids in Pagsanjan for 50 centavos, peered into the slumbering crater of Taal volcano, and rushed to Bicol to watch Mayon's fireworks.

For Book II of the *Readers,* Mendez translated Rizal's *A La Juventud Filipina,* an ode for which the national hero had won first prize at the age of eighteen. Dr. Clemencia Joven Colayco, well-known professor of education at the University of Santo Tomas, considers Mendez's *To the Filipino Youth* the best of all the translations of Rizal's ode. She included it in a textbook, *Viewing the World of Letters,* Volume II (1966), which she published for use in Catholic high schools.[2]

Defending the Imperial Tongue

In the early 1930s the *Tribune* enjoined schools, civic associations, and churches to join the ongoing campaign against illiteracy. The key to literacy, as far as Mendez was concerned, was the English language. In an editorial, he sought to allay the fears of Jorge Bocobo, Dean of the U.P. College of Law, who had declared that he "had no sympathy for the family that uses a borrowed language in the home." Mendez addressed his good friend, the Dean:

> Dean Bocobo must understand that his children today go to schools in which English is the language of instruction and that by speaking to them in that language he is doing nothing but facilitating their training....
> We admire Dean Bocobo's steadfast idealism, but we hold that we are not selling our ideals when we choose to commune with the rest of the civilized world through a medium of expression as rich in the universal precepts of human justice as it is practical in the scope of its uses.[3]

In a subsequent doublespread editorial, Mendez supported the proposal of the Constitutional Convention that English be made the official language of the Philippine Islands:

> It has been the language in our schools, the medium whereby we have kept abreast of the times. It has been the instrument of our contact with the rest of the world. Through it we have understood other nations and new horizons of knowledge have been opened to our minds....
> It is not correct...to suppose that English can blur the stamp of our soul. We want to meet the English-speaking Filipino who is not a Filipino in the innermost recesses of his heart, and who can claim without fear of successful contradiction, that his intimate conceptions of life are those of John Bull or of Uncle Sam.

Mendez went on to compare English with the Greek language during the glorious days of Hellenism, when "it quickened human knowledge" and became a disseminator of ideas for all men, regardless of national frontiers. Repeating Greek-language history in the twentieth century, English had "passed into the common inheritance of mankind."[4]

Six years later, Mendez was to argue in favor of Tagalog as the national language, but that belongs to another chapter in his career. (See Chapter IX.)

The Public-School System

Mendez's defense of English as the language of instruction was closely linked with his faith in the public-school system in the Philippines. He had faith in its democratic tradition, its efficiency as an administrative form, its high standards of instruction, and its unprecedented success in producing an enlightened citizenry. He recalled the early months of the American occupation, when children had to be "captured" from their homes and compelled to go to school. In the third decade the picture was radically different—children were flocking to the public schools as they would to a playground. No other country in the Far East could boast of a similar record in free education in the past thirty years.[5]

Unfortunately, a new problem had arisen—thousands of children were being turned away annually for lack of classrooms, and teachers were working to the bone on starvation wages. The Legislature proposed what Mendez thought was a curious solution: first, the introduction of the double single-session in the elementary schools, thereby forcing the teachers to work double-time; and second, the reduction of the teachers' wages to a rate below the minimum of ₱40 a month.

Mendez reacted to the proposal with a plea on behalf of the long-suffering public-school teacher:

> The way to do justice to the teacher is not to flatter him but to understand him as he should be understood—as a human being living his life in a world of reality. ... To know him as such is to realize that he is not a mechanical man satisfied to adhere to rules of classroom pedagogy for which he receives his monthly pittance.
>
> He does not, for one thing, want our sympathy. All he seeks is justice. All he desires is the conviction that he is UNDERSTOOD, that he is not merely POSSESSED, by the government that hires him...that he is an individual with feelings and ambitions, and that he has his self-respect to maintain.[6]

Mendez attributed the teachers' plight to the dependence of the educational system on doles from the Legislature. As soon as Governor-

General Frank Murphy arrived in 1933, the *Tribune* greeted him with a doublespread editorial appealing to him, among other things, to do away with the existing order in education, which allowed the school system to suffer in the "perennial give and take of our politics."

Mendez called Murphy's attention to the long hand of politics as it stretched even to the realm of higher education:

> The University of the Philippines has always been at the mercy of our political conveniences. The president of that institution cannot displease our powers that be. He must kowtow to the legislature or get nothing.[7]

U.P. Beloved

Mendez's fears for the financial fate of the U.P. were justified by events that took place in 1933, when the appropriations committee of the lower house slashed the U.P. budget by ₱300,000. The general belief was that Palma's strong partisan leanings during the national debate over the Hare-Hawes-Cutting Law (see Chapter V) had hurt Quezon's pro-independence efforts, thus bringing about the decapitation of even Palma's own salary. It was also true, however, that owing to hard times, the U.P. president had voluntarily reduced his salary the year before and that the faculty had responded to his call for austerity by turning off their electric fans.[8]

But what really infuriated Quezon was a remark that Palma had reportedly made about him—that he was not a Filipino "in face and heart" (*"de cara y corazon"*). This bit of political gossip set back the U.P. by one-third of its annual appropriation and left Palma with no choice but to resign.[9]

Disappointed in the treatment that his alma mater was getting from the legislature, Mendez attributed it to the fact that Palma was more of a politician than an educator. He gave the U.P. president credit for being an efficient administrator, citing the impressive buildings and massive pillars that graced the campus on Padre Faura. But when Palma offered to resign, Mendez saw no reason to hope that his resignation would not be accepted.

Mendez's view was that the only way to free the University from its political fetters was to make it self-supporting. Arguing the case for academic freedom, he asked, "What will the students in our highest seat of learning think of their president, or even a member of their faculty, if they suspect that he addresses them with mental reservations and that he is fettered by loyalties to political gods in whose hands lies the financial destiny of their alma mater?"[10]

But since a self-supporting state university was impossible, the next alternative was to minimize friction between the U.P. and the state by appointing a nonpolitical president. That opportunity came when the Board of Regents set about the task of selecting a successor to President Palma.

In "The Educator's Turn at the Helm," one of Mendez's many essays on education and the university, he offered his definition of an ideal U.P. president:

> Whoever is chosen must, first of all, be an educator, with a reputation as such not only in this country but abroad. We mean by an educator a man who has dedicated the best years of his life to the training of our youth and whose outlook on life is that of an exalted teacher rather than a politician or a mere specialist in one branch of learning.

A university, Mendez added, must be a place for "pure study, and an educator's hand must guide this recession from the crowd's ignoble strife into the calm of philosophical contemplation and the devotion of scientific research." Academic freedom must never be sacrificed "in the interminable clashes of mundane interests."[11]

But he also cautioned the academic community against the ivory-tower mentality. He cited national service "through a constant reorganization of knowledge and the intensification of research" as one of the roles of the university. The danger in a university's being merely encyclopedic was that an accumulation of facts might have no practical value for the country.[12]

When Jorge Bocobo was chosen U.P. president in December 1934, Mendez depicted his election as "the culmination of a career dedicated to the moral uplift of the youth of the land...the rightful reward to a man who has identified himself with the cultural progress of his people and their fight for national ideals." Mendez considered it significant that a product of the public-school system had been chosen to occupy the highest educational post in the nation. "His is the achievement the richest of the land might envy."[13]

Ye Olde Student Power

The difficulty of divorcing higher education from politics had been proven even before the Palma *faux pas*. In late 1932, the House of Representatives was treated to a mild dose of student power which proved beyond a doubt that U.P. students, for better or for worse, were destined to have a say in affairs of state. The incident also proved, however, that without the support of a free press, student power might have been confined to the campus instead of reaching the doorsteps of the legislative building.

For some months the budget committee of the lower house had been working hard to reorganize the government in order to do away with extravagance, inefficiency, and bureaucracy. Everyone was resigned to the fact that the pruning knife was going to slash the pay envelopes of all government personnel, from high officials down to janitor. (See "The Salariat," Chapter III.)

Imagine the shock of the nation when a tip to the T-V-T publications exposed the sneaky insertion in the appropriations act of a rider which would provide each member of the House of Representatives with the lump sum of ₱2,000 for clerical help, postage, stationery, and traveling allowances. The representative was not even obliged to account for the sum at the end of the year. Mendez viewed the plot as "A Betrayal of the Public Trust" and nicknamed the rider "bootleg item 85."[14]

The *Tribune* scoop filled the front pages, the editorials, and the Public Pulse for about two weeks. The result of the exposé was the decline and fall of "bootleg item 85" in record time, within a week of its discovery.

In a vengeful mood the "bootleggers" attacked the "sensational press" and alluded in no subtle tones to the wealth of the Roces family. To this *ad hominem* argument the *Tribune* editor replied:

> We have kept faith with the people in exposing what in the darkness of secrecy the representatives attempted to do. We prevented what would have been an outrage against the interests of the people. . . . This is our crime and in admitting this guilt we rest our case. Let the people decide.[15]

The highlight of the episode was the demonstration staged by students from Manila colleges and universities. Led by Wenceslao

Vinzons, president of the U.P. Student Council, they gathered at the Mehan Gardens and marched to the legislative building, carrying placards that read "Condemn the House of Mis-Representatives" and "Bootleg Salary Increase!"

Replying to charges that the students had gone out of bounds, Mendez asserted in an editorial that student indignation against perpetrators of wrongdoing in the government should not be repressed:

> It should be permitted to take its course, to recapitulate in its fire and fervor the unexpressed indignation, also, of the public. Better, indeed, that it be the chosen channel for the expression of mass reaction to political crimes. Better, indeed, that it be in the vanguard, than that in the forefront the fulmination of the mob should be substituted. One can reason with the first; the second can only be clubbed into submission.[16]

Student power had arrived.

But the editor was not content to leave it at that. In closing the "bootleg" incident with a doublespread editorial, he warned the youth not to let their "new-found power" go to their heads:

> The nation's leaders have taken cognizance of your action, you young men of the universities.
>
> They, men of experience in the affairs of the nation, men wise in the ways of the world, possessed of a knowledge far beyond yours... have seen fit to come to you and to make explanation.
>
> It would be fatal, both to yourselves and to your country, for you to take this action on their part as an admission that you have greater power than they have in the councils of the nation.
>
> It would be fatal to predicate on this action of theirs the conviction that you can run this country. You are from now on a power to be reckoned with; but you do not yet run your country.[17]

"A power to be reckoned with"—prophetic words, indeed.

V

ON WITH THE DANCE!

It would take an electronic memory machine to retrace the movements of Filipino newsmen as they shift from one journalistic position to the next and from one newspaper to another. But one event that every prewar newsman remembers is the *rigodon* in which Carlos P. Romulo and Mauro Mendez were the star performers.

Rumors circulated in July 1933 that Romulo had received an offer he could not refuse, namely, to become publisher of the M-H-M chain (*Mabuhay-Herald-Monday Mail*) then owned by Joaquin Elizalde. Romulo's right-hand man returned to the *Herald* ahead of him. On July 16, 1933, the name of Mauro Mendez disappeared from the *Tribune* masthead. The following day the *Herald* masthead contained the name of Mauro Mendez as managing editor.

Exactly a month later, Romulo returned to the Quezon fold as publisher of the M-H-M. Shortly after, the Spanish-language *El Debate* was added to the chain, making the D-M-H-M one newspaper larger than the T-V-T and ready to do battle with the latter over Quezon and the independence question. Mendez was appointed managing editor of the D-M-H-M syndicate.

His return to the Herald meant an improvement in his lifestyle. He had never enjoyed a paid vacation at the *Tribune* unless he was in bed with the flu. Working far into the night and crawling into bed at two or three in the morning was not his idea of being a family man. Sometimes he would be shocked out of his sleep at six a.m. by a phone call from Mr. Roces, wanting to know why he had been scooped by another newspaper.

Since the *Herald* was an afternoon daily, the pace was hectic for only three or four hours in the morning, and Mendez could rush home to play with his newborn twins, Ruben and Eloisa. He eventually had six children—three boys and three girls, with the twins in the middle—making him feel superior to Carlos P. Romulo, who had four boys, and Anacleto Benavides, who had four girls.

At the D-M-H-M, Mendez had the added experience of becoming an instructor in journalism. His classroom was his office, and his students were professional writers enrolled at the University of Santo Tomas. Journalism classes at U.S.T. were modelled after the system at Northwestern University in that the students learned their craft right where the action was.

One of Mendez's students was Teodoro F. Valencia, who was to become one of the most widely-read and influential columnists after the war. Classes were conducted on a seminar basis, recalls Valencia, with Mendez dangling his leg over his armrest and chatting about the manners and mores of previous editors. Valencia came to know him well, as his student, his colleague, and later as his classmate in law school. He noted Mendez's qualities—"the human touch, the sense of humor, the sense of wonder, and that all-important journalistic ingredient, curiosity." [1]

From Mendez's glass-enclosed office, he could look out on a large room that housed the D-M-H-M's madding crowd. In the center of the room was a long semi-circular table for Hernando J. Abaya, Jose A. Lansang, Jesus M. "Fatso" Intengan, and Carlos Quirino. Ex-*Graphic* editor Vicente Albano Pacis, now *Herald* city editor, worked at his own table facing that formidable array of deskmen. The office was a hive of typewriter noises and nicotine emanating from business manager Modesto Farolan (future presidential press secretary and diplomat), Antonio V. Arizabal (another postwar press secretary), Hermenegildo Atienza, Jose de la Cruz, Pete Villanueva, Montano Nazario, Ramon Torres (*El Debate* editor), and Amado Hernandez (*Mabuhay* editor). Emmanuel Pelaez, who was to become Vice-President of the Philippines in 1961, was a cub reporter for *El Debate*.[2]

Aside from Godofredo Rivera's "Believe It Or Not," the *Herald* carried Arthur Brisbane's "Illustrated Weekly Editorial." In need of another energizer, Romulo recruited his former student, wavy-haired Salvador P. Lopez, better known as S.P., who had just earned his master's degree at the U.P. S.P. began a daily column timidly titled

"So It Seems," which became the number-one rival of Fred Mangahas' *Tribune* column, "Maybe."

But there was nothing timid about S.P.'s adventures as a newsman. He covered the eruption of Mt. Mayon from an airplane and rushed posthaste to Mauban, Tayabas, to report on a tidal wave that had nearly engulfed the town. He returned to Manila partly by train and partly on horseback. It was the first time he had ever touched a horse.[3]

The Hare-Hawes-Cutting Brouhaha

The year that M.M., C.P.R., and S.P. began working together at the *Herald* happened to be the climax of a turbulent chapter in Philippine history. For the first time since the American occupation, the Filipinos had received a definite offer of freedom in the form of the Hare-Hawes-Cutting Act. The offer sparked a political and personal battle over the pros and cons of accepting the Act, a battle in which the press was embroiled, for it was a war of words.

Mission after mission had gone to the United States seeking independence, only to get the run-around in Washington. Thus, in 1932, when the so-called Os-Rox mission, headed by Senator Sergio Osmeña and Speaker Manuel Roxas, was offered the Hare-Hawes-Cutting Act on a silver platter, they decided to take it. From as far away as Manila, Quezon could smell the noxious odor of the bill. He instructed the mission either to ask for immediate independence with no strings attached, or to postpone action until the installation of President Franklin D. Roosevelt in January 1933. The mission closed its collective ears to Quezon's instructions.

Even before the Roosevelt administration was sworn in, the bill was enacted into law. Its implementation, however, was to hinge on its acceptance by the Philippine Legislature or by the Filipino people in a plebiscite, should the Legislature agree to call one.

In March 1933, a frantic Quezon rushed to the United States as fast as the waves could carry him. The news of April 30 was that Osmeña and Quezon were "in open clash" in Washington. Osmeña warned that the U.S. would stay in the Philippine Islands forever if the law was rejected.

In June, Quezon and the Os-Rox mission, with Carlos P. Romulo between them, packed their bags and sailed home together.

They argued on the bounding main and continued their argument as soon as they landed.

The Quezon group maintained that both the political and economic provisions of the Hare-Hawes-Cutting Law were outrageous, but the Os-Rox mission insisted that there was no alternative, and that under the circumstances which attended its passage, it was a fair and just law. Politically, the Law provided for a ten-year transition period before the granting of independence, during which the U.S. President would retain the power to approve or disapprove all amendments to the Philippine Constitution and to control the Islands' bonded indebtedness, currency, and foreign affairs. The United States was to retain land or other property that its President was to designate in the Philippines for "military and other reservations."

The economic provisions allowed a quota of only fifty Filipino immigrants per year into the United States during the Commonwealth period. Unlimited quantities of American goods could enter the Islands duty-free, but duty-free Philippine products, the mainstay of the nation's economy, could enter the U.S. only in limited quantities.[4]

These were among the stipulations that inspired Mauro Mendez to label the Hare-Hawes-Cutting Law "autocratic":

> Throughout all of its provisions our interests are placed in a position of secondary importance, while those of America are considered paramount. And yet, we have been made to feel that we should be grateful, that we should grab this crumb of bread from the banquet of America's selfish interests or lose every chance we have in this world to enjoy our birthright to be free and independent.[5]

The archipelago in general and the Nacionalista party in particular were split into the *Pros,* who welcomed the H-H-C Law, and the *Antis,* who wanted to junk it. Brilliant minds were lined up on both sides of the Great Divide: Resident Commissioners Camilo Osias and Pedro Guevara, Floor Leader Pedro Sabido, Ruperto Montinola, Jose P. Laurel, Benigno Aquino, Rafael Palma, Maximo Kalaw, and Gregorio Perfecto on the Os-Rox side; and Claro M. Recto, Lorenzo Sumulong, Quintin Paredes, Elpidio Quirino, Jorge Bocobo, General Emilio Aguinaldo, and Bishop Gregorio Aglipay on the Quezon side.

A League for the Acceptance of the Hare-Hawes-Cutting Law was organized, among whose members were prominent Nacionalistas in the Senate, U.P. President Palma, and Dean Kalaw. Professor Austin Craig lectured against the H-H-C Law at the U.P., and Salvador Araneta sent articles to the press condemning it. Commissioner Osias and Senator Quirino debated the subject before 1,600 city-school teachers at the Plaza Hotel. Others, less illustrious, wrote letters to the editor.

Passions ran high and throats ran dry over the issue. One dark July afternoon, 6,000 rejectionists ignored a menacing rainstorm and marched to the Luneta, accompanied by 28 bands of music. Cebuanos came all the way from the South, bearing paper flags imprinted with the handsome Quezon face. Quirino, Paredes, and Lope K. Santos managed to address the crowd, but before Quezon could open his mouth, the clouds doused him with cold rain.[6]

Students, of course, were not to be out-talked by the politicians. The U.P. *Pros,* consisting of Wenceslao Vinzons, Ambrosio Padilla, Arturo Tolentino, and Estanislao Fernandez, debated with the U.S.T. *Antis* headed by Narciso Pimentel, Jr., Teodoro P. de Vera, Sofronio Quimson, and Rafael David. When Manuel Roxas, the U.P. students' idol, was ousted as Speaker of the House, thousands of students demonstrated for him and carried him on their shoulders to the Luneta.[7]

The U.P. Alumni Association protested the students' involvement in the demonstration, and Dean Bocobo was constrained to issue guidelines on their behavior at parades and rallies of a non-academic nature. "A sense of fitness based upon the ethics of the gentleman and the gentlewoman should be and must be in the final analysis the basis for the action of the students and faculty of the University," said the Dean.[8]

In Quezon's opinion, President Palma himself had violated that injunction by attacking him personally in the guise of academic freedom. Palma turned in his resignation and announced that he was "quitting politics forever."[9]

D-M-H-M and H-H-C

On July 20, 1933, four days after Mendez became *Herald* editor, his first doublespread editorial appeared in the newspaper. Titled "Children of Hate," it deplored the personal turn that the conflict had taken, and criticized the Acceptance League for calling upon the people to rid themselves of what the League called "a leadership devoid of orientation, pernicious and irresponsible."

The illustration by P.V. Coniconde, art director of the D-M-H-M, showed Quezon's monumental head frowning stolidly on a hilltop, while Lilliputian people clambered among the rocks, screaming and tearing at his ears and hair. The editorial, as well as subsequent ones, was translated into Tagalog by Amado Hernandez for the *Mabuhay,* under the byline of Mauro Mendez.

During the fiery months when the nation bickered over the independence question, Mendez wrote approximately 70 editorials on the Hare-Hawes-Cutting Law for the *Herald* and the *Monday Mail.* He reminded the readers repeatedly that this was a fight over principles, that every point should be discussed "in the light of pure reason," and that if they lost sight of the vital points and saw only the human faults of the *dramatis personae,* they would be "lost in confusion" and "bungle" their destiny.[10]

Mendez admitted, however, that the Quezon image was irresistible to friend and foe alike:

> It is proof positive of Mr. Quezon's strength as it is of the malice of his foes that the Hare-Hawes-Cutting Law cannot be viewed by most of us without seeing, superimposed upon that law, the image of Mr. Quezon. Our very political atmosphere is permeated with Mr. Quezon and our political mentality is full of him.[11]

It was an uphill battle for the D-M-H-M and Quezon, considering that the T-V-T and the *Bulletin* were allies on the *Pro* side. "Representative" Andoy, a fictitious provinciano whose "Adventures in Manila" were featured regularly in the *Sunday Tribune Magazine,* explained in several issues why he favored the H-H-C Law.[12] On the other hand, the *Herald*'s Juan de la Cruz, speaking for Mauro Mendez, was an eloquent spokesman on the *Anti* side.

One editorial took the form of a soliloquy by Juan, the unassuming man in the *salakot,** viewing the H-H-C controversy from the perspective of his nipa hut:

> To me, simple that I am, the case is also quite simple... this is not the independence that our martyrs and heroes died

---

* Native hat made of squash gourd.

fighting for. I know that there are many strings attached to this law and that what gave it to us is not the same spirit which gave the Declaration of Independence to America and the world.

After citing the objectionable features of the Law, Juan declared that he could see no reason for the histrionics of the "political prophets." Camilo Osias, for one, had predicted that unless the law was accepted, "rivers of blood" would flow through the land. Juan de la Cruz contrasted the current politicians with the heroes of the past:

> Where some of us now must proclaim their patriotism to the four winds of heaven, our forefathers simply adhered to a rigid code of self-denial; and where today some of our self-styled popular idols declare that our rivers might turn to rivers of blood, our ancestors simply fell in the night with none to do them reverence.
>
> Theirs were the simple virtues of life, the ideals that did not have to be expressed with grand gesture of melodrama and studied appeals to the psychology of the crowd. Their thoughts did not have to be embellished with flourishes of oratory because they were thoughts born of truth rather than of the convenience of passing moments.[13]

On October 17, 1933, after months of melodrama, Senator Osmeña presented his resolution to the Legislature, calling for the acceptance of the Hare-Hawes-Cutting Law. The Legislature rejected it, and the Law was declared officially dead—"assassinated" was how the defeated faction put it.

The Tydings-McDuffie Law

After the rejection of the H-H-C Law, Quezon formed another independence delegation to the United States. He invited Osmeña to join him, but Osmeña politely declined the invitation. However, he saw Quezon off at the pier, an act of chivalry for which he received editorial praise from the *Herald*.[14]

Unfortunately, Washington's take-it-or-leave-it attitude put Quezon in a position that made the previous mission snicker, "I told you so!" Finally, after much haggling on Quezon's part, Senator Millard Tydings and Rep. John McDuffie offered him an amendment to the Hare-Hawes-Cutting Law. They changed the all-embracing provision for the designation of "military and other reservations" into the more specific "retention of naval reservations and fueling stations." The new bill also provided that within two years after the grant of independence, the American and Philippine governments were to conduct negotiations "for the adjustment and settlement of all questions relating to naval reservations and fueling stations of the United States in the Philippine Islands...." [15]

Quezon returned home with the Tydings-McDuffie Law to replace the deceased Hare-Hawes-Cutting Law. On May 1, 1934, the Legislature called a special session and approved the Law without a dissenting voice. It was Quezon's victory again. As Vicente Madrigal once remarked, "resisting President Quezon was like bucking a hurricane. So persuasive was he that he always had his way."[16]

Even before the acceptance of the Tydings-McDuffie Law, Mendez may have been in a quandary. He had supported Quezon from the start and had helped him sway the Legislature and the public to his side. But the D-M-H-M was obviously powerless to demolish the inequities that had moved wholesale from the old law to the new one. Already the anti-Quezon guerrillas were snorting that the Hare-Hawes-Cutting Law by any other name was the Tydings-McDuffie Law, and so forth. The Minority gleefully planned to hurl this issue at Quezon in the elections of 1934.

What the D-M-H-M did, therefore, was to soften the sting of the Tydings-McDuffie Law by emphasizing the advantages of the military amendment. In the previous year, Mendez had, through the voice of Juan de la Cruz, expressed this opinion of the military reservations clause in the Hare-Hawes-Cutting Law: "I have yet to hear of an independent state that remained contented in the shadow of alien fortresses...."[17] Now he pursued the same line of reasoning to prove that far from being trivial, the amendment in the bases provision clarified a question of "territorial integrity." The previous law would have coerced the Philippines into an outright donation of "military and other reservations" to the United States for that country to have and to hold as long as she wished. "The American flag, according to the sense of the Hare-Hawes-Cutting Law, would be supreme over the reservations, so that anything America might want to do within the specified areas would not be ours to dispute." The new law, on the other hand, would limit the kinds of reservations to be acquired and would allow the Philippines to renegotiate the terms of the agreement to satisfy the nation's idea of sovereignty.[18]

As the noted political scientist, Vicente Albano Pacis, has since pointed out, the amendment "had the effect of restoring to the Philippines all land and property reserved under Section 5 [of the Hare-Hawes-Cutting Law] except only naval reservations and fueling stations." [19]

Mendez also warned that should Philippine international interests conflict with America's military designs, the presence of her fortresses here would constitute a danger to Filipino lives:

> Manila would be within reach of Corregidor's guns to lay waste any moment, not to mention the dreadnaughts and destroyers and submarines that would be stationed permanently in Manila Bay. There is Camp Stotsenburg in Pampanga, right in the very heart of Luzon; Fort McKinley, a scarce twenty minutes' ride from this city; and Fort Santiago in Intramuros, to mention only a few of America's strongholds in this country at present.
> Is it possible that to the defenders of the Hare-Hawes-Cutting Law in its entirety the presence of these fortresses here presents no significance at all? Is it possible that even in their elementary logic they can not see anything incompatible in such fortresses with their conception of national freedom? [20]

In short, Mendez summed up all the arguments that anti-bases proponents were to cite in the '60s and '70s. But he himself was to change his mind on the same subject after the Second World War, when the specter of international Communism reared its nuclear head in the Far East. What he least expected, however, was to find himself up to his neck in the bases controversy 31 years after the passage of the Tydings-McDuffie Law. (See Chapter XIII.)

Woman Suffrage

The campaign for independence in the early '30s was fought on two battlegrounds, male and female. While the men fought for freedom from colonialism, the women fought for freedom from male chauvinism.

In 1931 a bill granting Filipino women the right to vote was approved with a comfortable majority in the lower house, but the

Senate killed it with a stroke of the pen. The following year the bill was revived in the upper chamber, but the senators continued to sit and even doze on it.

Governor-General Murphy, like all his predecessors, stood four-square behind the bill and encouraged the ladies to continue their campaign with the same persistence and dignity that they had shown in previous years. The senators, however, assumed that their womenfolk were not seriously interested in suffrage. While suffragettes in western countries marched in rallies and carried placards, their Filipino counterparts resorted to tea parties.

But the National Federation of Women's Clubs, headed by Mrs. Pilar Hidalgo Lim, was just as concerned as the men over the possible outcome of the Hare-Hawes-Cutting Law. If a plebiscite was to be held, they felt entitled to a voice in it. "We are not below the men intellectually," said Mrs. Lim in a tactful understatement.[21] As a matter of fact, she had long proven her intellectual prowess as a U.P. mathematics professor of Mauro Mendez and Carlos P. Romulo.

A few enlightened senators were in favor of granting the vote to their wives and even to their mothers-in-law. But when the proposal was raised, the Senate shoved it aside once more and resumed its polemics over the Hare-Hawes-Cutting Law.

The Mendez-Mendez marriage of true minds immediately went to work. "Sumulat ka ng editorial!" said Pacita, and Mauro complied, producing seven of them between August and December 1933, to say nothing of other pro-women editorials written before that year and after. In a forceful *Monday Mail* editorial, he condemned the Filipino male's treatment of woman as a form of "benevolent slavery," "conceived in the fetishism of our aborigines, that she is a piece of property to have and to hold."[22]

A doublespread *Herald* editorial showed a man in a white suit, standing on the left side of the page, facing a woman in a *terno,* standing on the right side. The left column recited the typical masculine arguments against woman suffrage, and the right column was a point-by-point rebuttal.

The man argued that to allow woman to vote would be to "despoil" her of her feminine virtues, her Maria Clara purity. Her vote would merely duplicate those of her husband, her father, and her brother. She would be the cause of disputes on the political field, being a troublemaker by tradition. It was a woman who betrayed the Katipunan to the Spaniards. Adam lost his Paradise because of Eve.

The woman replied that the man's views were selfish and sentimental platitudes; that men had made a mess of their own politics; that their home finances would go to pieces without their wives' budgetary skills; that the Katipunan was betrayed by a man, not a woman; that Adam had not the strength of character to refuse an apple.

"You have educated us," argued the Filipina, "and yet you would deny us the reward of our education. . . . you would rather give to an unprincipled cochero the prerogatives that you deny us." [23]

Fortunately for the Filipino women, no plebiscite was held on the Hare-Hawes-Cutting Law, and they were saved the disgrace of being kept out of the voting booths. With the Law out of the way, the Senate now had the leisure to reconsider the suffrage bill. The first thing the senators did was to insert an amendment to the bill, providing that if it was passed into law, it would not be effective until four years later, in 1937 to be exact, unless special elections were held in the intervening time.

Although Mendez chided the Senate for its delaying tactics, the suffragettes were thrilled when Governor-General Murphy signed the bill into law on December 6, 1933. Among the ladies who put on their best ternos for the Malacañang ceremony were Mesdames Aurora Quezon, Pilar Hidalgo Lim, Pura Villanueva Kalaw, Asuncion Perez, Sofia de Veyra, Josefa Jara Martinez, and Josefa Llanes Escoda. Paz Policarpio Mendez refused to make a fuss over a long-delayed right, and chose to report for work at the U.P. that morning.

Governor Murphy signed the law with Mrs. de Veyra's pen at 11:07 a.m., and by some miraculous intervention of the stars, the cabinet clock in the room stopped ticking at that precise moment. When Murphy returned the pen to Mrs. de Veyra, she insisted that he keep it as a souvenir of the clock-stopping occasion. It was such a touching scene that Secretary Jorge Vargas was overwhelmed and contradicted himself: "Personally I am not in favor of the bill but I'm glad that the women are at last unshackled." [24]

The guests received commemorative badges with the compliments of the D-M-H-M newspapers. Mauro Mendez wrote "Our Women Triumphant" for the front page of the *Herald,* paying high tribute to the Filipino woman in history:

Symbolically, the Filipino woman has been the guardian of the nation's Key in our past history. Then Christianity came to give her the Prayer Book, and after the Prayer Book came the Book of Knowledge which opened before her eyes new horizons of understanding. Now, as the final testimony of our recognition comes the Ballot—the symbol of her rights and the standard of her ascendant role in the drama of our destiny.[25]

The Filipinas voted for the first time in 1935, when they ratified the constitution of the Commonwealth. Ironically, this same constitution took away their voting rights and made them fight the suffrage battle all over again. But that is another sad story.

VI

CONSTITUTION AND COALITION

Despite the financial vicissitudes of its different owners—Madrigal, Elizalde, Jorge Araneta—Mendez's years with the D-M-H-M syndicate were the most productive in his editorial career. Even without his byline, his trademarks were unmistakable: an incisive style spiced with humor and irony; historical resumés; scholarship without pedantry; literary allusions woven into the texture of his prose; and a passionate dedication to the common weal.

In April 1934, he wrote an essay on "The Mob in History," a doublespread editorial that moved an American in Cebu, who signed himself "The old man of the mountain," to write him a letter overflowing with praise.

The essay had been inspired by a protest march held by Mr. Mendez's pet peeve—the cocheros of Manila. In tracing the history of mob rule in various countries, Mendez conceded that democracy had its weaknesses, one of which was that it granted too much liberty to the individual, "and too much liberty is libertinism—parent of human disintegration." In the case of a dictatorship, the mob was the whole nation itself, bowing to an absolute power who was "more or less master of the situation." In a democracy, however, mobs could develop here and there without being controlled. In the Philippines the supreme example of the uncontrollable mob was the gang of cocheros who plied the streets of Manila.

Cocheros had been involved in many crimes and disorders, but there was no way of keeping track of them because they carried no licenses. In April 1934, a movement was begun to require them to register at the City Hall and to pay a moderate fee, in the same way that automobile drivers had to pay a fee before they could get their licenses. The proposal was backed by the community, but the cocheros banded together, defied City Hall, and demonstrated in the streets. "So the councilors capitulated," said Mendez, "and to this day our cocheros ply their trade with the privilege of not being known individually to our authorities for the convenience of law and order in this community."

Why did the municipal councilors give in? Because they were afraid to lose the cochero vote, said Mendez. "For if anything, the cochero vote was MOB VOTE, symbolizing the tyranny of a class over the general welfare of the City of Manila."[1]

After reading the editorial, the "old man of the mountain" wrote him this letter:

> Bravo! Mr. Editor for your fine editorial of April 25th on the "traffic cruelty" problem of the city of Manila.... Surely a few more editorials on "mob rule" like this one will cause Philippine posterity to rise and call you blessed indeed.
>
> We have personally noted your high-powered editorials the past year—Have sent some to the U.S.A. as proof of the caliber of the newspaper men of the Philippines. The editorial column together with a couple of your columnists—make your newspaper "first class." It is for this page I chiefly buy it. But this a la Brisbane even out Brisbanes him.... I say that in "power of expression and *true* idealism" you have no superior. I do not know who you are. It is enough that you possess that powerful weapon called the genius of inspiration which so surely can mould enlightened public opinion....
>
> I'm not so young anymore—and I wish I could join you in the great crusade for a clean, intelligent and efficient government.... But we are with you and salute you.

The Ideal Democracy

Part of the Mendez crusade for a "clean, intelligent, and efficient government" was a series of about 60 editorials on the constitutional theme, written between June 1934 and May 1935. His objectives were to encourage a nonpartisan election of convention delegates, to acquaint the citizenry with the significance of framing the constitution, to comment on the various provisions while they were being drafted into the document, and finally, to urge the Filipino people to ratify the finished product.

Notwithstanding his hatred of mob rule, his first suggestion to the Constitutional Assembly was that they design a government in line with the Jeffersonian dictum that that government is best which governs least:

> Without any desire on our part to tell the delegates to the Constitutional Assembly what to do, we would suggest that the ideal democracy for this country is that in which there will be little government and abundant trust in the initiative of our citizens.
>
> An elaborate government system is not compatible with public efficiency. Common man resents too much interference. He wants simple justice and simple dealing. Legalistic red tape is repugnant to his temper.[2]

Mendez believed that the most direct bearing of the constitution on the Filipino people lay in Article III, or the Bill of Rights, which stipulated that no man was to be deprived of his life, liberty or property without due process of law; that the sanctity of his home would not be violated; that he would enjoy freedom of speech and the right to petition for redress of grievances; that he would enjoy liberty of conscience without interference from others; that he would not be imprisoned for debt or subject to any form of involuntary servitude. "It is the freedom that makes of his home his castle—the castle in which, no matter how poor he may be, he is the sole knight and his own master."[3]

A Unilateral Peace Pact

The only thing that disturbed Mendez in the deliberations of the convention delegates was what he called their "anti-war emotionalism." He thought it was unrealistic and even pathetic of them to include in the constitution a categorical renunciation of war "as an instrument of national policy." The phrase was borrowed from the Kellogg Pact of 1928, a grandiose and ineffective multilateral agreement to outlaw war.

First of all, said Mendez, a renunciation of war would tie the hands of the nation in the future, when war might be either necessary or inevitable. Secondly—and this was the pathetic part—an antiwar proclamation from a weak country was superfluous, for obvious reasons:

> ...it goes without saying that if a country like Belgium, for instance, or Siam, or the future Philippine Republic, should assure the world that it wants no war, the world would believe it. The assurance in such a case is the condition itself—the condition of weakness, in the military sense, that makes aggression impossible.

To offset possible charges that he was a warmonger, Mendez clarified the distinction between a constitution and society, between dream and reality:

> This is not a defense of war, but it is necessary that we understand that the forces producing war are not within the orbit of a *magna charta*. A constitution is one thing and society is another. The former embodies the architecture of government and the ideology of that government; the latter is something vital—the organism of the people's dynamic force.
> ...To make it [the Constitution] the symbol of our dreaming would be to write it into puerility. And what, in the light of contemporary tendencies, is a declaration against war in general but an idle dream?[4]

But nondelegate Mendez was overruled, and the constitutional convention went ahead with its renunciation of war. Mendez reacted with a concise satire labelling the antiwar declaration a "Unilateral Peace Pact," a "stupendous" repudiation of tradition that went far ahead of England's Magna Charta, the American Constitution, and France's Declaration of the Rights of Man.

> An assembly of Filipino constitutional delegates, with one dash of the pen, has declared the millenium. What no nation has done, except perhaps in peace treaties that have turned out to be "scraps of paper," we have done. There shall be no war, as far as this Pearl of the Orient is concerned, and that is all.
> The lame renounces his right to run in a race, the blind to swap blows with a prizefighter. For the same reason, the man who is unarmed solemnly declares to his foe, who is armed, that he does not like fighting. All of which are obvious, and

our delegates, in writing as obvious a fact as our helplessness in our constitution, have written our unilateral peace pact.[5]

Tilting at Windmills

The ratification of the constitution on May 14, 1935, paved the way for the election of officials who were to head the Commonwealth government. Quezon, of course, had made up his mind to become President. Rather than run the risk of being defeated by the Os-Rox camp, he invited Osmeña to become his running mate. In June, Quezon's Partido Nacionalista Democrata and Osmeña's Partido Nacionalista Democrata Pro-Independencia joined hands in a coalition party, thereby putting an end to the tongue-twisting distinction between them.

The election results were intriguing, to say the least. Osmeña polled 117,000 more votes than Quezon, leading even the non-Cebuanos to wonder what would have happened if Osmeña had run for President on his own ticket.

What made the political scenario interesting, however, was not the coalition victory but the tragic-comic overtones of the opposition's defeat. General Emilio Aguinaldo provided the tragedy, and Bishop Gregorio Aglipay supplied the comedy. Mauro Mendez functioned as narrator and commentator—a one-man Greek chorus, as it were—with some of the most pungent prose to emerge from his typewriter.

The T-V-T either maintained a discreet silence or limited its political editorials to bland and indifferent remarks. The *Tribune* was then more actively involved in a campaign of a feminine sort, the T-V-T-sponsored Women's First National Popularity Contest. Among the leading contenders were Mrs. Aurora Quezon, Mrs. Alicia Quirino, Mrs. Aurora Recto, Dr. Fe del Mundo, and Mrs. Carmen A. Melencio. The winner was the charming Mrs. Melencio, and her prize was a round-trip ticket to China and Japan.[6]

On the other hand, Mrs. Melencio's father, General Aguinaldo, was making his last trip down the political highway. Even before the ratification of the constitution, the General had made it known that he intended to run for the presidency on a platform of "complete and immediate independence." The birth of the new opposition, the Partido Filipinista of the *Veteranos de la Revolucion,* was announced with the unfurling of the revolutionary flag and the proclamation of the magic Aguinaldo name.

Unlike its T-V-T counterpart, the editorial department of the D-M-H-M annotated the presidential race with enthusiasm. Mendez opened the drama on April 11, 1935, with a prologue entitled "The Historic Present."

> It is said that when elephants are dead, they still remain standing. We have no way of verifying the truth of this belief because we happen to live in latitudes not inhabited by pachyderms, but we know that we have men in this country who think they can stand on their feet and command the electorate, even when they are politically dead.

This was not an attack on the General's age, for Mendez had always believed in arguing on the basis of principles rather than personalities. He knew that one defeat at the polls was no guarantee of political death: "the repudiated man can live again by the miracle of new principles that are capable of moving the passionate multitudes."

But Aguinaldo's battlecry was as out of date as Patrick Henry's "Give me liberty or give me death!" The Tydings-McDuffie Law was a *fait accompli,* and Aguinaldo's pledge to shorten the ten-year transition period to three years was, in Mendez's words, "tilting at the windmills of long-forgotten sentiments."[7] What the Commonwealth would need was a concrete program of economic survival during the transition period, not a quixotic return to the past via an emblem that belonged in the nation's museum. Aguinaldo went barnstorming through the Islands with the historic flag, and Mendez feared that curious spectators, by repeatedly handling it, would turn it into a rag.[8]

Mendez posed the following questions to the sentimentalists who viewed the Aguinaldo formula as "the very lamp of Aladdin":

> Can the splendors of our Revolutions yield to us the magic formula of solution to our problems of today? Can a relic alone of our epic yesterday perform the wonder of organizing the Filipino nation out of its present difficult circumstances?
>
> We have figures of venerable faces who played their part with courage in that great conflagration of energy remembered in our history as our Revolution. That was forty years ago. Now, does it follow that the warriors of forty years ago are the statesmen of this day?

> Every period in a people's life is more or less a transition. The change is perpetual in the vital currents of a nation, and the eternity of no human institution is guaranteed. Art, politics, philosophy, tradition are going through an endless process of transformation.
>
> No man can live in the past and be with us in a historic sense, for life does not mean isolation in an island of Time, and History is nothing if not progressive. We cannot remain rigid against the everchanging circumstances of the cosmic world.[9]

Instead of helping his cause, Aguinaldo's image-makers succeeded in making him look ridiculous. His campaign manager insinuated that when the General underwent an appendectomy some years before, someone had attempted to "eliminate" him by leaving a roll of gauze in his interior. The satirist in Mendez rose to the occasion, treating the incident with overblown gravity as a question of "deep historic interest." Who had tried to kill the General?

> His rivals of revolutionary fame had themselves long been eliminated. When the famous Aguinaldo appendix was removed, those rivals were already in marble—Bonifacio, sword in hand, in the act of uttering the First Cry, and Luna, with folded arms, looking down upon his smaller contemporaries with doubt in his eyes.
>
> As for Apolinario Mabini, the Sublime Paralytic, whose voice has that insistent power of addressing our consciences from the depths of the Past, in the midst of our selfish ambitions of the present, he also had already long been dead.[10]

Dissatisfied with the way the campaign was being run, some of the General's leaders deserted him one by one. But the show had to go on, and the assassination theme had to be pursued to its logical conclusion. Barely a week before the election curtain rang down, the stage resounded with threats from the Aguinaldo wing that Quezon was not going to be elected President in spite of his sure victory. An *Aguinaldista* was planning to assassinate him[11]—whether with a pistol or with a roll of gauze, nobody knew.

After waiting in vain for Aguinaldo to issue a formal denial of the threat, Mendez repaired to his typewriter for a dissertation on terrorist tactics and the "politics of despair":

We must bear in mind that we are not living under a military dictatorship. The assassinations recorded in our history were perpetrated during a regime of war. The victims were defenseless; the dictator had his way.

x x x x x x x x

What punishment could there be for the assassins of Bonifacio and Luna? What courts of justice could have tried them for their cowardly acts? And who was the judge to impose on them the sentence of the law?

The peculiar privilege of a dictator, added Mendez, is that he may turn lawless without having to account for his acts. He must answer only to his conscience, a conscience hidden in the most infinite recesses of his being. He suffers alone; ghosts of his dark past haunt him even in the morning light, and nobody sees them but himself. "The ghost of Banquo appeared only for Macbeth."

Under a civil regime, however, a repetition of the Bonifacio and Luna episodes would surely land the assassins in Bilibid's electric chair. Mendez suggested that the culprits proceed with their attempt to repeat history. "Perhaps the men who have not paid for those crimes will pay at last." For, as Macbeth himself realized, "walang utang na hindi pinagbayaran."[12] ("No debt is ever unpaid.")

Murder in the Independent Church

One presidential aspirant who was not afraid of Bilibid prison was Bishop Gregorio Aglipay, candidate of the newly created Republican Party. "I will instruct my men to murder election inspectors who commit frauds," announced the holy man. "I am willing to enter Bilibid for a just and worthy cause."[13]

"From Pulpit to Soap-Box" was how Mendez described the Bishop's descent into the political arena, a realm where angels usually feared to tread.[14]

Aglipay pledged his efforts to save the nation from a "despotic administration" and to chop off the "tentacles of the bureaucratic octopus that oppresses our national life."

"A Theseus out to slay a horrid Minotaur," observed the *Herald* editor admiringly.[15]

Aglipay: "I want an independence that will make us all happy."

Mendez: "The independence that will make us all happy is one which will make us forget all our responsibilities. All we have to do is elect Bishop Aglipay: Providence will take care of the rest."[16]

To be sure, Aglipay was perhaps the first to see the humor of his situation. As Mendez himself admitted, the Monsignor was a "jolly fellow."

> His antics, his utterances are entertaining. He regales his hearers with good cracks; they laugh, they cheer; the bishop feels success; and the morning after the night before, he issues a statement to the press assuring himself of victory.

For showmanship, Mendez compared Aglipay to the great Charlie Chaplin, who made the largest income in Hollywood by "tickling humanity's ribs." The difference was that Chaplin was not a candidate for the presidency of the U.S.A.[17]

Pilots of the Ship of State

Mendez dropped the comic irony whenever he wrote of his candidates for the leadership of the Commonwealth. He interpreted the Quezon-Osmeña alliance as a "truce" and as a refusal to quarrel over a "dessicated issue." Together, the "men of the hour" were "determined to pilot the Commonwealth ship of state through the unsettled weather of its maiden voyage."[18]

It was unnecessary for Mendez to duplicate the pro-Quezon overkill of the Hare-Hawes-Cutting era. "A statesman needs no dramatization," he wrote, "because he stands on his own merits." Without waving a flag or shedding a tear, Quezon laid his plan before the electorate: a program of social reform and spartan self-discipline during the transition decade.[19]

A little more editorial drumbeating was called for in the Osmeña case, for he was a transplant from the defeated minority of the Partido Nacionalista. What weighed heavily in his favor was his role in the country's postrevolutionary efforts to regain its self-respect. In Mendez's editorial, "Statesmen of Peace," he pointed out that Aguinaldo had delivered the country into the imperialists' hands in 1901 as a tribute to "American magnanimity," and then had gone into retirement, only to re-emerge in 1935 to "banish American tyranny." Quezon and

Osmeña, on the other hand, had given themselves, "body and soul, to the conquest of difficulties inherent in a colonial existence."

In his appreciative analysis of Osmeña's acceptance speech, Mendez reviewed the events of the 37 years that had gone by since the collapse of the Revolution: the slow grant of civil rights, the bumpy road to autonomy, the struggle for a definite independence measure that would replace the vague promises of the Jones Law. Osmeña was among the statesmen who played a great role in overcoming those difficulties:

> The political struggle has been long and at times bitter, but our men went into it with grit and fervor. Prejudice had to be overcome; misrepresentation had to be fought—the kind of misrepresentation that pictured the very leaders of our Revolution as so many bandits and the Filipinos as savages in G-strings. This unfortunate propaganda is a thing of the past, but what finally defeated it was not the silence of the survivors of 1898's disaster, but the labors of our statesmen of peace.
>
> Senator Osmeña's acceptance is a plea for these statesmen of peace, who seek no vainglory but merely the recognition of just minds. . . . We of the present have lived with them through the decisive crises of our political struggle, and what is more, we know that they have not deserted us in our difficulties.[20]

On the eve of the elections, the *Tribune*'s doublespread editorial reminded the people to vote, but not whom to vote for. The *Herald*'s "Last Call," meanwhile, was a bit of eleventh-hour politicking for a crucial cause:

> Nothing counts in the last analysis but the intelligent vote. The ballot cast for the mountebank is an instrument the voter turns against himself; it is not merely wasted but employed to undermine the foundations of good government. It is not his right alone that the citizen outrages when he votes for the wrong man deliberately, but the right of his nation as well to exact loyalty from him as a citizen.[21]

Having accepted a clearly defined program of self-government under a constitution of their own making, the people intended to push it through. Such was the basis of Mendez's candid hint that the victory of the coalition superstars was a foregone conclusion.

The first to congratulate the champions for their sensational success, even in the traditionally oppositionist city of Manila, was Bishop Aglipay. Mendez gave him an editorial pat on the back for his sportsmanship, remarking that the Monsignor had "transfigured himself in the public eye." Aguinaldo, however, behaved "like Rip Van Winkle," except that unlike the protagonist of that famous legend, the General refused to believe that he had overslept. He insisted that he had been tricked, and demanded that his charges of election frauds be transmitted to President Roosevelt.[22]

Despite threats of revolution from the *Veteranos* in Kawit, Cavite, the inauguration of the Philippine Commonwealth took place peacefully on November 15, 1935.

VII

THE COMMUNIST BEAR HUG

Filipino literature in English bloomed at a prolific rate during the fifteen-year period immediately preceding the Second World War. Contemporary critics have noted, however, that prewar fiction in general is detached from the socio-political realities of its time, somewhat like Amorsolo paintings of the planting season viewed through the rosy haze of his palette.[1]

For insights into the era's sordid side, expressed in a literary medium, one would have to leave fiction and turn to journalism. Mauro Mendez's editorials, for instance, were written in the thick of the crises, especially during the economic depression of the early thirties. Among the issues that disturbed him most deeply were peasant unrest and the threat of Communist subversion.

Detente in '33

Communism was then a global monolith dominated by the heavy hand of the Soviet Union. Filipino delegates had attended Communist-sponsored labor conferences in Canton and Moscow, and groups of Filipino worker-pensionados had undergone indoctrination at Moscow's University of Toilers of the East.[2]

For a while, Mendez was confident that Communism would never take root in the Philippine Islands, despite the activities of propagandists who preached "the paradise of a Soviet state" among farmers and factory workers. He thought that Filipinos could easily discern the tattered "scarecrow" cloaked in Red rhetoric. In the first place, the Filipino farmers and laborers, unlike the prerevolutionary Russian peasants, could appeal to a democratic government for redress of grievances against oppressive landlords and employers. In the second place, the Filipino's family values, his religious upbringing, and his attachment to his possessions would inhibit him from swallowing the "quack nostrums" of Communism.[3]

Mendez was aware, however, that the "doctrines of Sovietism as transfigured in the language of their apostles" were destined to thrive in the fertile soil of poverty. What he deplored was the way "the shadow of the red flag of violence" appeared wherever there was human distress.[4] It appeared in Cuba in 1933 while that island was in the throes of a political convulsion. "And shall we shut our eyes to the Red threat that is sweeping the plains and cities of tortured China?" he asked.[5]

In spite of his anti-Communist sentiments, Mendez applauded the news that diplomatic relations between the United States and the Soviet Union were to be renewed after 16 years of alienation. First of all, he reasoned, the Russians constituted "a big branch of the human family" and could not, as such, "be ignored without seriously unbalancing the universal equation." The second and greater advantage lay in Moscow's promise to observe the ethics of international relations and to desist from "its underhanded methods of exploiting the discontent of the masses." The new atmosphere of frankness and tolerance would make Communism less appealing to those who were attracted to its hidden delights.[6]

Recognition of Soviet Union, he continued, did not mean that capitalism would soften its stand against Bolshevism. Rather, the capitalistic world might "correct its own methods to meet what may be reasonable in the Soviet formula of social welfare, while at the same time allowing the ludicrous and fantastic claims of that formula to follow their natural course to inevitable discredit."[7]

When Washington and Moscow formally reopened diplomatic relations in November 1933, the *Herald* celebrated the occasion with a stirring editorial, "Hands Across the Sea." Mendez saw the historic handshake as the beginning of a "new era in international affairs," a clearing up of a horizon which had been "blurred by the clouds of misunderstanding" since the overthrow of the Czars in 1917.

He regarded that overthrow as one of the inevitable events in the history of mankind:

> The conspiracy which ended in the slaughter of the Czar and his family was the conspiracy of the common people, of the

masses of the Russian population who had groaned under the lash of a profligate Aristocracy. It was a conspiracy which had been gathering momentum in every street corner of Moscow and St. Petersburg, in the prisons and the St. Helenas of political offenders, in the hives of oppressed laborers, where the Trotskys and the Lenins and the Stalins of Marx the Prophet preached their doctrines at the peril of their lives.[8]

This viewpoint was unusually sympathetic, coming as it did from an avowed anti-Stalinist who loved the literature of Chekhov and Tolstoy, and who mourned the growing callousness of the "sentimental Russian soul." But Mendez had always had a soft spot for the downtrodden. Reading some of his pro-labor editorials, one would have thought that he was a potential Communist. For example:

> The mental horizons of our laboring classes are expanding daily. Our workingmen are developing a consciousness quite the opposite of the sense of property of our capitalist class. This consciousness will be a driving force in a fight for new rights, perhaps the attainment of that Marxian ideal of men's common ownership of the earth and their common right to the management of public enterprises.[9]

Glad Tidings for Labor

Ever since his *Tribune* days, Mendez had advocated the creation of a labor portfolio in the Cabinet, and when the lower house proposed such a department in 1933, he supported the proposal with all the eloquence at his command. When the Eight-Hour Labor Law and the Labor Compensation Act were passed in November 1933, he wrote several jubilant editorials on the benefits that labor would enjoy. One editorial concluded on this triumphant note:

> The Legislature...has set the pace for the emancipation of our masses from ignorance and penury. It has raised the banner of Labor as against the absolute rule of Capital. It has served notice that henceforth the workingman in the Philippines shall not groan under his employer's feet.[10]

For several months Mendez remained in the optimistic mood of "Hands Across the Sea." He continued to think that with Russia keeping her part of the agreement with the United States, the "Red

Menace" in the Philippines would die a natural death, and that "law-abiding Labor" and "enlightened Capital" would coexist in peace forever.

In this idealistic frame of mind he objected when the Constabulary commander in Iloilo ordered the seizure of all red flags displayed by labor leaders during a parade in February 1934. Mendez reasoned that the Philippines was bound by its colonial ties to adopt the American government's official attitude toward Moscow. He believed that laborers should be allowed to parade the streets with as many red flags as they could carry; however, these flags were to be "understood properly as symbolizing no longer a revolt against the government but rather as a standard serving only to identify a certain school of political thought."[11]

In April of that year Governor-General Murphy ordered the parole of three Bilibid prisoners who had been convicted for being Communist agitators. In the same benevolent mood, Mendez suggested that other prisoners serving terms for the same offense be paroled as soon as possible. His argument, again, was that the government policy under which those convictions had been obtained needed revision in the light of the new relationship between the United States and the Soviet Republic. "If these agitators who have just been paroled are made to understand Moscow's pledge of honor, they will cease preaching violence, although they may still remain Communists if that is their desire."[12]

To his surprise, the three prisoners refused to be paroled. He then realized that they intended to renew their subversive activities as soon as they had served their sentences. Surprise turned to indignation. "To them," wrote Mendez, "it does not mean anything that the Soviet government has pledged its word not to disturb America's peace with the wild doctrines of its propagandists; it means little to them that as a possession of the United States, we come under the terms of the Soviet-American agreement."[13]

It took a strike at La Minerva Cigar Factory in 1934 to make the *Herald* editor lose all his illusions about Moscow's honor system.

The Sovietization of Labor

Mendez was not against strikes per se. He admitted that they were necessary in order to bring "predatory interests" back to their senses.[14] However, he distinguished between a strike by laborers with a valid cause, and a strike fomented by Communist rabble-rousers. The August–September strike at La Minerva Cigar Factory, led by Communist Pedro Ocampo, belonged in the second category. Its aim, according to Mendez, was to prove to Moscow that Philippine labor was on its way to being "successfully Sovietized." He quoted an April broadcast to Communists all over the world, calling for "sixteen weeks of intensive demonstrations and strike agitation to culminate in a general strike on August 16," the very day that the Minerva strike began.[15] The strike instigators made no secret of the fact that they had received funds from Shanghai, which funds had in turn been supplied by Moscow. The Philippine government had acquired translated copies of leaflets openly calling for the overthrow of both capital and the state. Unknown to Mendez, the local Communists had also been receiving aid and comfort from the American Communist Party.[16]

The Philippine cigar industry was then suffering from the depression that had affected all other industries. To make things worse, American cigar manufacturers had opened a campaign for curtailment of cigar importations from the Philippines. In view of the situation, Mendez could see no logic in a suicidal strike. He had previously stressed that because labor had a right to share in the profits of capital, "it must also suffer the consequences of industrial failures ... it is labor's concern as much as capital's that the world's industrial advancement should continue without any serious disturbance."[17]

But since Sovietization thrived on serious disturbances, the strike dragged on through wind and rain. Secretary of Labor Ramon Torres appealed to the strikers to submit their grievances to his department instead of to their Communist sympathizers, but to no avail. The Manila Tobacco Association, on the other hand, refused to recognize the Communists who tried to sponsor the strikers' demands.

Tired of walking the streets with empty stomachs, some of the strikers trickled back to work at the end of August. La Minerva then decided to increase their salaries, but this development only incensed the remaining strikers. Despite the Governor-General's appointment of a neutral mediation board, violence erupted on September 17 between the strikers and the policemen on guard at the factory premises. Four of the strikers were killed, and 17 others, including ten policemen, were wounded.

One of the wounded men was a non-striker whose abdomen had been penetrated by a bullet. Upon being interviewed by a *Tribune* reporter, he revealed that he had traveled all the way from a Laguna barrio after reading in the *Taliba* that "the poor laborers were not fairly treated by the capitalists." He had gone to the Mehan Gardens, where the strikers had assembled for a tempestuous meeting, and he had followed the marchers to the factory on Azcarraga. "I did not know there was going to be fighting," he told his interviewer.[18]

Mendez blamed the "Irresponsible Press" for aggravating "class enmity" among the people. He pointed to the September 19 *Taliba*, which had as its banner headline, "IPAGHIHIGANTI ANG MGA PATAY." ("The dead will be avenged.") At the top of the page, in smaller type, was another banner: "HIHIGPITAN NA ANG KILOS NG MGA WELGISTA.") ("Strikers' movements to be placed under strict control.") With inflammatory headlines such as these, it was not surprising that the provinciano had rushed to the city to aid his fellowmen. In the seclusion of his barrio his only connection with the outside world was his vernacular paper. As Mendez pointed out:

> Daily he has been fed by this newspaper with stories and editorials that make him feel he can not trust the government, that the government is in the hands of plunderers, and that the courts of justice are a mockery and a farce. Daily he has brooded over what has been pictured as his hopeless situation, and daily his grievances, fancied though they are, have grown to greater proportions the more he ponders over them after reading the daily outpourings of his vernacular paper.[19]

During the violence of September 17, the Communist leaders escaped from the scene of the strike. Their absence enabled the Secretary of Labor to reconcile labor and management, at least for the time being. Three days after the riot, the cigar makers returned to their cigars.

The funeral for the four dead strikers was attended by a crowd estimated at 10,000 and a wary police escort of 300. The mourners waved red flags, and the women wore nonfunereal red. A few days later, Pedro Ocampo, the "riot-and-run Communist," as Mendez called him, was captured personally by the famous General Basilio Valdes.[20]

Crusade against Communism

In the absence of a governmental instrument with which to combat "insidious propaganda," Mendez proposed the appointment of a Director of Public Information who would be in charge "not only of guiding public opinion along the safe paths of democracy but of detecting such opinion as may endanger that democracy." He cited Pedro Ocampo as an example of the "actual danger of the uncontrolled demagogue to our common tranquility... a man who abused his liberties at the cost of the lives of four strikers and the blood of many others."[21]

An Office of Public Information would be responsible for enlightening the laborers on the Communistic way of life:

> Perhaps the best way to show our laborers the futility of Communism is to enlighten them on its propagandized merits that they may judge those merits themselves. Perhaps it would be well to open their eyes to the peculiar fact that Communism has to make its way through our social order in an insidious way, that like a disease it must develop treacherously through our system until it attains its ends with the death of that system.[22]

In Mendez's crusade against Communism, one of his goals was to promote better relations between labor and capital by constantly reminding them that each would be lost without the other. Although he wrote more editorials in behalf of labor, he interspersed them with praise of capital—"the kind of Capital that has vision, not the kind that is self-centered and avaricious," the capital that considers labor as its "indispensable partner in the promotion of our common prosperity."[23]

Mendez also ridiculed Moscow's claim that as the godmother of Communist parties around the world, she was entitled to their eternal homage. In November 1934, the Third Internationale of Moscow celebrated the thirteenth anniversary of the Bolshevist revolution by appealing to the world's proletariat to unite in a "solid front against capitalism." Another Utopian dream, scoffed Mendez as he predicted a clash between nationalism and proletarian internationalism:

> Will Japanese be loyal to Russia and turn their backs on their Mikado? Will Germans abandon their watch on the Rhine and watch the Volga instead?

What Messiah is this co-called Third Internationale to draw all the "toilers" of the world into one union transcending racial frontiers and overcoming all sentiments of patriotism?

Even religion, he continued, the only force that should have united all of mankind in one bond of love, had "never been strong enough to overcome the nationalistic embitterments that beset the world." How presumptuous of the "prophet Marx" to think that his doctrine of class hatred, "implacable and harsh," could succeed in doing what the "Galilean gospel of peace and good-will" had not yet accomplished.[24]

Late in 1934 a report from Moscow disclosed that leading officials of the government's textile trust had embezzled huge amounts of money by manipulating their books. Ironically, the same embezzlers had previously been rewarded for being efficient public servants. Mendez cited this incident as proof of "What the Bolsheviks Forgot," namely, that the "proletariat is made up not of angels but of men, and that... given the same facilities that the capitalist enjoys, the workingman can be as venal as his employer." By making the state "the supreme capitalist," the Soviet system had fallen into the same errors of the capitalist system that it condemned. The advantage of a democratic government was that there was "a higher state to check the abuses of the capitalist system."[25]

The abuses of the Soviet system, however, continued unchecked. Such a situation was fraught with danger for a totalitarian ruler like Josef Stalin, Mendez pointed out. "The great mistake of the tyrant who suppresses public opinion is that he deprives himself of the only means of knowing whether his subjects obey him because they have faith in him, or whether they simply submit to him in fear."[26]

Finally, Mendez attacked the Marxist cliché that the state would wither away under conditions of perfect equality among men. Equality was possible only in a juridical sense; in a social and absolute sense, it was an absurdity. No country could eliminate ranks unless it was a "hopelessly plebeian" "underdog's country."[27]

Cooling the Hotbeds of Discontent

But Mendez knew that no amount of counterpropaganda would help the government's cause unless it carried out a long-range program for the amelioration of the masses. He wrote many editorials prodding the authorities to alleviate the misery in the slums, those "hotbeds of discontent...where human bitterness is in eternal ferment."[28] He attributed the restlessness of the populace to the "drudgery, the penury, and the lack of light in the social depths. Poverty is the greatest enemy of organized society."[29]

For the sake of the peasantry, he recommended the breaking up of large estates and public lands and the encouragement of homesteads for small farmers:

> Our soil is our common inheritance, and our duty is to ensure for every one who may feel the inclination, his own small farm to cultivate for his benefit and for the common wealth. That would be not only ensuring the stability of the great mass of our people but stabilizing the foundations of our economic system.[30]

Still another object of his campaign against social evils was the eradication of usury. This was the same practice that had aroused young Mendez's wrath, when, at the age of 19, he had published his vehement poem, *Who Are the Usurers?* ("The greedy vampire of the poor," "Shylocks vile," etc.) Two decades later, the usurers were still thriving, and Mendez, now 39, was still fuming over "the heartless Shylocks who reign supreme over our people who are in need."[31]

Lastly, Mendez reminded the wealthy class that unless it mended its selfish ways, it would have only itself to blame for a Communist take-over. "The distressed men and women who are driven to Communism are not of the arguing class," he warned. "They believe what they see, and that is all." He therefore asked the rich to stop the social extravaganzas that could only "suggest to the common man's mind the enrichment of a few and the impoverishment of the anonymous crowd.... It is up to Wealth itself to correct the impression that it is the cause of Poverty."[32]

Mauro Mendez as pensive U.P. graduate. (1918)

Tribune *staff members and foreign guests at panciteria. From right, counterclockwise: Manuel Villa-Real, Pedro Aunario, Carlos P. Romulo, guest, Alejandro Roces, Jr., guest, Lawrence Thibault, Mauro Mendez, guest, and unidentified newsman. (Late 1920s)*

Mauro Mendez in his office at D-M-H-M Publications. (1934)

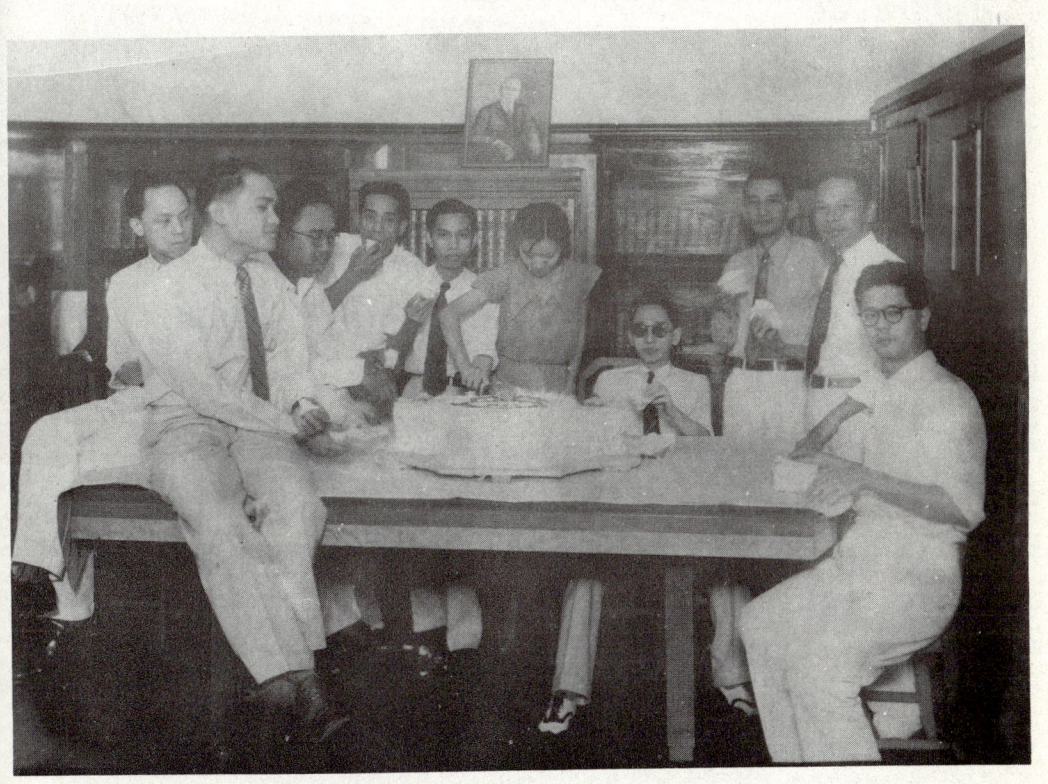

Staff of Philippines Herald *enjoying someone's birthday cake. From left, clockwise:* **Salvador P. Lopez, Jose A. Lansang, Sr., Jesus Ma. Intengan, Vicente Ferrer, Fortunato Gupit, Enriqueta David Perez, Vicente Albano Pacis,** *unidentified newsman,* **Modesto Farolan, and Mauro Mendez.** *(1935)*

PAGE 14 — THE TRIBUNE: FRIDAY, SEPTEMBER 2, 1932

A Tribune Editorial

The Salariat

So the People Ma Know

There is a term in modern sociology that is used to describe what was in other times known as the landless, the masterless—something typifying complete dispossession; total lack of property, of assets, of all resources but those of body and mind.

The word-coiners who have been proclaiming a new social order as a panacea for all earthly ills have gone back to ancient Rome for the designation of this class, and have called it the *proletariat*.

It was not a happy thought. The proletarius of the noisome alleys of the Rome of the Caesars was regarded as the lowest and meanest of the destitute, whose fault lay not in his destitution, which was a misfortune, but in the remarkable preference he showed for the squalor and vice that are the concomitants of poverty, and in his flat refusal to try and raise himself out of his environment. It is a term that could scarcely, with justice, be applied to the laborer of today, who always has his eye on the well-being beyond his daily squalor, to which his children, if not he, will in time attain.

But the word has become *synonymous*, rightly or wrongly, with a class—the class of the poor whom, the *scriptures say*, we shall always have with us.

Mankind grows, and its life, individually and in the mass, becomes daily more complex. New types, new classes are evolved. Under the exigencies of modern civilization a new class has arisen in all advanced countries, among them the Philippines. This class we may call, for our purposes, the "**salariat**."

As modern libertarian thought movements progressed, it has become the custom to represent the *proletariat*, in rags, its back bowed under the burden of the whole structure of humanity.

Amorsolo, in the illustration on this page, depicts the newest application of the same idea—no less true because of its newness.

Instead of the staggering wage-slave, with the globe borne Atlas-like on his bowed back, the artist has shown us what is an infinitely more immediately true picture; that of the government salary-slave, supporting on his shoulders the massive structures that represent the complex bureaucratic government to be found in every nation in the world today, not excluding the Philippines.

Let us digress a moment and see what it is that has brought this newly-created class, this salariat, into prominence among us today.

There is before the legislators of our land the important problem of the reorganization of government. The topheavy structure which in times of prosperity we have built must be better balanced. There must be a better proportion established between the base and the tower. To this end, it seems, we are planning to cut both at the base and at the tower.

In other words, we are planning to abolish posts in our government, both at the top and at the bottom, without considering that the elimination of a few ornate cornices and capitols might detract from the appearance of the building, but that the taking away of a proportionate number of foundation stones will endanger its stability and the safety of its inhabitants.

It is in connection with this proposed shifting of the materials of which our government structure is built that the salariat figures most prominently.

Now, as distinguished from the proletariat, what is the salariat?

Here we have, not the unthinking mob of the destitute, easily led by platitude-mouthing demagogues, but a class composed of intelligent, well-informed men, trained for the work they do and for no other, and, above all, loyal to the principles and traditions of the body which they serve —the government.

And it is approximately two thousand of such men that it is contemplated to turn out into the streets.

Every class in a nation fills a definite place in that nation. What is the place filled by the Salariat in the Philippines? Without going into a detailed discussion of the subject, we can safely say, we believe, that the place is a most important one.

Our people is mainly agricultural, with an upper crust, if we may call it that, of wealth. Between the two, and forming the cement which binds them together, is this class of the salariat, mostly risen from the foundation layer of the farmers. In all countries which have attained success, it was the middle class that was responsible. That is a fact that needs no further demonstration.

The salariat is the strong, substantial, conservative middle class of the Philippines.

It is the class, as long as it remains a class, that stands for order and stability. It is the class that sticks most closely to its traditions of family, of a decent respect for the forms of life, for the edicts of the law. It is the class that is distinguished for its unfailing loyalty to constituted authority. It is the class least likely to be affected by subversive doctrines spread by irresponsible, self-seeking demagogues. It is the class on the loyalty of which the government as at present constituted can always depend.

And it is the class which it is now proposed to break up, by throwing a goodly portion of it into the streets, and by demoralizing the fragment which will remain.

It is proposed, in short, to take away from it the belief in the soundness and stability of the government to which it has consecrated its existence.

Let us consider an example of such a class, broken by the exigencies of a change in government, by the rigors of an economic debacle.

We have seen many important social movements of late. We have seen the proletarian aroused in a nation of 160 millions, and we have watched that nation go from the tyranny of an autocracy to the oppression of an autocratic class.

We have, on the other hand, seen a class of salaried men, the equivalent of our own "salariat," unite under the leadership of a forceful character, and bring a great nation to the verge of civil war, because the gods by which they stood, the traditions which they loyally maintained, were shattered before them.

The Nazi movement in Germany is not a movement of the proletariat. In sharp opposition to the Bolshevist movement of Russia, it is the embodied protest of a middle class, once strong in its support of a government which stood by it—now equally strong in its determination to get its rights. And it is not the unthinking surging of a demagogue-led mob. It is the considered, determined drive of intelligent men, who feel that only by following a demagogic personality along lines of violence, if need be, can they have their rights restored to them.

This is what a strong middle class, when it has lost its feeling of loyalty to constituted authority, can do. Six thousand men, literate, thinking, intelligent men, with families dependent on them, devoted to a government, cannot without serious menace to that government be thrown out of employment by the government which they have served the greater part of their adult lives.

From the beginning, the TRIBUNE has advocated what it has sincerely believed to be a proper and just reduction of government expenses, and with it, an equitable reduction of government salaries. From that stand it has not receded, nor does it recede.

We have advocated drastic cuts in the excessive salaries of the higher government officials. The government has effected cuts in the salaries of all officials and employees.

Although we have gone on record as opposing reductions in the salaries of the lower-paid employes, we concede that there was a real necessity for it. In this we are supported by the victims of the reduction themselves. It was no less an authority than Governor General Roosevelt who called attention to the praiseworthy attitude of all the government personnel in the face of the forced cut.

But precisely because of this attitu the part of every government servant, the ₱12,000-a-year department secreta the ₱40-a-month clerk, we believe tha lawmakers, in their laudable scheme reorganizing the government, should tate before lopping off activities and b ing up a class of loyal, conservative, d ed citizens which it has taken a gener to build up.

Because, once destroyed, that class not for many generations be rebuilt; a the meantime, it may form a powerfu telligent nucleus for a movement th fects of which may be far-reaching not in a pleasant sense.

We have heard much of the need of a stron anced middle class in our citizenry. We have hear parisons between the Philippines and other cou We have bewailed the lack of such a class, becau have had no group of solid, responsible farmers or men or merchants to constitute it.

And all the time under our very such a class was quietly, unobtrus building itself. Now that it is built, trying to break it down.

We do not believe that the 6,000 governmen ployes whom it is proposed to oust will unite to group for the purpose of attacking the governmen believe that their patriotism and loyalty will be against the call of the agitator.

But we do believe that in justice to them, a the greater protection of the government, their ch interests, their welfare, should be safeguarded. Th ernment in its anxiety to avoid bankruptcy may their salaries further—but only if absolutely nece there are other ways to avoid going into the bank receiver; other economies, and principally going af evaders who are many, and finding new sources of r —but the government should not, must not, for safety, turn on the very men to whom it owes much stability.

The man in the illustration, the sal carries a tremendous burden on his carries it well. He will not carry well if the government takes a notion off an arm or a couple of legs.

Brisbane-type editorial essay written by Mendez for the Tribune *and illustrated by Pablo Amorsolo.*

THE MONDAY MAIL

AT THE CROSSROADS

October 23, 1933

Senator Sergio Osmena, a recognized statesman of his nation, may be said to be standing today at the crossroads of his political career. At this very hour it is likely that he has made up his mind regarding the momentous question now before his people—that of asking the Congress of the United States to grant them their independence.

His colleagues of the Minority have given Senator Osmena free hand to decide whether to go or not to go with the new Independence Delegation which is soon to sail for the United States. Thus that Minority reiterates its confidence in him because of his wisdom and his long record of statesmanship.

His is a very difficult task. To begin with, he came back to his country one of the staunchest champions of the Hare-Hawes-Cutting Law. This Law has not deserved the approval of the Legislature. The sentiment of the people has been decidedly against it.

Senator Osmena, in other words, has found that opposition to the Law in the Philippines is responsible for the fact that he is now of the Minority upholding views which his own party has discredited. And he cannot say that this opposition is the product of partisan prejudice after he himself has seen how the Law has been dissected and how every detail of it has not escaped the public notice.

Understanding Senator Osmena as a human being, the public will appreciate his vigorous defense of the Law even after it has been clearly disapproved by the Legislature. The public, aside from that, will grant that his convictions on the Law are patriotic and

Illustrated editorial typical of those written by Mendez for the D-M-H-M newspapers. Illustrator: P.V. Coniconde.

Mendez, manager of the National Information Board (second from left), beside Elpidio Quirino, Secretary of Interior, at a provincial reception for the latter. (1937)

N.I.B. manager Mendez (center) with colleague Hernando J. Abaya (left) and Felipe Jose. (1937)

Mr. and Mrs. Mauro Mendez at the Manila Hotel. (1940)

The Khaki Crowd, 1945. Press Secretary Mendez in oversized helmet, with President Sergio Osmeña, U.S. Army officer, and members of U.S. Army press corps.

Mr. and Mrs. Mendez with General Carlos P. Romulo. (1948)

VIII

SAKDALISM AND SOCIAL JUSTICE

After the strike at La Minerva, the Philippine Constabulary spent more than a year tracking down Teodoro Asedillo, one of the strike leaders who had disappeared during the violent confrontation at the factory. A former schoolteacher and chief of police, Asedillo achieved legendary fame in the hinterlands of Laguna and Tayabas, where he spread the gospel of the Katipunan ng mga Anak Pawis, a Communist organization. Thievery was the least of his reported accomplishments. He also had to his credit the killing of municipal officials, policemen, and members of the Constabulary.

On December 31, 1935, an informer led Lieutenant Jesus Vargas and his men to Asedillo's highland retreat. He was shot dead at dawn just as he emerged from his hut to prepare his breakfast. Despite news of his death, the superstition persisted that he was still laughing somewhere in the mountains.[1]

To demolish this myth, the Constabulary made a traveling exhibit of Asedillo's remains for two days. "Not only the simple folk of Laguna and Tayabas saw that picture of atrocity with revenge," remarked Mendez with a shudder, "but Manila also—the metropolis of our so-called civilization—had its full share of the morbid delight." In his opinion, a wooden box marking the end of the bandit's career "would have sufficed to show that the paths of criminal glory lead but to the grave."[2]

On January 17, 1936, the *Herald* headlined a scoop on the imminent surrender of another brigand, Nicolas Encallado, a veteran of the Revolution and erstwhile comrade of Asedillo in the Anak Pawis. After his surrender to the Tayabas governor, "Capitan Kulas" was received by President Quezon in Malacañang. Then he returned to Tayabas in the presidential limousine, escorted by Governor Maximo

Rodriguez. A crowd of one thousand came out to greet him, marveling at the change in his appearance.

"Like a conquering hero," commented Mendez in his sardonic editorial, "The Return of the Native":

> After the hair-cut, the shave, and the shampoo at a first class barber shop, after the audience with the Commonwealth's great and near-great, after discarding the shabby and unwashed clothes of his hunted life in the Sierras and putting on the boots of civilization for the first time in many months—after all these, what was lacking for a fairy tale?
>
> And thereby hangs the tale for every potential bandit in this country. After defying the law from the mountain fastnesses, after compelling the armed forces of the State to go out on a manhunt of costly proportions, and after giving the public an exhibition of contempt and mockery of constituted authority, a bandit may surrender and afterwards live in a fairy tale. We should next consider the possibility of including this tale in our readers for the public schools.[3]

Some weeks later the radical community was overheard discussing plans for erecting a monument to Teodoro Asedillo. Mendez wondered if the inspiration had come from the "solicitude of Tayabas' Public Servant No. 1" toward "Kulas" Encallado. In an article written for the *National Review,* Mendez depicted the episode as a chapter in "our own contribution to the general history of human stupidity.... From now on let us see to it that our dignified authorities are not forced to offer themselves as *compadres* to bandits in a futile effort to compromise with lawless elements."[4]

The Sakdalistas

In the 1930s the landed gentry in Laguna and Tayabas used the name of Asedillo as a *panakot,* a Philippine version of the big bad wolf or the bogeyman who would come and get any child who refused to behave. Children also used to peer nervously out of their windows to watch the Colorums, underground peasant societies of long-haired men with bolos tucked into their pants, marching in the streets at twilight. Mothers and nursemaids used the image of these phantom figures to frighten the young ones. Another threat that sent the children scurrying to bed was, "Ayan na ang mga Sakdalista!" ("The Sakdalistas are coming!")

To the aristocracy, the word *Sakdalista* was synonymous with *bandit*. The fact, however, was that the Sakdal was a legitimate political party with a wide following among the disaffected masses. What gave it the status of an outlawed society were its antiplebiscite campaign of 1934 and the misguided "revolution" of May 1935.

While the constitution was in the making and the Quezon-Osmeña coalition was being forged, the Sakdal party was laying the ground for its own version of an independent Philippines. On May 2 and 3 a horde of Sakdalistas attacked several towns in Cavite, Laguna, Bulacan, and Rizal. One of the groups captured the municipal building of San Ildefonso, Bulacan, and hoisted their red flag as a signal for the proclamation of the "Philippine Republic."

It was a short-lived insurrection. After a two-day clash with the Constabulary, 57 Sakdalistas were dead, 36 were wounded, and hundreds of others were behind bars. Among those jailed was a chieftain who had detained a helpless government employee at the Malaria Control Field Laboratory in San Jose del Monte, to prevent him from warning the central government of the uprising.

And it was just as well that communication lines to Manila had been virtually cut off. Everybody was out of town during the rebellion—the acting Governor-General, the entire Cabinet, and even the chief of the Constabulary. "Many had succumbed to the lure of 'inspection trips,' for which, be it said, our men in the government seem particularly over-anxious," remarked Mauro Mendez wryly. "Not having been informed that the Sakdalistas would strike, our high officialdom perhaps were not to blame for seeking relief from the torturing heat of the nation's capital."[5]

His facetious tone was no mask for his alarm and indignation over the ill-fated mutiny, particularly in Santa Rosa, Cabuyao, and San Ildefonso—"those three fiascos of demagoguery," as he called them. Two months before the Sakdalista outbreak, he was irritated by the party's call to boycott the May 14 plebiscite. "By what logic can our agitators come to the verdict that the constitution should be rejected?" he asked. "Why should we reject the guarantee of due process of law, freedom of speech, the prohibition of involuntary servitude, and the sovereignty of the people?"[6]

Actually, the Sakdalistas were not against the constitutional guarantees but against the Tydings-McDuffie Law, the unequal distribution of landed wealth, and the perpetuation of American colonial values. Renato Constantino, in *The Philippines: A Past Revisited,* expresses the opinion that the Sakdal movement, "despite its opportunist and fascist-inclined leadership was a genuine expression of protest and a milestone in the politicization of the people."[7]

Mendez was not blessed with the hindsight that now views the movement as a "milestone in politicization." From where he saw it, the uprising was nothing but a tragic waste of human lives and a proof of provincial illiteracy. Only illiteracy of the most pathetic kind could have convinced the Sakdalista rank and file that they could vanquish the Philippine Constabulary and even the U.S. Army with their bolos and one-shot revolvers. Only delirious ignorance could have conjured up the image of their leader and liberator, Benigno Ramos, returning from Tokyo with General Artemio Ricarte on board a Japanese warship escorted by Japanese planes. "That San Ildefonso proclamation of the Philippine Republic marks the mental level of the so-called radical agitation in this country today," scoffed Mendez.[8]

The Forgotten Village

Despite his exasperation, he could understand why the Sakdal movement had attracted the peasants. He took exception to an opinion expressed by Senator Juan Sumulong in his article. "After the Coalition, the Deluge." Sumulong objected to the Quezon-Osmeña team on the ground that it was an alliance between the "intelligentsia" and the "Philippine plutocracy." The laboring classes, "be they called Socialists, Sakdalists, or Communists," were left out and were likely to become restless.[9]

Mendez's opinion was that the coalition was irrelevant to social unrest. "Experience shows that parties will come and parties will go, but radical preachers will carry on forever. The phenomenon of social unrest is more fundamental than the alignment of parties for strategic reasons."[10]

Since Communism and Sakdalism were second cousins, so to speak, Mendez traced their roots to the same source: the poverty of the masses, aggravated by lawmakers' amnesia. He pointed to the fact that "our political parties have not kept their ears to the ground close enough to feel the pulse of the masses... the acquaintance of our politicians with the *tao* in the street has been more or less a seasonal affair."[11] He painted the familiar pre-election picture—generous candidates buying *cedulas* for their constituents and making merry in the huts of the poor—followed by the post-election syndrome: "Promises are forgotten. . . . State dinners, balls, and receptions become the order of the day."[12]

Unlike the forgetful politicians, the Sakdals showed fraternal concern for the masses, talking to them "in their own intimate language—the language of their needs and feelings." After the winning candidates "had settled down to the pomposity and glitter of their position in the capital, the preachers of discontent remained with the people and have remained with them ever since."[13]

In a masterpiece of irony entitled "The Forgotten Village," Mendez mocked the legislators who had a habit of vetoing bills designed to uplift the lowly barrios. He enumerated the needs of these simple folk:

> Here are some of them: a village school, a road to the town, an artesian well, and perhaps a puericulture center. Does the forgotten man get all these? Yes, he does, perhaps.
>
> He gets, for instance, a school of bamboo and nipa; perhaps the last typhoon has blown off its roof. There is a road leading to the aristocratic town five kilometers away; fortunately, the village man has a carabao to walk the stony *via crucis* for him.
>
> Perhaps there is an artesian well, and perhaps there is none. The water of the river hard by will do for the present; it has served the purpose for years anyway.
>
> A puericulture center? That is decidedly a luxury. The sanitary doctor who happens by once in a blue moon is enough. He can at least look over our barrios' well-known methods of waste disposal.
>
> Yes, the village man gets it—that is, the mouthpieces of our special interests in the nation's capital remember him when, embittered by his fate, he springs into the limelight, bolo in hand, to air his grievance. . . .
>
> This village man, now turned a "sakdalista" with an eye on the hoards of commercialized interests and therefore a menace to the stability of money-making enterprises, then becomes the object of effusions on the "welfare of the people."
>
> The tumult and the shouting die on the sakdalista front; the money-making enterprises are safe again! The machines of

commerce are reinforced to mitigate the lack of human brains. The machines roar their message of greed and gain!

Where is the village man? Back in the dust and penury of his obscure nook. Back in his nipa shack, by the dilapidated barrio school and the stony road, to ruminate again over the irony of fate.[14]

Senseless Combustion of Energy

Since illiteracy added fuel to the flame of discontent, Mendez stressed the importance of adult education, along with the education of the youth, as one approach to the Sakdalista problem. It was necessary to teach the masses that they could correct the errors of political men via the ballot, the organ of their collective will, instead of resorting to the violence of the feeble *paltik*. If he thought of politicalization at all, it was always in terms of the democratic process.

Whether the Sakdalistas were interested in the democratic process was open to question. On the eve of the plebiscite a rumor spread that they were planning to sack the city of Manila and to dynamite the Legislature, Malacañang Palace, the Philippine National Bank, and the insular treasury, so that the voters would be forced to stay indoors. But voting day dawned without so much as the pop of a firecracker. "God's in his heaven and all's right with the world," rejoiced the *Herald* editor on May 14, 1935.

In late July, the Constabulary commander in Bulacan recommended pardon for 74 Sakdal followers who had been sentenced to a period of from two to four years in prison. Governor-General Murphy, after consulting with the Secretary of Justice, decided to heed the commander's advice. Murphy was criticized, but Mendez supported his decision, for it was clear that those poor unlettered men knew not what they were doing when they captured the municipal building with their homemade weapons.

> Now, in all common sense, why punish these men for all that senseless combustion of energy? Is it not clear that what they need is light? And where could that light be? In the dungeons of Bilibid or in the educational institutions of the State? Let us be stern to those who deliberately fooled those 74 Sakdalistas, but to these 74 misled men let us be just as Gov. Murphy has been just.[15]

The denouement of the Sakdal drama came when, despite its anti-American stance, the party joined forces with the defeated presidential candidate, General Aguinaldo, and the remnants of his group. Together they announced their plans to march to Manila during the inauguration of the Commonwealth and to elevate their protests against the Philippine government to American high officials who were coming for the ceremony. Mendez was driven to ridicule the whole troop of "malcontents" for their "infantilism" in running to the Americans.[16]

But the demonstration failed to materialize. Four years later Benigno Ramos was convicted in four cases of estafa, after having collected funds for an "independence campaign."[17] Despite sporadic threats to rise in arms again, the Sakdalista party eventually passed away.

Quezon Attacks Poverty

But socio-economic unrest continued to be a blight on the Philippine landscape. Time and again Mendez would warn the Commonwealth government that its major task was to win over the common man through a comprehensive and long-range program of amelioration.

Writing for the *National Review,* he cautioned the state against falling into the tragic error of Narcissus, the error of living "absorbed in the image of its splendor...in what it imagines itself to be, rather than what it really is." Recalling the pompous inauguration of the Commonwealth, he wrote:

> ...let that lavish display of our vanities be a thing of the past; let the splendor of our external glories give way to a little more determination on our part to live the internal richness of our soul.
>
> Where is that soul? Not in the super-efficient departments of the Ayuntamiento and Malacañang, not in the glamor of our social triumphs, but in the vast throng of common men, often inarticulate, that walks the streets of our industrial centers or inhabits the forgotten barrios of our provinces.[18]

President Quezon knew that a discontented populace was a threat to the stability of state and throne. After his election he announced that the theme of his inaugural speech would be the problem of poverty. Mendez agreed in an editorial that the President had chosen the best way to open the Commonwealth regime. Unless poverty was attacked at its very roots, Philippine society would be in a state of perpetual peril, "for order is not possible with its members in an ugly mood." The reason was obvious:

> The only condition in which it is possible for the select minority to advance the cause of organized Society is its ability to count on the adherence of the majorities; when these majorities are miserable, every word and act of the select few places that few in imminent jeopardy. As long as there is discontent in the depths, all government becomes merely a pose.[19]

Quezon launched his well-known Social Justice program at a time of severe economic depression in the provinces, when wages were only 60 centavos a day in areas near Manila, and 40 centavos in the Ilocos region.[20] At the outset of his regime he fixed a minimum wage for laborers hired for public works but fixed no such minimum for laborers in private industry. He hoped that capitalists, as a matter of sentiment and not of law, would follow the government's example of their own accord. Mendez added his own appeal to private business to "relinquish temporary benefits and prepare the ground for permanent harmony with their laborers." Instead of waiting for labor to demand its rights, "we should grant those rights without its asking for them."[21]

But sentiment was slower than the law, and the President eventually had to convince the National Assembly to fix the minimum wage for all laborers at not less than ₱1.00 a day in the provincial districts and ₱1.25 in the municipalities. He also worked for an inheritance law and an increase in the taxes levied on the higher-income brackets.[22]

To prove the sincerity of his compassion for the poor, President Quezon fraternized with leftist intellectuals such as Crisanto Evangelista and Guillermo Capadocia of the Communist Party, and Pedro Abad Santos of the National Socialist Party. Mendez, however, continued his anti-Communist crusade in the press, not sparing even the less radical Socialist Party, which, he said, "should properly be called the Bolshevist Party with a bourgeois at its head."[23]

But even as he attacked Stalinism in all its forms, he continued to warn the moneyed class that unless they followed His Excellency's advice to donate a portion of their wealth to their respective communities, they would go the way of the Russian Kulaks, those "conscienceless property owners" of the Tsarist era, who were responsible for having precipitated "the greatest class war in history."[24]

Games Filipinos Play

With his characteristic objectivity, Mendez looked at the other side of the poverty question and blamed it partly on Filipino prodigality, laziness, love of gambling, and the fact that "One's most distant relative may always be depended upon to save him from starvation."[25]

During off-harvest seasons, he added, many men would rather snore than make themselves useful, "not even planting camote in their yards to give their diet a variety, or clearing the rubbish in those yards and shaking off the dust of ages that has settled thick on the roofs and walls of their houses."[26]

He pointed to certain towns along the provincial highways north and south of Manila, where the early-morning traveler was greeted daily by the spectacle of able-bodied men petting their roosters by the roadside. "These are moments of transcendental calculations," mused Mendez. "In the daily preoccupations of these men, they are the algebra."[27]

Later in the afternoon the able-bodied men would repair to billiard halls, cabarets, and roadhouses, there to drown their cockfighting sorrows in beer, or to engage in gunfights over taxi-dancers. From time to time, news of a fatal gun duel would reach the front pages of the newspapers, and a stern-faced town official would padlock a cabaret or two. But after a while, the *municipio* would miss the revenues from these establishments and the ill-starred cabaret would open its doors again.[28]

Then there was the jueteng plague, which afflicted many a fun-loving pauper in Manila and the neighboring provinces. Every street corner had a friendly collector, noted Mendez, who called on his customers daily "for their regular contribution to the cause of their own impoverishment."[29]

If a prospective bettor was unsure of his lucky number for the day, the jueteng agent would guide him by interpreting his dream of the night before. Each dream had a number assigned to it by a book of dreams. Thus, the customer's financial status would depend on whether he had dreamed of, say, a serpent or his pet pig.

To keep the poor people hopelessly addicted to the numbers game, the jueteng capitalist would occasionally manipulate the *tambiolo** and announce that Ginang Anungalan of the slums was richer by five pesos. Consequently, the rest of the neighborhood would be inspired to try their luck.

A curious situation, indeed, observed Mendez. "Jueteng, like art, may be called a product of leisure; but whereas people of leisure cultivate the arts, people who are poor cultivate jueteng."[30]

Mendez blamed this state of affairs on the lack of a "vigorous national policy" regarding the future of the provincial communities, save one—a policy of *"laissez faire"* in permitting the population to "drink, dance, and be merry. It shows that our liberties are not menaced, including our liberty to go to the devil. Ours is a happy lot, indeed, and let's make the most of it."[31]

---

* The dropbox containing the bettors' numbers

IX

THE COMMON TOUCH

In November of 1936 Mendez's dream of a governmental information office became a reality when President Quezon created the National Information Board under the Department of Interior. Mendez was a logical choice for manager of the Board, since the idea was the *Herald*'s editorial brainchild. He resigned from the D-M-H-M, bringing with him his favorite newspaperman, Hernando Abaya.

The National Information Board was the first precursor of today's Department of Public Information. Its duty was to disseminate information regarding the Commonwealth government via print media, film, and radio, thereby hoping to end what Mendez had once referred to as "the alienation of the barrio citizen from the affections of this glamorous capital city."[1]

Former Secretary Narciso Ramos recalls his association with Mendez during the early years of the Commonwealth:

> I began dealing extensively with Mauro Mendez when I became Congressman for Pangasinan. He had been pressed into government service by President Manuel Quezon, as Director of Public Information. Again he was a pioneer, struggling against difficulties that would have defeated lesser men. Exploiting the novel information medium of the motion picture, with but a handful of assistants and pitifully limited funds, he was in the forefront of the campaign to bring the government closer to the people. I can still see his spare frame, moving among the people in the towns and in the barrios, among his projectors and his rolls of film and his portable screens, showing the people what their government was doing for them and what *they* could do for their country.[2]

Mga Balitang Pangbayan

The National Information Board published two pamphlets in English: *Our Government—What It Is Doing For You,* written by Hernando Abaya for local consumption, and *The Philippines,* written by Jose Q. Dacanay and exported by the thousands to the United States, where it was in great demand as the most authoritative source of information about the Islands. The N.I.B. also put out the *Aklat ng Mamamayan* (*Citizens' Handbook*) and a small periodical, *Mga Balitang Pangbayan* (News for the Nation). Translated into three major Philippine languages, the *Aklat* informed the citizens of their rights and responsibilities, the political and economic advantages they enjoyed under a peaceful and democratic government, and everything else the radicals forgot to tell them.

Aside from inspiring love of country and respect for the office of the President, *Mga Balitang Pangbayan* dispensed the latest news relevant to the needs of the masses, generally calculated to counteract subversive propaganda. "₱40,000,000 ibibili ng mga asienda!" announced the maiden issue on July 10, 1937. In line with its land reform program, the government was ready to pay for the remaining friar estates which had not yet been purchased for the tenants who had been tilling them.

Another morale booster was the news that the Philippines was making progress ("sumusulong, umuunlad") as proven by the rising birth rate and the building boom. In an underpopulated archipelago it was necessary to be fruitful and multiply.

It was apparent from *Mga Balitang Pangbayan* that the government was at last carrying out a definite policy aimed at uplifting the provincial communities. Secretary of Interior Elpidio Quirino had appointed a commission for every province, to be in charge of a clean-up and beautification campaign, the improvement of roads, highways, and sources of drinking water, the building of playgrounds, and the encouragement of a vegetable industry in every backyard.

The only bad news in the *Balita*'s maiden issue came from "Mosku" via United Press. "Ito ba ang 'paraiso ng maliliit'?" ("Is this 'the paradise of the little man'?") There was no mistaking the Mendez voice behind the question. One item from Moscow was that in the small Siberian community of Svobodny, 44 men and women had been executed by a firing squad. In another town twenty spies and saboteurs had been liquidated after having been declared guilty of planning to set up their own republic under the aegis of a capitalist country.

Here was a moral lesson for the Sakdals:

> Ano ang ipalalagay ninyong nangyari marahil sa mga Sakdalista kung sa Rusia nagsipag-alsa? Ang lahat ng mga pinuno ng Sakdal at ang kanikanilang mga kabig o tagasunod ay walang salang pinahanay marahil sa isang bakod na bato at pinagbabaril nang walang ano mang paglilitis. Gayon pa man, kahi't isang Sakdal ay hindi ipinabaril pagkatapos ng kanilang pagsusuwail dito. At hindi lamang ito, kundi, walang ipinasok sa Bilibid nang hindi muna nalilitis at nabibigyan ng pagkakataong makapagtanggol sa kanilang sarili sa harap ng hukuman.

> (What do you think would have happened to the Sakdalistas if they had revolted in Russia? All of their leaders and their followers would surely have been lined up against a stone wall and shot without any trial whatsoever. And yet not a single Sakdal was shot after their uprising here. Moreover, not one of them was imprisoned in Bilibid without having been given a trial and an opportunity to defend himself in court.)

"Apostle of Malacañang"

Leon Ma. Guerrero, Jr., a young writer for the *Philippines Free Press,* gave Mauro Mendez the sobriquet "Apostle of Malacañang." In a profile of Mendez, Guerrero wrote, "By written word and word of mouth this brisk bright apostle of Malacañang spreads a gospel of sweetness and light."

There was no doubt that *Mga Balitang Pangbayan* was outright propaganda, but as Guerrero put it, "Conditions in the Philippines are such...that even propaganda is welcome in the remote barrios where government-slanted news is better than no news, and where a supervised knowledge is better than ignorance." He added that before the information office was created, the barrios were "a virgin field" for subversive pamphlets and periodicals. "They were received and read with such alarming enthusiasm that there could be only one explanation for it: anything to read was welcome, any news was correct news, and if the reading matter and the news happened to be Reddish, that was just too bad for the government because it was going to be believed."

When the Philippine press asked itself "jokingly" if it would soon have to submit to the blue pencil of the Board, Guerrero allayed their fears: "...propaganda in the Philippines is far from the censor stage. Malacañang's apostle must concentrate on information before he can think of reformation.... Apostleship is a long way from the Inquisition."

Mendez denied that there was any censorship in his work, even when the government took over the news broadcasts over KZRM-Radio Manila. His purpose was informational, educative, and even entertaining, after a fashion. The People's Hour, a 45-minute broadcast every Saturday, combined music and news, featured short patriotic playlets on the lives of national heroes, and invited guest speakers, usually government officials, to chat on topics of timely and vital importance. To lure the masses away from jueteng and allied vices, Mendez planned to organize a troupe of actors who would stage patriotic dramas in the provinces.[3]

Jose Luna Castro, in an article on "The Radio and the Masses," commended the N.I.B. radio programs for supplying the masses with "accurate, unbiased information, simplified without having to pass through the emasculating process, and sent out quickly before it would be useless to mull over it and before the ambitious agitator would have enough time to interpret, in the subversive manner, the issues involved."[4]

Mendez himself spoke over DZRM, in no less than Tagalog, on the necessity of living "by that most unerring of all laws, Common Sense." He appealed to his listeners to avoid class intolerance, and "to erase all demarcation lines that might lead to the fragmentation of our society....No government that we know of has ever succeeded on any other basis than the unqualified support of the people." [5]

Ang Wikang Pambansa

As manager of the National Information Board, Mendez traveled frequently in the provinces, usually with Secretary Quirino and sometimes with Mrs. Mendez. One of the things he realized during his contacts with the masses was that English was not destined to be the national language of the Philippines.

In 1937 President Quezon proclaimed that Tagalog was to be the basis of a language that would unify the multilingual archipelago. In April 1940, he authorized the publication of a dictionary and a grammar book based on Tagalog. In the same month Mauro Mendez went on the air to defend his native tongue.

The occasion was a language debate during the Town Meeting of the Air, a regular Sunday evening program over Radio Manila. The proposition was, "Resolved: that Tagalog should be the national language of the Philippines." Mendez defended the affirmative side, while Antonio Estrada, U.S.T. professor and *Herald* columnist, argued for English. Leon Ma. Guerrero, Jr., was moderator, and Federico Mangahas, then editor of the *Herald Mid-Week Magazine,* was interrogator. Guerrero introduced Mendez as a product of a public-school system that used English as the language of instruction.

Mendez defended Tagalog with lyric eloquence:

> The language of a nation is not its mere caprice; there is something more than the wishes of mice and men in the fact that human thought has had to be expressed. It was no accident that we were cradled in a language of our own; in the plan of our existence, that language is an essential force, one of the really sublime things that have a reason to exist. For it has affected our inner lives from the very beginning, accumulating upon our soul the impressions that identify us as a people.

He pointed to our forefathers and heroes who wrote "the epics of our history" in Tagalog. "In the blood of these illustrious Filipinos, Tagalog lived gloriously. We can say, indeed, that they expressed what they felt, and felt what they lived because their language was their own."

He admitted that the English language was admirable for its "grace and dignity," and its "enrichment of our store of ideas." He saw it as "our best bid for participation in the commerce of mankind." But "we were born for the Philippines first and for the world second."[6]

The Tagalog press was amazed. A week after the Town Meeting debate, an editorial appeared in one of the Tagalog periodicals, praising Mauro Mendez as a "magandang halimbawa," a beautiful example:

> ...isa-isang inilahad ni G. Mendez ang makabayang matuwid na diya'y kasama na ang pagsasantabi ng kanyang sariling kapakanan, sapagka't gayong siya'y supling ng paaralang bayan,

nabuhay, nabubuhay at kaipala'y mabubuhay sa wikang ingles, yamang siya'y makata, mamamahayag at manunulat sa wikang ingles. . . .[7]

(Mr. Mendez has promoted the national cause, setting aside even his own personal interests. A product of the public schools, he has lived by and will perhaps continue to live by the English language, inasmuch as he is a poet, a journalist, and a writer in that language.)

A Case of Abduction

"Young, ambitious, full of ideas" (as Leon Ma. Guerrero, Jr. described him), Mendez taught English at the Philippine Law School even while he was managing the National Information Board. One day he decided to resume the law studies he had dropped twenty years before. There were two compelling reasons for his decision to pursue the study of law. A lawmaker whom he had chided in editorials for having introduced a bill that stood to favor his personal interests had brushed the editorials aside with the remark that Mendez was not a lawyer anyway and knew not whereof he spoke. The other reason proceeded from his participation as assessor in a sensational trial, when his recommendations were assailed in some legal sectors on the ground that he was not a lawyer when he made them.

No court case during the Commonwealth titillated Manila society as much as the trial of Josefino Cenizal, a handsome musician and U.P. law student, who was accused of serious illegal detention. His alleged victim was a pretty 19-year-old U.P. coed, the daughter of a Manila councilor.

The pair had eloped and were married in a civil ceremony in June 1939. They lived together in Tanza, Cavite, until her father took her away by force. One morning in July the young lady and her sister went to an Echague bakery to buy bread. Cenizal appeared at the bakery the same day and allegedly abducted his struggling wife. The prosecution charged that he beat her black and blue in the face and then released her after three days. She filed charges of serious illegal detention against him, and the trial of the decade began.

At the request of Eliseo Ymson, attorney for the defense, the municipal board appointed two assessors to sit at the trial. The *Free Press* described them as "elderly, erudite Pedro Aunario, editorial writer of *La Vanguardia,* and quiet, pleasant-faced Mauro Mendez, former managing editor of the DMHM newspapers and now Manager of the National Information Board." [8]

The use of assessors was similar to the jury system in the United States. One of the differences was that assessors were drawn from a list of 25 residents of Manila, chosen by the municipal board for their high qualifications, being "best fitted by education, natural ability and reputation for probity to sit as assessors in the trial of actions." They earned a fee of ₱5.00 per court session.

Although either party in a court case had the right to have assessors, they were very rarely employed in Philippine courts. Mendez and Aunario were the first assessors to be employed in the past twenty years. Their duty, as defined by the Code of Civil Procedure, was "to sit with the judge upon the trial of an action and to advise him in the determination of all questions of fact involved therein." The final responsibility for the decision, however, rested with the judge.

If the assessors were of the opinion that the judge was mistaken in his appraisal of the facts, they were to explain the reasons for their dissent in writing. If the case was appealed, the higher courts could review the facts, giving as much weight to the dissenting views as they were entitled to in order to render fair judgment.[9]

Hundreds of spectators, including many giggling women, filled the narrow courtroom during the Cenizal trial. Public opinion appeared to lean in favor of the distraught "abductor," especially when he declared that he was still in love with the girl who had filed charges against him. The justice of the peace who had married them in June testified that the ceremony had proceeded normally and without disturbance. Witnesses, including an unbiased milkman and a houseboy, had noted the loving relationship between the couple—"tumutugtog ng piano at naghahalikan." [10] ("Playing the piano and exchanging kisses.")

Pre-"abduction" letters written by the lady were read in court, letters which, to the ears of assessor Mendez, "were redolent of affection," with "the rosy promise of love between the lines." One of the letters alluded to Cenizal as a "magnificent brute." The "brute" himself told the court that his lady-love had once offered him some prunes, whereupon he had given her his own version of "prunes"—a kiss on her lips. After hearing this testimony, romantic Manila thrilled to the sound of the word "prunes" for the next few weeks.

Believing that the lady had been "abducted with her consent," both assessors recommended acquittal for the accused. To their astonishment, the judge pronounced him guilty and imposed a sentence of from four to ten years in Bilibid for "slight" instead of "serious" illegal detention. Mendez was so upset by the decision that he vowed never to assess a case again.

Because of the widespread interest in the trial, the *Herald* printed portions of Mendez's dissenting opinion.[11] He cited conflicting testimonies of the supposed victim and her witnesses, and discrepancies in their statements, as the basis for his recommendation for acquittal. His memorandum carried such whimsical titles as "The Tryst at Dainty Bakery," "Interlude on Hollywood Drive," "The Bahay Kubo Prison," "Enter the Milkman," "Love Sweeter After a Quarrel," and so on.

Publication of the memorandum provoked an exchange of words in the Spanish-language press between the assessors and ex-Representative Manuel V. Gallego, lawyer for the prosecution.[12] Defending the judge's decision, Gallego wrote a long and caustic attack on Mendez and Aunario, pronouncing their nonlegal opinions fit only for a literary contest:

> Un asesor que no es un abogado no puede alegar tener mejor conocimiento que un juez-abogado que ha estudiado las leyes.
> Es una triste coincidencia el que los asesores escogidos sean ambos hombres de letras, y por lo tanto impresionables por naturaleza. Es una cosa ser escritor, y otra, ser analizador de hechos de acuerdo con la ley. El arte de escribir puede ser innato, mientras que la habilidad de interpretar las leyes se adquiere.[13]

> (An assessor who is not a lawyer cannot claim to have more knowledge than a lawyer-judge who has studied the law.
> It is an unfortunate coincidence that the assessors chosen were both men of letters and therefore impressionable by nature. It is one thing to be a writer and another thing to be an interpreter of facts according to the law. The gift for writing may be inborn, while the ability to interpret the law is acquired.)

Mendez dispatched a quick reply to *El Debate:*

> Este asesor jamas ha pretendido asumir el papel de abogado y mucho menos el de juez. No ha interpretado ley alguna, excepto, quizas, la porcion aquella de la Declaracion de Derechos de nuestra Constitucion, que se refiere a la libertad individual y al debido proceso de ley, que, en mi opinion, incumbe tanto

a mi, como ciudadano de esta Mancomunidad, como el Sr. Gallego. Un poco de sentido comun es todo lo que se requiere para comprender los articulos de la Declaracion de Derechos.[14]

(This assessor has never pretended to assume the role of a lawyer, much less of a judge. He has not interpreted a single law except, perhaps, that portion in the Bill of Rights of our Constitution, which refers to individual liberty and due process of law, which, in my opinion, concerns me as a citizen of this Commonwealth as much as it concerns Mr. Gallego. A little common sense is all that is required to understand the articles in the Bill of Rights.)

At the same time Don Pedro Aunario issued his own statement in *La Vanguardia*:

Estoy mas convencido que nunca de que Cenizal no es culpable, y si tuviera que preparar mañana otro informe sobre el caso, pediria veinte-mil veces su absolucion. Si estuviese profundamente convencido de que es culpable, por el honor de mis hijas yo pediria sin remordimiento su condena. Soy padre de siete niñas a quienes amo mas que mi propia vida.

(I am more convinced than ever that Cenizal is not guilty, and if I had to prepare another brief on the case tomorrow, I would ask twenty-thousand times for his acquittal. If I were deeply convinced of his guilt, for the honor of my daughters, I would ask for his punishment without remorse. I am the father of seven girls whom I love more than my own life.)

Two years later the Court of Appeals reversed the verdict of the lower court and acquitted Cenizal in a decision based largely on the assessors' findings—"las opiniones de los dos asesores y sus observaciones de buen sentido comun..."[15] ("the opinions of the two assessors and their common-sense observations.")

By then, Mendez was well into law school, determined that nobody should ever again accuse him of being a nonlawyer.

Preview of an Air Raid

In 1940 politics began to rear its ubiquitous head at the National Information Board. Although Mendez and Quirino were close friends, they disagreed over the functions of the Board. In a memorandum filed with the National Assembly, Mendez stated that "the Secretary of Interior, whether he likes it or not, contracts political obligations for which the bureau may be asked to give its share of satisfaction."[16]

Mendez was subsequently transferred to the office of the President, with the ever-present Hernando Abaya as his technical assistant. He organized a press section in Malacañang and became, in effect, the first presidential press secretary, although that title was then nonexistent. He edited the *Official Gazette,* improved the style of the presidential messages, and wrote some of the messages himself.[17]

In 1941 a new government office, the Civilian Emergency Administration, was hastily created in response to the growing Japanese menace. The National Information Board was transferred to the C.E.A. and Mendez was appointed head of the publicity department, in addition to his position as Malacañang press officer. Thus, he found himself working with his former staff again, but with a less cheerful objective this time. His office was in charge of preparing the civilian populace for war by teaching them the art of survival, such as how to build air-raid shelters and how to behave in the event of an air attack. In the daytime the people dug trenches in their backyards and piled sandbags around them. On scheduled evenings they turned off their lights for blackout drills, their eardrums throbbing nervously to the screech of an air-raid siren.

Mendez occupied his new position in an anxious mood until the genuine air raid on Pearl Harbor on December 7, 1941.

X

ON THE WARPATH

Shoulder to shoulder, Dictatorship and Militarism are stalking through Europe today, casting their shadows upon the continent like sinister omens of death.[1]

* * * * *

The Japanese tidal wave is a force that is bound to determine the future course of history.[2]

As astute observer of the geopolitical scene, Mauro Mendez filled the editorial pages of the *Tribune* and the *Herald* with his analyses of world events and international relations. In Europe he saw what he called the "goose-stepping infantries" of Hitler's Germany and the "spaghetti-eating Black Shirts" of Mussolini's Italy as the most monstrous threats to peace. Closer to home, he foresaw the Imperial Army of Dai Nippon lording it over the Far East.

The Japanese Tidal Wave

It surprised him that so many Filipinos in the early '30s seemed blissfully unaware of Japan's gigantic schemes for empire. It was written "in the drama of Japanese destiny," he wrote, "this desire for the pomp of power," this "ascent of the imagination to the topmost peak of international supremacy."[3]

Not that he blamed Japan for wanting to extend her frontiers. In 1935 her birth rate was 250 babies per hour, or a total of over two million additional Japanese for that year alone. "We must look at Japan in the light of her population problem, if we are to understand her greatness and her distress," he wrote. "The rest of the world might well tremble before this greatness because not mere ambition or megalomania, but the law of necessity—the law of history itself—has made it possible and will continue to make it possible."[4]

From time to time Tokyo would assure Washington and Manila that Japan would respect the sovereignty of an independent Philippines, and that she desired only peace and friendship with the rest of the world. But Mendez's suspicions mounted with every friendly word uttered by a Japanese spokesman. There was increasing evidence of militarism in Japan, especially when the Diet voted one billion yen for the Imperial Army in 1934. "Would it be beyond the range of possibility for bayonets to carve a little empire out of our national territory?" inquired Mendez. "Who can forget the Chinese 'melon,' for instance, and the way it has been sliced, although the Chinese patrimony is clear upon the map of the world?"[5]

Along came Resident Commissioner Francisco Delgado with his assurance that Japan would not invade the Islands because she would be too busy with Manchuria, rebaptized "Manchukuo," for the next 50 years. Furthermore, said the Commissioner, the Japanese had always preferred temperate climates, and the heat of the tropics would not appeal to them.[6]

Mendez found "this prescription for the health of the Japanese" quite amusing. "The Japanese will agree with our climate if they should choose to come here," he said. "Even Americans have found conditions here congenial enough for their health. There is nothing wrong with our climate: it is and will always be good enough for any people, especially for people who must move out of a congested country."[7]

The best evidence that the Japanese had adjusted to Philippine weather conditions was their formidable presence in Davao. A decade before the war began, half of the fertile land in Davao was owned by Japanese. Fifty to seventy percent of the hemp output was the product of Japanese industry, and even the plantations which appeared to be owned by Americans and Filipinos were being worked by Japanese hands. Davao instead of Manila was the site of the Japanese Trade Commissioner's office. Mendez described Davao as a "miniature Nippon" and called the province "Davaokuo," a nickname that caught on among Filipinos who knew the history of "Manchukuo."

Mendez made this on-the-spot report on the situation in the South:

> The soul of Japan is in Davao as it is in Hondo or in Hokkaido. In that province the Shinto temple stands as the symbol of faith. There the schools are Japanese schools, teaching loyalties strange to ours, keeping alive traditions alien to the spirit of our land. The Japanization of Davao is an accomplished fact.[8]

Mendez placed the blame squarely on the Filipinos themselves:

> The story of Japanese prosperity in Davao is the story of the surrender of a national heritage, of unpardonable indifference, of shameful neglect. In it are reflected the procrastination of our government and the apathy of our people. Our generations to come will read in that story the dismemberment of their national domain and the barter of their rights.[9]

Nor was the Japanese threat confined to the hemp industry; the fishing industry was also in Japanese hands. Moreover, there was something sinister in the way Japanese ships and motorboats often intruded into Philippine waters on missions of a mysterious nature. For example, in September 1934, the steamship *Hayun Maru,* flying the flag of the Rising Sun, sailed into the waters of Palawan and was boarded by Filipino port officials for the usual inspection. Instead of submitting to the inspectors, the captain and crew attacked them. One was wounded and thrown overboard; the other managed to jump into the water before he was hurt. The ship then fled to its home port in Formosa. Only after insistent protests on the part of the Philippine government did Tokyo prosecute the offending seamen.[10]

The Fighting Spirit

Fear of the Japanese menace led the National Assembly to appropriate ₱18,000,000 for the nation's defense program, an amount that General Aguinaldo considered "excessive and unnecessary." He advocated, instead, cultivating the good will of neighboring countries. "There is at present a strong sense of international justice that will prevent an invasion of the Philippines," spoke the General.[11]

To which Mendez replied that in the light of current international relations, "blind faith" was the last policy to consider. "It would be foolish for us, however microscopic our place in the scheme of human destiny, to think we can remain unscathed in the midst of the maelstrom of passions that besets the world."[12]

Mendez devoted his writings wholeheartedly to the defense program by encouraging young men to enlist, writing morale-boosting essays on the Philippine Army in history, and reiterating the need for maintaining national dignity through national defense. He took a realistic view of the world situation:

> This is a militarist world, a bourgeois world, taking to arms not for the love of fighting, but because it must fight; not as the warrior of medieval history who, from his castle, was carried to his grave full-panoplied for battle, but rather as a merchant building himself a fortress for the security of his interests.[13]

But there was not much the country could do with its weak defense system. Six years later the Japanese tidal wave engulfed the Philippine Islands.

One of the first Manila buildings to be directly hit by a Japanese bomb was the *Herald* office. The colored bulbs of the D-M-H-M initials, a familiar landmark in prewar Manila, never lit the evening sky again.

Yellow Interlude

As soon as war was declared, Mendez and family joined the exodus from Manila and fled to San Isidro, Nueva Ecija. When news of the Japanese landing in Pangasinan reached their ears, they rushed back to Manila and camped with relatives on Taft Avenue, Pasay. There they watched the enemy march triumphantly into the open city of Manila.

The day after the Occupation began, the Mendez family driver, whom they had left in their San Juan home as caretaker, went to Taft Avenue before dawn with the terrifying news that some Japanese soldiers had gone to the house to pick up Mr. Mendez. The driver told them that the family had left for parts unknown.

Mendez then decided to hide in another house in Paco, where nobody would have thought of looking for him. To make himself less accessible, he spent plenty of time in third-class moviehouses near by, sitting in the dark among the bedbugs and watching reruns of Tagalog pictures and western movies over and over again. To disguise himself, he grew a beard of a most unusual kind. Instead of being soft and wavy like his hair, it bristled on his chin like the quills of a porcupine.

After six months, it looked as if the Japanese were going to stay much longer than the Filipinos had expected. Mendez was getting tired of his claustrophobic existence; he also wanted a shave very badly. His wife decided to seek advice from Justice Jose P. Laurel, who was later to become President of the puppet Republic. He suggested that her husband throw away his anti-Japanese writings and remain out of sight.

Mendez himself, whiskers bristling, took the risk of going to Malacañang to see his friend, Jorge B. Vargas, then Chairman of the Executive Commission. Vargas asked him if he was willing to work for the government, but Mendez replied that he only wanted to be left alone.

Vargas suggested that he see Mr. Enrique Imamura, the Japanese liaison officer, who was married to a Filipina and whose daughters were friends of the Mendez girls. A cultured gentleman, Mr. Imamura was entirely different from the soldiers who slapped Filipinos in the streets. He told the Mendezes that they could go home and that the Japanese would not bother them. Grateful to Imamura, Mendez packed his family into a *carretela* and journeyed home to San Juan.

Like most Filipinos during the war, the Mendezes settled down to a life among *camote* patches and poultry. They also managed a *sari-sari* store on their front porch. When the schools opened in 1943, Mrs. Mendez resumed her teaching at the Centro Escolar University, while the ex-Apostle of Malacañang sold candy and cigarettes. The merchandise included his wife's jewelry and used ternos, the family furniture, and an antique gold watch given him by his father-in-law. During his spare time he wrote a novel—his first and last—about the war, filling page after page with denunciations of the Japanese and their Filipino cohorts. Unable to maintain an aesthetic and psychic distance from his subject matter, he told his wife that he would wait ten years before looking at the novel again.

One evening Pacita received a phone call from her close friend, Mrs. Asuncion Perez. Would she and Mauro please come over for a *merienda* the next day? The *merienda* turned out to be a secret meeting to organize a home guerrilla unit affiliated with Marking's Guerrillas. Mr. and Mrs. Mendez were designated "major" and "captain," respectively, titles which would have amused them if the situation had been less grim.

Two couriers of the Perez unit traveled to and from the mountains with letters, coded messages, and donations of cash, medical supplies, and clothing collected by other members. Agustin and Yay Marking sent messages signed "King Arthur and the Shipmate." Yay's personal letters to Pacita were signed "Amazon." The Mendezes used the pseudonyms "Elias" and "Solomon" for Mauro, and "Victoria Tapang" for Pacita. She was inspired by the "V for Victory" finger sign with which Filipinos used to greet each other during the Occupation.

"Victoria" wrote to "Amazon" in January 1944:

> Elias calls this era the yellow interlude. In a way I am glad all this happened if only as a revelation of the true character of our people and of ourselves. . . . So many people, especially newspapermen, are now in the government, because, as they say, 'we have to live.' Yet here we are, still breathing, still spiritually free, never so sure of ourselves as in these days.

The Puppet Press

During the Occupation, Mendez received several job offers but he turned them down because they all involved working for the puppet regime. In a letter to Yay Marking in December 1943, Pacita wrote, "Solomon often plays hide and seek with people who are anxious to have him on the same boat."

Mendez either feigned illness or told his friends that as a matter of principle he could not accept the offers. Arsenio N. Luz, then chairman of the Board of Information, seemed most anxious to have Mendez work with him, but the latter wrote this answer to "dear Arsenic":

> I beg to be excused from taking any part in the project you discussed with me the other day. I have no quarrel with your technique: I think it is excellent, if you have the right men who agree with you. As for myself, I am not convinced about the things you propose to sell, and without conviction I cannot hope to convince others, much less a public inclined to doubt everything they see and hear under the present setup. So it's bound to be an uphill job for your organization as I see it. Without the "steam" behind it, the machine may not go. In my opinion, publicity these days cannot amount to much, and the less our public men say, the better for them. A Free Press is the fundamental

thing. It is only when such a press exists that publicity may come to the people with the impression of fairness.

Mr. Luz was to use this letter in his defense when he was tried for collaboration after the war, claiming that if he had been a traitor, he would have reported Mendez to the Kempei-Tai.

To a public accustomed to the prewar newspapers, the puppet press was a farce. Rather than see his property go up in smoke, Alejandro Roces, Jr., had surrendered the T-V-T to the Japanese as soon as they set foot on Manila. "It was the mainstay of the family fortune," Mendez was to recall later. "The old Roces had fastened all his interests upon it, and when the Japanese took it over in 1942 Roces was so deeply moved that he is said to have shed tears. It was as if a part of his being had been taken from him, for the T-V-T was his own creature and he loved it."[14]

The *Tribune* staff met their usual deadline on the first day of the Occupation, but the paper's theme and tone changed overnight. From then on, it sang hosannas to the Rising Sun:

> That great Asian people, the leader nation of Greater East Asia, has grasped our outstretched hand to guide and to assist us. However high the mountains, and how deep the sea, the journey toward Our Tomorrow can no longer be interrupted.[15]

The *Tribune* informed the public that "self-censorship" was being practiced by the T-V-T, "although the censors still review the articles every night, being on the lookout for anything that might not be in consonance with the policies of the Japanese."[16]

The censors not only "reviewed" the articles; they actually wrote some of them under the bylines of their Filipino employees. On one occasion, a certain Mr. Matsunaga wrote an article with the byline of newsman Armando Malay, spelled "A. Maray." Mr. "Maray" was once severely reprimanded for handling the Emperor's photograph casually, without the reverence deserved by a supposedly direct descendant of the Sun Goddess.[17]

"New Philippines Forever in Old East Asia!" was one of the daily *Tribune* slogans. The Imperial Army, however, suspected that 99.9 percent of the Filipinos longed for the old Philippines. In January 1943, the military authorities ordered the alteration of all short-wave radio sets so that they could pick up broadcasts only on the medium-wave band. The purpose was "to safeguard the Philippine public from the influence of fabricated enemy propaganda."[18]

Two days later, the *Tribune* announced with pride that 1,405 applications for short-wave alterations had been received, indicating that the people were "cooperating." Like countless others, Mendez did not cooperate. He continued to keep his ears tuned to short-wave news about the war. His only entertainment consisted of daily meetings with friends and neighbors for the exchange of foreign news and underground information that he could pass on to the resistance movement.

In August 1944, the colonizers began to lose their Imperial calm. Manilans were ordered to undergo a five-day defense drill in case of an attack by "the Anglo-Saxons." The *Tribune* revealed that American planes had bombed Davao, raining "death and destruction upon innocent Filipino civilians and destroying cemeteries and farm crops." On September 21, Manila "received its baptism of fire from American planes."

President Laurel proclaimed a state of martial law beginning September 21. On the 29th, with the concurrence of the National Assembly, he declared war on the United States and Great Britain. Despite the growing tension, the puppet press continued to play up the demoralization and imminent defeat of the anti-Axis camp: "U.S. Task Force Crippled." "Desperate Enemy Suffers Disaster."[19]

While "panic-stricken enemy planes" were allegedly being shot down, the *Tribune* bannered a desperate gesture of Nippon charity—a loan of twenty million yen to the P.I. But at that stage nobody cared for that kind of money; there was plenty of "Mickey Mouse" currency literally floating in the streets. While the "arch-enemy of the Asian peoples" had begun "to violate our land with bullets and bombs," the people were told to prepare for a nationwide celebration of the Republic's first anniversary on October 14. On the 16th a truck belonging to the Hodobu, the Department of Information, toured Manila to distribute "extras" informing the citizens of the "success" of war operations. Attached to the truck was a giant streamer with the sign, "U.S. HEAVILY BEATEN!"

Three days later the last issue of the *Tribune* featured a front-page photo of a falling enemy plane, supposedly shot over Manila and leaving a trail of black smoke on its downward flight. It was the perfect emblem for a dying newspaper. The next day General MacArthur landed in Leyte.

In the second week of October 1944, Mendez received a phone call from his friend, Pio Duran, who had been circulating in Japanese society. Duran was a member of the dreaded Makapili, an association founded by Benigno Ramos of Sakdalista fame. The Makapili was responsible for pointing out Filipinos in the resistance movement and having them liquidated. Duran advised Mendez to leave town because his name was on the blacklist. By then the Kempei-Tai had intensified its antiguerrilla operations. Mr. and Mrs. Cirilo Perez, Mr. and Mrs. Antonio Escoda, and other guerrillas had been brought to Fort Santiago in August, and only Asuncion Perez had been released alive.[20] The two men who had acted as emissaries between the Mendezes and the Marking couple had also been arrested and liquidated.

One early morning the whole Mendez household, including the dog, the cat, and the turkey, boarded a truck and headed for San Isidro to wait for General MacArthur.

XI

LET FREEDOM RING

A few days after his return to Manila with the liberating forces, Brigadier-General Carlos P. Romulo sent a messenger to San Isidro with an invitation for Mendez to meet him in Tarlac. It was a joyous reunion, a night filled with laughter and nostalgic chatter until sunrise. That same evening Romulo invited him to join the staff he was organizing to represent the Philippines in the United Nations. It was a tempting offer, but Mendez said he would finish his law studies first and join the Philippine Mission later.

With the Commonwealth government firmly re-established, Mendez returned to work. He rode a bicycle to Malacañang every day until he was appointed Undersecretary of Information, whereupon he was provided with an army jeep. Members of his staff included Raul Manglapus, a well-known guerrilla leader, and Philip Buencamino III, a survivor of the Bataan death march.[1]

Postwar Malacañang was a rhapsody in brown, swarming with Filipinos in khaki uniforms donated by the U.S. Army. Many of them could produce guerrilla certificates at the drop of a helmet. Before long, it became a joke to boast, "I, too, was a guerrilla."

Mendez was particularly irked by well-known collaborators who claimed that they were *guerrilleros* during the Occupation. He dismissed them as "alleged generalissimos of dubious underground movements."[2] Future Manila Mayor Arsenio Lacson, then the author of a racy no-byline column called "Open Secrets" in the *Philippine Press*, remarked that "after Manuel Roxas and Hilario Moncado made public their unsurpassable records as Generalissimo and four-star general respectively, no one else has had the courage to make public his underground activities. As a matter of fact, Mauro Mendez has never had the daring to disclose that he too was a guerrilla major."[3]

When the guerrilla organizations filed claims for backpay, "Major" Mendez refused to join the bandwagon. "I didn't join the underground to get paid," he said.

The Information Explosion

Postwar Manila was in high spirits despite hard times. The purchasing power of the peso was only one-third of its prewar value. The Emergency Control Administration (E.C.A.) was created to ration rice and bread and to keep prices down. One of Mendez's chores was to assure the nation that it was not going to starve and that nobody need worry about the rice shortage. Recalling the three years of hunger during the Occupation, he said, "We can eat camote again; what is more, we can plant it again in all our backyards."[4] Public reaction—typical Filipino humor—was that E.C.A. meant "Eat Camote Again."

Although the information office was then attached to the Department of Public Instruction, Mendez's work was a continuation of what he had been doing before the war broke out. But he was much busier after the war, especially with press relations. As soon as Manila showed signs of normalcy, a free press re-emerged from the ruins in all its prewar glory. At one time there were more than 20 different newspapers to delight a populace that was hungry for the truth.

It was the first big heyday of Philippine columnists, all of whom had something to say about "the ubiquitous information undersecretary" and "the self-effacing assistant of Don Sergio."[5] According to the *Manila Chronicle's This Week* magazine, "An old hand in the newspaper game, Mendez won the warm sympathy of the Malacañan reporters, and soon the doings of President Osmeña and the various departments in the Commonwealth received a big play in the local dailies."[6] Lacson's "Open Secrets" remarked that one could judge "the ups and downs of the President from the smile or scowl on Mauro Mendez's bespectacled face."[7]

Resident Commissioner Romulo wrote Mendez from Washington in August 1945: "It does not surprise me at all that you and Osmeña should be pals. He represents the almost extinct type of Filipino gentleman that my father and your father were."

On August 6, 1945, a letter in defense of President Osmeña appeared in *Time* magazine. Entitled "Healthy Statesman," it was signed by "Maury" Mendez (*Time*'s spelling) in reply to an article in a previous issue in which the President was described as "greying and ailing." "Mr. Osmeña is greying but not ailing—far from it," wrote "Maury." "I have had the privilege of working with him every day, Sundays and holidays included, and my observation is that he has never been more fit in his career than at this time." The letter added that Osmeña was undisturbed by the "rigors of the presidential post" and that he was ready to "shoulder the heavy burdens of the Commonwealth reconstruction and rehabilitation program.... Mr. Osmeña's perfect health is due to his methodical existence and his complete abstinence from all forms of excesses."

News of Mr. Osmeña's good health did not dim Senate President Roxas' visions of occupying Malacañang. Osmeña was then 67 years old, and the opposition bloc of the Nacionalista Party was planning to make his age an issue in the campaign to install Roxas in his place.

To the Roxas faction, Mendez's appointment as Undersecretary of Information seemed to be bad news. Perhaps they remembered the Hare-Hawes-Cutting debate, the Quezon-Osmeña victory in 1935, the apostleship in Malacañang. As a press-relations officer and publicity agent, he was a man to reckon with. *The Newspaperman,* a magazine published and edited by prominent newsmen, rated him "one of the big guns of Philippine journalism."[8]

From June to September 1945, Osmeña submitted Mendez's name to the Commission on Appointments six times, and six times it was "shelved" for future discussion. The Roxas group was powerful enough to keep the case "in cold storage," as one paper put it.[9]

The controversy was interesting for the light it shed on the pros and cons of a Department of Public Information. Senator Mariano Jesus Cuenco said that the information handed out by Mendez's office was "biased and slanted." Speaker Cornelio Villareal branded the Department of Information a "Department of Political Propaganda smacking of Nazism." Senator Roxas agreed with his colleagues but later changed his reason and gave the polite excuse that an information office was unnecessary in peacetime. He cited the fact that the United States had dismantled its Office of War Information on V-J Day.[10]

Expressing "shock" when the Commission on Appointments first set the Mendez nomination aside, a reporter for *This Week* remarked:

"Roxas felt that in the fight for the Commonwealth presidency he would be at a disadvantage because Osmeña had somebody to boost him. Another reason for Mendez's blackballing was that the former editor was too intimate with reporters who get much inside stuff from him."[11]

An anonymous writer of an editorial squib wrote about having informed a "member of the local house of lords, who stands high in the Commission on Appointments," that the Mendez office was not an Osmeña creation:

> And being one of those who believe that the late President Quezon could do no wrong, he was simply stunned when we demonstrated to him that his late idol created the office of information—first as an office of special services, and later office of information and public relations. Save for the difference in name, Mendez is occupying the office Quezon created in Washington in 1942 to "collect, collate, and disseminate information about the Philippines and the Commonwealth government."[12]

The Tagalog press also expressed itself strongly on the case of *Kalihim Mendez*. Lope K. Santos, editor of *Ang Bayan,* deplored the fact that the commission, on the pretext of applying the letter of the law, was inclined to reject Mendez's appointment. Santos wrote: "Dinaramdam naming ang pangalan at katungkulan ni Mauro Mendez, na kung sa kakayahan, karangalan at katapatang-loob ay hindi matatawaran ng sinuman, ay isa pa ngayong nagiging sangkalan at tuntungan ng masamang lakad ng pulitika sa Pilipinas."[13] ("We regret that the name and position of Mauro Mendez, whose qualifications, integrity, and sincerity cannot be questioned by anyone, have become a tool for the machinations of Philippine politics.")

The *raison d'etre* of a Department of Information was best explained by Abelardo Subido, editor of the *Manila Post*. He admitted that such a department could be used as a propaganda tool, "but in a country where freedom of speech and press and freedom to criticize are the boon of the citizens, in a country where the opposition is an active check on the ruling party, this danger is easily forestalled."

"An independent Philippines," continued Subido, "needs organized publicity, not only to promote her trade, commerce and industries, but also to win her the recognition and regard of sister countries, and enhance her innate prestige and dignity."[14]

Finally, word of an impending confirmation reached Mendez through the grapevine of the Fourth Estate. Some newsmen who covered the "house of lords" told him that Roxas was merely waiting for him to plead personally for the confirmation. Never! said Mauro Mendez, not even if he had to lose his job and eat camote again.

Not to be outfoxed by the commission, President Osmeña appointed Mendez his press secretary, the first in the Philippines to hold that title. He carried the item of an undersecretary, but his salary was drawn from the President's funds. Naming him "Man of the Week," the *Chronicle*'s Sunday supplement rejoiced that "handsome, curly-haired, be-spectacled" Mauro Mendez was now "out of the range of the Congressional big guns."[15]

The Os-Rox Split

In January 1946, Osmeña made a half-hearted decision to run for President against Manuel Roxas. To preserve his health, as well as unity in the Nacionalista Party, he had considered withdrawing in favor of his old friend, but some of his colleagues warned him that his failure to run would open the door to all sorts of nuisance candidates. The party would thus be more fragmented than ever.

If the Roxas faction, then known as the Liberal Wing, had any fears that the Mendez press relations would help Osmeña remain in power, they were groundless. It was impossible to boost a candidate who was not really interested in the presidency, and who refused to meet his opponent on the campaign trail. The President felt that his long record of public service was too well known to repeat. To remind the voters of Osmeña's existence, Mendez distributed 1,000 copies of a twelve-page biographical sketch that he had written himself. The title was *Sergio Osmeña—Highlights Of A Leadership Unequalled By That Of Any Living Filipino*.

The biographer knew his subject well. Fifteen years before, on September 9, 1931, he had written a front-page journalistic essay for the *Tribune* on the occasion of Osmeña's 53rd birthday. Even then, Osmeña was the archetypal Filipino statesman, exuding dignity through every greying hair. By 1946 the aura of dignity had increased around his silver head; it was difficult to imagine him running, literally or figuratively. As expected, the Liberals made capital of his wrinkles, and the Chief Executive did nothing to erase the suspicion voiced by

Arsenio Lacson that he had "one foot in the grave and the other on a banana peel."[16]

By comparison, Manuel Roxas was dramatic, ebullient, and imaginative. Nobody expected him to reach the grave ahead of Don Sergio, but then, as General MacArthur had often said, Osmeña was "slow."[17] (Aside from Roxas, two other Philippine Presidents were to die ahead of him—Elpidio Quirino and Ramon Magsaysay.)

One of the campaign gimmicks circulated by the Roxas headquarters was the draft of an undated letter allegedly sent by the late President Quezon to General MacArthur during the war. Quezon thought that Roxas had been captured by the Japanese, and feared the worst for his protégé. Part of the letter read:

> The news that Roxas fell into the hands of the Japanese has broken me almost completely, for I suspect that after his insistent refusal to be President of the Philippines the Japanese might murder him.
>
> But oh, how proud I am of him! I almost envy him for he had occasion to do just what I wanted to do myself—tell the Japanese that we want nothing from them.
>
> If Roxas has been murdered he is the greatest loss that the Filipino people have suffered in this war. He can't be replaced and I don't know how long [before] the race will produce another Manuel Roxas.

Subsequent research has proven that this letter was never sent and that its inclusion in Quezon's autobiography was an error on the part of those who continued the unfinished book.[18]

Mendez, for one, refused to take the letter at its face value. He produced an answer in a full-page advertisement that included excerpts from Quezon's tributes to the statesmanship of Sergio Osmeña, as well as the press secretary's own evaluation of the Quezon letter:

> The letter of the late President Quezon was written when Quezon was under the impression that Roxas had been captured by the Japs, put to the torture, and killed.
>
> But—
>
> Roxas had surrendered. Roxas was not being tortured—on the contrary, the Japs were pampering him. Roxas accepted high posts under the Japs, signed the Jap-sponsored Constitution, and gave his assent to the declaration of war on the United States.

Would Quezon have written that letter after Roxas had done all that? He would have denounced him instead! To say that he would have approved all that Roxas did is to impeach both the patriotism and the wisdom of our late great President.[19]

But Roxas was ready with letters from American commanders of guerrilla organizations, acknowledging him as head of the resistance movement in the Philippines. He denied having been captured by the American forces during the siege of Baguio, insisting that he had escaped to the American side. At any rate the issue was academic, for General MacArthur, an old Roxas friend, had cleared him of all charges even before the People's Court was convened to try the collaborators. The Filipino people, worshippers at the MacArthur altar, buried the past and swept Roxas into office.

The Morning Sun

Before the Osmeña defeat, columnist Pedro Padilla observed that the presidential press secretary was not at home with politics:

> Mendez is essentially a literary man. I think he is doing violence to his self-respect whenever he works himself up into a frenzy over things that he knows exclusively belong to politics.
> Mendez simply doesn't have the political temperament.
> Let me give an instance. A few days ago an afternoon paper printed an indirect answer to one of Mendez's press releases. The paper made the gratuitous remark that he was not of sufficient stature to be taken seriously. And did Mendez fume!
> Well there you are. Does Mendez think he can play with fire without getting burned?
> No. He'd better go back to journalism. He is more at home there.[20]

A similar left-handed compliment was voiced by another columnist: "A friend of ours in the Chronicle is rooting for Roxas because the victory of Roxas will be a gain for Philippine journalism—Mauro Mendez will again be available for that kind of militant writing that he is cut out for in the first place."[21]

The prediction was accurate. On May 18, 1946, "The Jaywalker" of the *Daily News,* a young columnist who signed himself "T.F.V." (Teodoro F. Valencia) made this announcement:

> Our good friend Maury Mendez will soon put out a daily which he has chosen to call *'Manila Morning Sun.'* ... This was the original name of the *Daily Standard* but people were sensitive about *Sun* even before the general elections. The Nacionalistas were afraid then that it would be discovered that some of their ways resembled the tried and true policies of the Rising Sun.
>
> The *Manila Morning Sun,* so Mendez swears, will be strictly, absolutely, positively, and definitely non-partisan. ... We take Maury's word. But let's see.

On May 22 the maiden issue of the *Morning Sun* was on the newsstands, proclaiming its motto, "All that's news under the sun." Mendez's associate editors were Ernesto Rodriguez, Jr., a colleague from the prewar *Herald,* and Zacarias Nuguid. Rodriguez wrote a column on "Politics and Politicos," and Jose L. Guevara presented the lighter side of things in "Sunny Side-Up."

Mendez objected when newsmen described the launching of the *Sun* as the "birth of a new opposition daily." "Yes, we are the opposition—to all wrong," he answered. "The shortest route to a journalistic funeral is partisan politics."[22]

Letting bygones be bygones, he put Roxas' picture on the front page of the *Sun*'s maiden issue. On July 4, 1946, on the inauguration of Philippine independence and of Manuel Roxas as first President of the Republic, Mendez conceded that the new Chief Executive was a "man of broad ideas, a leader of great breadth and capacity." In his editorial for that day the ex-press secretary pledged his support of the man against whom he had campaigned.

Mendez's first *Morning Sun* editorial, "Our Daily Bread," was a tribute to the Filipino newspaperman:

> While the human motive is not always pure, we submit that a newspaper is too serious a proposition to be the object of mere adventure, and the men who go into its publication, openly and without fear, have the presumption of good faith in their favor. The responsibility they assume is too heavy to be toyed with lightly, and the day they break faith with the public, that day they are finished.
>
> We like the public to believe that the men who "sweat it out" in the newspaper office are out to prove—as they are proving—that free men are the mainstay of public opinion, just as free men and good men are the foundation itself of all civilization....

The Filipino newspaperman does honor to our citizenry. We submit that he possesses the fundamental common sense of the race, that he is God-fearing, that he is eminently true to the oath of his profession.

It was a compliment to the countless writers perspiring in the countless newspaper offices in the land. "Mauro Mendez is a free man again," crowed Ernesto del Rosario of the *Chronicle*. "His first editorial in the maiden issue of the *Morning Sun* yesterday gave us goose pimples. The Press really can be greatly powerful as long as newspapermen remain free."[23] As a former captive on the staff of the Occupation *Tribune,* del Rosario knew whereof he spoke.

A week after the *Morning Sun* went into circulation, Mendez received a cordial letter from Dr. Pedro T. Orata, one of the country's foremost educators. Orata had missed one issue of the *Sun* and wanted a copy reserved for himself. "It is my intention to keep a complete file of your paper because of the editorials which appeal to me," he wrote. "I like the way you keep both sides clear and your putting the responsibility on the people to see both sides. This is what we call in education 'being critical and fair.' "

"Sun Beams"

The publication of the *Morning Sun* marked Mendez's first return to verse-writing since the early 1930s. The daily editorial page featured his sprightly "Sun Beams," a short verse-column that chattered of all that was news under the sun.

The "Sun Beams" were hastily composed; once in a while Mendez would scribble them while he was at the press, waiting for proofs to be run off.[24] Some of the verses were witty; others were clumsy. All were satiric in content and style.

Side by side, the editorials and the "Sun Beams" often balanced each other by touching on the same subject, the former in a serious manner, the latter in a humorous vein. An example of such a subject was the notorious Bell Trade Relations Act sponsored by Missouri Congressman Jasper Bell. Mendez wrote strongly against it because of its "parity" clause, which gave the Americans a free hand in exploiting the natural wealth of the war-ravaged Islands. To him the economic consequences of parity would be "the stark evidence of what independence is not, rather than what it is."25

Roxas wanted the Bell Bill approved, and after much vacillation, the House of Representatives gave in to the President. Mendez commented on the event with a verse beginning with this mock imitation of Thomas Gray's *Elegy Written in a Country Churchyard*:

> The Congress tolls the Bell of happy days,
> The party sheep dissent and then agree,
> The Prexy hears the yes, yes from his place
> And nods assent to Julius and to me.*

Drawing the Amnesty Line

Another topic that recurred in the *Sun*'s editorials and their accompanying "Sun Beams" was the question of whether amnesty should be granted to collaborators. Mendez was naturally against a general amnesty for collaborators of all stripes. He suggested that the public "draw the line between those who collaborated politically within the bounds of human reason, and those who saw eye to eye with the enemy and gloriously went out of bounds."26

Two weeks after he wrote this, the nation was gratified to learn that the Japanese lieutenant-general who had killed Justice Jose Abad Santos had been arrested. Mendez took this opportunity to eulogize the late Secretary of Justice by contrasting his martyrdom with the comfort enjoyed by the collaborators who were now the objects of a clamor for amnesty.27

The collaboration-amnesty theme received ironic treatment in the "Sun Beams":

> Someone who always talked aloud
> Did say in language clear,
> That Filipinos should be proud
> The Japanese were here.

---

* The original stanza from Gray:
> The curfew tolls the knell of parting day,
> The lowing herd wind slowly o'er the lea,
> The plowman homeward plods his weary way
> And leaves the world to darkness and to me.

(In the parody, "Julius" is a reference to Commander Julius Caesar Edelstein of the American Embassy, a close friend and adviser of Roxas.)

> He thanked the Japs who came to crush
>   Imperialism's might,
> And said 'twas sad he had to rush
>   Another's war to fight.
>
> He called all that a rotten game
>   In ire that made us quail,
> Now watch him play a humbler game
> **And get out free on bail.**[28]

Unmoved by verses, editorials, and anti-amnesty rallies, President Roxas granted amnesty to all collaborators without drawing any lines. Soon after, he also granted amnesty to guerrillas who had committed crimes supposedly in pursuance of the resistance movement.

Huks to the Left

The Hukbalahap guerrillas, however, were not to be dismissed with a simple grant of amnesty. To them the end of the war was only the beginning of another battle to raise the red flag of Communism over Central Luzon. President Roxas' biggest headache was the fratricidal war between the Huks and the Military Police Command, better known as the MPs.

From Mendez's standpoint, the Huks added a new complication to the old problem of agrarian unrest. Having lived in Huklandia during the last months of the Occupation, he viewed the organization with mixed feelings. Some of the people he knew in San Isidro were tenants who had become Huks and who walked freely in and out of the Policarpio ancestral home, where the Mendezes lived with a tribe of relatives.

Every evening after supper, some townsfolk would come to the house to fetch Mendez for their regular get-together at a corner store. In the darkness lit only by their cigarettes, they would gossip about the world situation. Instinctively acting out his role as information officer, Mendez was always the center of attention. Aside from the usual friends, his listeners included the neighborhood Huks and their rivals, the USAFFE guerrillas.

His brother-in-law, Marcelo Samson, was a relative of Nueva Ecija's Huk chieftain, Juan Feleo.[29] On one occasion, Feleo invited Samson to a Huk meeting in barrio Pulo, and Mendez went along to "cover" the event. He noted that while his own shortwave newscasts came from American sources, the Huks' underground leaflets, also based on shortwave communiques, used the Moscow dateline. But Communism was the least of his worries at the time, for Russia was an ally of the United States against the Axis powers.

It was against this background that Mendez viewed the Huk problem right after the war. When the government called for immediate disarmament of the Huks, he felt some sympathy for them:

> First to draw sword against the sons of heaven, the men of Taruc and Alejandrino defied the anti-arms orders and picked up the quarrel with the foe in the hill and the jungle, in barrio and city, in every place where a blow for freedom could be struck, and death for fascism.
>
> The Huks were hunted far and wide, put to the most inhuman torture and death when captured, but they fought on and on, until the yellow invader learned to fear and respect them. It was clear to the Japanese that this was the best organized resistance they had to contend with.
>
> And so, these are the men we are seeking to disarm now. From their hands we would receive the arms which they risked life and limb to snatch from the enemy—the same arms, in most cases, for which so much Huk blood was shed.[30]

Mendez suggested that the government at least pay for the arms surrendered. What the government would lose in pesos, it would gain in peace and security. "Most of the present holders of unlicensed firearms are people in need, and only sentimental reasons might dissuade them from giving up their prized possessions."[31]

At the same time Mendez echoed what he had often said in his prewar editorials, namely, that there was no made-to-order cure for social unrest. He cautioned the people against being deluded by "grandstand play" such as peace parades and front-page pictures of Secretary of Interior Jose Zulueta receiving rifles and carbines from the Huks. Zulueta was then in charge of the pacification campaign, and he figured prominently in Mendez's "Sun Beams." For example:

> The tempo of the MP's ire,
>   The anger of the Huks
> Seem more convincing than the fire
>   In Joe Zulueta's looks.
>
> We get them here, they fire them there—
>   It's very hard to tell

> Which way it's going, foul or fair,
>   But Pepe says it's swell.
>
> Fight, brothers, fight; on with the row,
>   Let war be unconfined!
> If all the arms come back to Joe
>   Can more be far behind?*

Now and then the government would announce a breakthrough in the peace campaign. The Huk spokesmen would come to Manila and join the pacification chiefs at a sumptuous meal, during which they would talk of ending the bloodshed. Meanwhile, Secretary Zulueta informed the President that he had spent ₱60,000 on the building of cantonments in which the Huks were to register their arms.

Mendez looked askance at the cantonments project. A "lauriat," in his opinion, would be more effective:

> For all we know, chop suey may get
>   The peace we have not won,
> That better than cantonments yet
>   Is plain pancit canton.[32]

Newspaper Blues

While Mendez was working on the *Morning Sun,* he was also vice-president of the Philippine Newspaper Guild and head of the U.S.T. School of Journalism. Norberto de Ramos, U.S.T. registrar, was impressed with the way Mendez discharged his duties:

> His quiet but effective classroom manner and meticulous correcting of every error of his students, had a tremendous impact upon those who wanted to learn from him. His students in journalism and law at the University of Santo Tomas, for instance, learned the art of the profession with the Mendez imprint. For to Mauro Mendez, the professor's chair was not only for the learning of his students; he also considered teaching as a mission that a pro-

---

* Another instance of Mendez's flair for parodying his favorite poets. In the second stanza "foul or fair" is derived from Shakespeare's *Macbeth:* "Fair is foul and foul is fair." "On with the dance! Let joy be unconfined" is perhaps the most famous line from Byron's *Childe Harold's Pilgrimage,* Canto IV. "Oh Wind, if Winter comes, can Spring be far behind?" is the last line of Shelley's *Ode to the West Wind.*

fessor must profit from by continuous studying and researching in order to guide his students to wider horizons and a deeper understanding of basic principles.[33]

At an age (50) when most people would have put their schoolbooks behind them, Mendez was still studying. In 1946 he received his law degree from U.S.T. and reviewed for the bar examinations. In November of that year he passed the bar with a rating of 83.85 percent, the highest of the ratings obtained by the ten newspapermen who took the same tests. He went on to get his Master of Laws at U.S.T., where he also taught some law subjects. Coincidentally, he found himself in the classroom as a student of his onetime cub reporter, Diosdado Macapagal.

Unfortunately, at about this time, the *Morning Sun* began to set for lack of funds. Many people asked for it at newsstands, but there were never enough copies printed to make it a going concern. Most of the other newspapers in the postliberation era met a similar fate.

"A newspaper cannot subsist on the stuff of dream," Mendez wrote a year later. "Of necessity it must count on some business organization if it is to survive." [34]

The idealist in him had always regretted the relatively low salaries of the newsmen during his time, and the dependence of the press on advertising support. At a conference on press freedom held in India in 1947, he suggested that newspapermen "pool their resources, then pull together." They would thus be share-holders in their corporation instead of merely hired men. "Only by having as writers men who are economically free may a free press become a reality." [35]

He called to mind an incident in 1935, when he had written an editorial on how appropriate it would be for Filipinos to wear *barong tagalogs* instead of cutaway suits to the inauguration of the Commonwealth. "Manila is not Tokyo, nor Washington, nor Paris. Here we don't shiver but perspire; here, indeed, we earn our bread by the sweat of our brows." He reasoned, further, that the cutaway was unsuited to Filipino customs and financial means.[36]

The following day a well-known American haberdashery and tailoring establishment on the Escolta complained that the editorial was "a direct assault on its business." The firm was making the tuxedos to be worn by high officials at the inauguration, and it was feared that no further orders would be received because of that editorial. The

Herald's business manager advised Mendez to take back his sartorial opinions or lose a substantial amount of advertising revenues. Swallowing his editorial pride, Mendez wrote an immediate follow-up, informing the public where to get lightweight woolen cutaway suits for the inauguration.[37]

This was the sort of business tyranny that made the Mendez blood simmer. Good motives and patriotic intentions meant nothing to advertisers. As he put it bluntly, "shorn of ideals, the newspaper is reduced to a sort of mercantilistic monstruosity." In his article, "Stalwarts of the Fourth Estate," written in 1947, he presented these cold facts:

> They who have not the letter of credit to buy the linotypes, the rotaries, the newsprint, and the ink, shall not inherit the kingdom of the Press. For them the pursuit of truth must be along harmless paths only. Theirs is not to question the good-will that draws the merchants, or, in a country so small as theirs, to incur for the hands that feed them the distempers of the gods.[38]

Political gods were another obstacle to the freedom and the stability of the Philippine press. Mendez attributed the financial difficulties of the prewar *Herald* to the interference of sugar barons and politicians combined. "Thus was the cause of journalism subordinated to ends strange to it. The ideals of legitimate newspapermen were placed second to the fortunes of personal politics and the goals of trade and commerce." [39]

He had served Quezon loyally and sincerely during his D-M-H-M days, but he had no intention of repeating history. In June 1947, the Liberal Party thought of publishing its own newspaper and began scouting around for an editor. Mendez was mentioned as the only candidate. Jose L. Guevara, then writing his "Post No Ill" column for the *Manila Post,* was among those who assumed that the Mendez appointment was inevitable: "My friend and former boss, Mauro Mendez, is being groomed for editorship of the Philippine Liberal, which, I understand, will serve as the mouthpiece...of the present administration. 'The Morning Sun will shine again,' as the song would put it." [40]

President Roxas made the offer personally to Mendez at Malacañang, in the presence of Mrs. Mendez. It was the first time she had witnessed a President fumbling for words. Mendez, for his part, was speechless.

"Money is no object," said Roxas. "You will have full financial backing." Sensing Mendez's hesitation, he added kindly, "You need not make a decision now. You may send me your answer later."

Mendez's answer was a humble "no." In his letter to the President he wrote: "I had not expected to deserve such generosity from you, and I need not say how deeply grateful and honored I feel. . . . I trust that you will not take this painful decision of mine as any hesitation on my part to serve you, for I know my duty and I know you are my President."

With that letter, Mauro Mendez made his last farewell to editorial writing.

XII

HANDS ACROSS THE SEA

The year was 1965, and Mauro Mendez, then Secretary of Foreign Affairs, was being interviewed by a reporter from *The Quill,* official organ of the professional journalists' society, Sigma Delta Chi. "I can remember when Romulo and I used to wrap up the papers to catch the early morning mail to Ilocos," he said. "Diplomacy couldn't have been farther from our minds."

Nonetheless, Mendez's experience as an editorial interpreter of world events stood him in good stead when he entered the foreign service. "I think a successful newspaperman would qualify for any important diplomatic assignment," he told his interviewer. "He is able to see things in a larger context, and this is valuable background." [1]

From the *Herald* alone, six men rose to high positions in the diplomatic service—Carlos P. Romulo, Salvador P. Lopez, Modesto Farolan, Vicente Albano Pacis, Narciso Ramos, and Mauro Mendez— a record unmatched by any other newspaper. S.P. Lopez has this explanation for the phenomenon of the journalist-diplomat: "Journalism is one of the best training grounds for diplomacy because it is a discipline that trains a person to be a generalist, to think broadly and liberally. The editorial writer develops breadth and universality, both of which are qualities of a good diplomat." [2]

Awakening in Delhi

Mendez's first sortie into international relations took place in March and April 1947, when he and his wife went to India as delegates of the Institute of Pacific Relations to the Inter-Asian Relations Conference. In a series of thirteen articles for the *Manila Times,* he wrote of the momentous meeting of representatives from 32 countries embracing more than half of the human race: "Emerging from the shadow of old imperialisms, a long-suppressed continent unfurled its colors to launch a movement of human integration without precedent in the memory of men now living." [3]

He described the thunderous cheers of the 50,000 people who filled the ancient fort of Purana Qila in New Delhi to watch Asian history in the making. "It was a setting by Destiny itself," he observed. "Never did so many hearts beat as one for a single cause, or so many eyes see so clearly but one fate, or so many ears hear so distinctly but one clarion-call, as on that occasion, under one canopy." [4]

His opening article, "Interview with Nehru," described how India's Prime Minister and "Man of Destiny" moved about "without the least ostentation, ever mindful of the hopeless misery of the millions of men, women, and children whose lives are, to use his own words, 'a slow merging into non-existence.'"

Rationing was strictly observed in postwar India. At Nehru's residence, Mendez received a "microscopic" cube of sugar in his teacup, for the Prime Minister's weekly ration had been used up.

"Of course you are entitled to exemptions from this rationing," suggested Mendez.

"Well, that is true. I may ask for exemptions, but one does not really care for exemptions," was Nehru's reply.[5]

A remark made by Romulo in a letter to Mrs. Mendez in June 1947, testifies to the pleasant impression left by the Mendezes on Pandit Nehru:

> Only yesterday at the cocktail party I gave in honor of Assistant Secretary-General Owen, I was speaking to Mr. Nehru, who entertained you and Mauro in his home in New Delhi, and he was singing your praises. That naturally made me very proud of you.

Another Indian whom Mendez met and wrote about was Mahatma Gandhi, then India's greatest living man. He was reclining on a big white pillow, facing the audience that had gone there to see him. A brief but meaningful dialogue ensued between Mendez and the Mahatma:

> "Mr. Gandhi," I began, "I am a delegate from the Philippines."

He smiled very cordially and we shook hands.
"The Philippines," I continued, "is now independent."
"Yes, yes, I know...but are you quite sure?" [6]

Skepticism about the Philippines' newly acquired independence was widespread among the delegates to the conference. Mendez reported that the Filipinos were greeted cordially but not with the cheering ovations that hailed the delegates from Indonesia and Vietnam. The Asians "love a good fight," he noted. They admired the Vietnamese and the Indonesians for opposing the imperialists from France and the Netherlands. "Nothing was more certain than that the delegates to the Asian Conference were not enamored of the British, the French, or the Dutch, and that on the testimony of their misdeeds there was ground enough for a common cause against all colonizers of the earth." [7]

On the other hand, the Philippine revolution against Spain had happened in a forgotten past. As far as the Asians were concerned, "the curtain had dropped forever on that heroic episode." All they could remember was the Filipino attachment to the American colonizer, an aberration that puzzled the rest of exploited Asia.

One of the accomplishments of the Inter-Asian Conference was the elimination of the word "Asiatic" from the "lexicon of the new Asia." Nehru entered his formal objection to the word, contemptuously used by the Western world, and asked that it be discarded. The delegates gave their unanimous assent, and thus the Asian conference stood out as a great landmark separating Asia's past from Asia's future.[8]

Another theme that emerged from the Conference was that the motley Asians were more likely to be unified by cultural cooperation than by the concept of "One Religion." Several delegates had suggested that "fundamentally, all religions are one, exactly as the human race must be one." Mendez was asked many times to cast his lot with "the apostles of One Religion" for the world, beginning with One Religion for Asia. But every time he asked which religion was to form the basis of the "divine amalgamation," the Hindus said, "Buddhism," and the Muslims said, "Mohammedanism."

Negotiations were then under way for the subcontinent's partition into Hindu India and Muslim Pakistan. The two religious factions were opposite poles, observed Mendez, and not even Gandhi's

Philippine delegation with their Indian hosts at the Inter-Asian Relations Conference in New Delhi in 1947. From left: Quirino Gregorio, Mauro Mendez, Prime Minister Jawaharlal Nehru, Mrs. Paz P. Mendez, Mme. Vijaya Laksmi Pandit (Nehru's sister) Anastacio de Castro, Jose Castro, Manuel Enverga, and Indira Gandhi.

Philippine Mission to the U.N. (1948) honors Amado Hernandez. From nato Constantino, Adriano Garcia, Victorio Carpio, Mauro Mendez, left: S.P. Lopez, Isaias Salonga (guest), Hernandez, Galo Ocampo, Re- Antonio Chanco, Jose D. Ingles, Pedro Abelarde, Col. Cesar Jimenez.

Mr. and Mrs. Mendez with five of their six children in Long Island. From left: Ruben, Mr. Mendez, Eloisa, Sylvia, Nina, Mrs. Mendez, and Carlo. Not in photo is son Manuel. (1948)

Mr. and Mrs. Mendez and S.P. Lopez with Mrs. Franklin D. Roosevelt at a party given by the latter in Hyde Park for delegates to the U.N. General Assembly. (1949)

Mendez speaking at committee meeting in former U.N. building in Lake Success, Long Island. (1949)

Mr. and Mrs. Mendez and daughter Sylvia, with Dave Boguslav of the Manila Times, *during the opening of the U.N. General Assembly in Paris in 1952.*

Mendez with Henry Cabot Lodge, Jr., U.S. Ambassador to the U.N. (1955)

Philippine Mission at U.N. meeting. Front, from left: Narciso G. Reyes, Mauro Mendez, Jose D. Ingles, Salvador P. Lopez, and F.E.U. President Teodoro Evangelista (visiting delegate from the Philippines). Behind, from left: Adriano Garcia and Victorio Carpio. (Mid-1950s)

Reception given by Indonesian Delegation to the U.N. in honor of President Sukarno (left) at Waldorf Astoria in New York. Beside Mendez (right) is Ambassador Thanat Khoman of Thailand. (1956)

Reunion of former Presidential Press Secretaries in 1958, when Minister Mauro Mendez was on home leave from Paris. From left: *Juan Orendain, Antonio L. Arizabal, Sr., Jose Nable, Vicente Albano Pacis, Mendez, Guillermo V. Sison, and party host Baldomero T. Olivera.*

Minister and Mrs. Mendez and daughters Eloisa and Nina on the Grand Canal in Venice. (1958)

Minister Mendez greets Laotian Ambassador to France, Prince Souvanna Phouma, at Philippine embassy reception in Paris. (1959)

Left: Minister and Mrs. Mendez at Heidelberg Castle in 1959, while retracing Rizal's footsteps through Europe.

Below: Minister Mendez (at right) with Pastor and Frau Gottlob Weber and the Webers' two sets of twin daughters at the vicarage in Wilhelmsfeld, Germany, in 1960. Marble plaque on table now hangs on vicarage wall to commemorate Rizal's stay in the same house.

persuasion and prayers could bring them together. "In the vision splendid of a One World which Gandhi said he would like to see realized during his lifetime, religion is not likely to be the leaven of unity. Every religion will tend to be self-contained, and when it becomes a way of life, it may prove to be a stumbling block to a One World." [9]

Mendez concluded his report with a look into India's future—"a giant may rise in Asia, and this giant will bear watching." [10] The prediction was fulfilled in 1974, when India, under the leadership of Nehru's daughter, Prime Minister Indira Gandhi, announced India's membership in the nuclear club of nations.

To New York, with Love

A year after the Delhi conference Mendez was ready to accept Romulo's invitation to join his staff at the U.N. It was also time to fulfill his promise to take his wife and children to the United States, a promise he had made in 1925, when Paz Policarpio forsook her Barbour scholarship on his behalf.

Forty newspapermen paid ₱2.50 each for a despedida luncheon in honor of their departing colleague. "When newspapermen pay for their meals, that is an event," commented the *Star Reporter*'s star columnist and editor, Vicente del Fierro. Nine newsmen delivered speeches after dessert, before singing the "Jolly Good Fellow" theme song.[11]

On September 1, 1948, Mendez and his family sailed for San Francisco on the *SS President Wilson*. He was afraid to take a plane because, as he was fond of saying, "You can't defy the law of gravity." The ocean voyage lasted almost three weeks, and everybody was seasick during the first week except the head of the family. He was not an ex-cabin boy for nothing.

From San Francisco they took a train for the four-day cross-country journey to the east, arriving in New York in a bedraggled state. They camped temporarily at the Langwell Hotel in the heart of Times Square. The hotel was a haven for Filipinos, who liked it not only for its proximity to the Great White Way but mainly because the management allowed them to pollute the air with the smell of home cooking. The corridors reeked of adobo and bagoong, enough reason for the Langwell to earn the nickname *Langaw* (fly) and even *Bangaw* (big fly).

School had already opened by the time the family arrived, so Mendez wasted no time teaching the children the intricacies of the subway system, they who had never gone to Quiapo alone. Later he took them to his favorite places—the Bronx Zoo, the Barnum and Bailey circus, Bear Mountain and Indian Point along the Hudson River. He was living his youth all over again.

One of the first places he visited was the campus of his alma mater on Morningside Heights. At Columbia he called on his friends for a chat about the good old 1920s. Some weeks later, at the invitation of Dean Ackerman of the Graduate School of Journalism, Mendez spoke to the students on the Philippine press before, during, and after the war. The Dean said that many of the boys had served in the Pacific and had a journalistic interest in all they had seen in the Philippines.

The Philippine Mission to the U.N.

The Philippine Mission to the United Nations was then housed on the 63rd floor of the Empire State Building. Romulo's star-studded staff included Salvador P. Lopez, Jose D. Ingles, Narciso G. Reyes, Renato Constantino, Adriano Garcia, Victorio D. Carpio, and Galo Ocampo. They were all neighbors in a new subdivision called Parkway Village in Jamaica, Long Island. The children grew up in an international community, for the village was leased exclusively to members of the diplomatic corps and employees of the United Nations.

The U.N.'s first home in New York was a sprawling building in the meadows of Long Island's Lake Success. It was there that Mendez found himself face to face with the Russians about whom he had written volumes of editorials. An incident that he later recalled with amusement took place when Russia's Foreign Minister, Andrei Vishinsky, while lecturing before a U.N. committee on the definition of aggression, accused the United States of having murdered General Emilio Aguinaldo. After the lecture, Mendez corrected him: "General Aguinaldo is very much alive and may be visited at his home in the Philippines." To his surprise, a friend later mailed him a newspaper clipping about the incident from, of all places, the *Glasgow Evening Citizen* in Scotland.

Mendez's modest role in the U.N. also made news in 1949, when the question of U.S. military bases in foreign countries came before the General Assembly's special political committee. The Soviet Union's Jacob Malik charged that the Philippines and Turkey were victims of American military domination. Both countries refuted the charge. Mendez explained that the American bases were not impositions on his country but were the result of a free decision of the government and the people.[12] By this time his position on the American presence had crystallized: he objected to American economic domination, but he held that the U.S. bases were essential to the balance of power in the Far East.

Mendez spoke in Spanish at U.N. meetings whenever the need arose. In November 1949, he delivered an extemporaneous speech at a meeting attended by many Spanish-speaking delegates. After the speech, Luis Fernan Cisneros, the Ambassador from Peru, shook his hand eagerly and congratulated him on his "magnifico discurso." Not satisfied with his verbal congratulations, Sr. Cisneros wrote him a letter the following day, profuse in Latin American "felicitaciones":

> Creo que usted hizo algo mas que intervenir con acierto en una tema transcendental de la angustiosa perspectiva del mundo. Usted concilio tan admirablemente con la ponderacion, la franqueza y la energia que produjo una interpretacion muy feliz de la madurez y la alta responsabilidad politica de Filipinas.
>
> Ademas, mi felicitacion se acrece por haber escogido usted la lengua de sus mayores para esta nueva confirmacion de la autoridad de su pais. La Comision debe de haberse dado cuenta de que ha querido usted mostrar, en ocasion muy oportuna, la raiz historica de su patriotismo. Y ha empleado usted el espanol con tal exactitud y espontaneidad que aquella raiz estuvo de relieve en todas las ideas y todas las palabras.

> (I believe that you did more than intervene successfully on a theme so transcendental as the distressing world situation. You mediated admirably with prudence, frankness, and liveliness, creating a pleasant impression of the Philippines' political maturity and high sense of responsibility.
>
> I am even more pleased by the fact that you chose to speak in the language of your elders during this confirmation of the authority of your country. The Commission must have realized that you wanted to show, on a very timely occasion, the historic roots of your patriotism. And you have used Spanish with such

precision and such spontaneity that all your ideas and your words stood out in bold relief.)

In 1953 Mendez was among the sponsors of the solution to the Puerto Rican problem, a settlement which made that island a Commonwealth, or Estado Libre de Puerto Rico, enjoying local autonomy, free trade with the U.S. mainland, and other benefits enjoyed by all other states in the Union, minus the burdens of taxation. For the Philippine role in bringing happiness to Puerto Rico, Mr. and Mrs. Mendez, together with Mr. and Mrs. Salvador P. Lopez, earned a second honeymoon on that Caribbean isle, courtesy of Governor Luis Muñoz Marin.

Mendez's assignment with the Philippine Mission was generally devoted to representing the Philippines at various meetings of the U.N. and ghost-writing speeches for visiting delegates from the Philippines, usually congressmen and senators. He sat on all the main committees of the General Assembly, such as the Sixth (Legal) Committee, as well as other committees—the Commission on Human Rights, the Economic and Social Council, and the Committee on Freedom of Information. He thus familiarized himself with practically all the issues that confronted the world body, including those that the general public seldom hears about, such as statelessness and stateless persons, tourism, and international criminal jurisdiction.

He was naturally most eloquent on the subject of freedom of information and matters concerning human repression in all its forms. In 1951 he was designated Philippine Representative to the U.N. Committee for Drafting a Convention on Freedom of Information.

In 1954, during a controversy on forced labor, he condemned countries where outspoken political dissidents were confined in slave-labor camps and reduced "to the category of beasts of burden, of guinea pigs, or of cannon fodder." "Where the essence of democracy exists, as in my country," he asserted, "the exchange of views and clash of ideas will remain untrammelled." [13]

In the same year, when he was part of the Ad Hoc Political Committee of the General Assembly, he spoke on the need for a free exchange of information among peoples. Addressing the Czechoslovakian delegate in particular, he said that the absence of a free press in totalitarian countries was an obstacle to peaceful coexistence. He challenged the Communist block to lift the iron curtain so that the world could see what went on in the "so-called paradise" of the Soviet Union and its satellites. In a free society the public was able to see through propaganda, but it was impossible to know the realities of life in countries shielded by the iron curtain.[14]

As a member of the Social, Cultural, and Humanitarian Committee, Mendez delivered a speech, explaining the Philippine stand on the self-determination of peoples. He asserted that some colonial powers had "plundered the resources of their colonies" while arrogating unto themselves a "messianic mission." The inhabitants of dependent territories, however, were now exploding the messianic myth by demanding the restoration of their fundamental rights. "The absolute truth," he concluded, "is that no people deserve to be subservient to an alien power as to the determination of what to do with the natural resources of their own land." [15]

In 1955 Mendez was elected Rapporteur of the Administrative and Budgetary Committee of the General Assembly. It was not as great as being U.N. Secretary-General, but he derived some comfort from a congratulatory letter written by one of his favorite colleagues, Narciso G. Reyes, who was then in the home office. Wrote Reyes:

> Congratulations again—on your election as Rapporteur this time. . . . Although the Secretariat is normally of great help, the final responsibility is yours. There's one consolation, though, for an Assembly Rapporteur. You can mount the plenary session rostrum more frequently than most chief delegates! It's nice to be up there, looking down on a prize assortment of VIPs, not to mention your fellow delegates in the Mission!

At that time Reyes probably had no idea that he was destined to be his country's chief delegate to the U.N. some twenty years later.

La Vie Parisienne

After nine years with the Philippine Mission, interrupted by a brief assignment in Washington, Mendez was appointed Minister Plenipotentiary to France. He sailed to Europe with his wife and his youngest daughter, Nina, better known as Popsy.

After a year, Popsy left Paris to go to college, making life quite lonely for the sentimental Papa. He had never been separated from all of his six children at the same time. Three years before, when he walked his eldest daughter up the aisle on her wedding day, his cheeks were soaked with tears.

Fortunately, there were more than enough diplomatic and cultural activities to keep the Minister and his wife from pining away in Paris. They also had interesting Filipino guests who either stayed in their apartment for days or dropped in to sample Mrs. Mendez's native cuisine, concocted out of French ingredients. "Oh how I enjoyed that,,paksiw,,!" wrote poet Jose Garcia Villa in a thank-you "comma" letter from New York.

Although Mendez had previously lived in Paris for four months, during the U.N. General Assembly of 1951–52, he had never ceased to marvel at the French. He loved to spend his idle hours at a sidewalk café, sipping tea and watching Paris go by. French diction intrigued him, and so did French currency. Whenever he boarded a bus, he simply held out a palmful of coins to the conductor and trusted the honest fellow to pick out the right amount. The Minister and his wife took their close friends sightseeing by public bus. "The Muse of Tourism is ever Mrs. Mendez's guide, and so we never go wrong," he wrote in a letter to his children.

To the Mendezes, the charm of Paris was enhanced by the knowledge that Rizal had lived there, had strolled along the same Champs Elysees and enjoyed the same shade in the gardens of the Tuileries. Paris was a perfect launching pad for a Rizaliana journey through Europe. Like a pair of bloodhounds, guided by what Mendez called his wife's "Rizaliana intuition," the couple spent more than a year following Rizal's trail on the continent, covering extensive ground not only in Paris but also Strassbourg, Ghent, Brussels, Heidelberg, and Wilhelmsfeld.

"All in all, it has been an extravaganza of motion, action, and sometimes grief and exasperation," wrote Mendez to his children in January 1960. "The title of the story is ALL FOR RIZAL. And all because that man was such a wanderer, covering the earth's vast spaces untiringly in the days when cars and aeroplanes weren't even dreamed of."

Wherever they went, Mendez was armed with Philippine cigars to give away. He used to hand out *Alhambra Coronas* and *Tabacalera Super Kings* even to complete strangers whom he met in train compartments. At the University of Heidelberg the librarian went out of his way to help them when Mendez gave him some Tabacaleras. In Paris he parted with most of his precious Coronas to please Monsieur Limet, a bearded septuagenarian discovered by Mrs. Mendez in the apartment building once occupied by Juan Luna and Felix Resurreccion Hidalgo. Limet, an artist who used to work for the great sculptor, Auguste Rodin, remembered having smoked Hidalgo's Philippine cigars, and he considered them the best in the world.

Wherever the Mendezes discovered an important former Rizal residence, the Rizal Centennial Commission authorized them to install a commemorative plaque. The first French building to be thus adorned was the clinic where Dr. Rizal had trained as an ophthalmologist under the famous Dr. Louis de Wecker. Salvador P. Lopez, then Ambassador to France, unveiled the plaque on Rizal Day, 1959, before an audience of Filipino residents in Paris.

In Ghent, Belgium, the Mendezes located the lodging house where Rizal had lived while his novel, *El Filibusterismo,* was being printed. The installation of a plaque at the lodging house elicited wide interest among the citizens of Ghent. The mayor was visibly honored by the fact that the Philippine hero had chosen to reside in the Belgian city, and requested that copies of the *Fili* be donated to the University of Ghent and to the public libraries. Minister Mendez distributed biographical data on Rizal to the reporters present, plus champagne and cigars to the guests.

Rizaliana in Wilhelmsfeld

The biggest event of all was the discovery of Rizaliana in Wilhelmsfeld and Heidelberg in late 1959. In June of that year the Mendezes had gone to Belgium to attend the wedding of Prince Albert and Princess Paula. On the way back to Paris they thought of stopping in Heidelberg to do some research on Rizal. Guided by a one-sentence reference to a certain village named "Wilhelmsdorf" in Retana's biography of Rizal, they inquired at their hotel where the village could be located. Their informant told them that there was a place called Wilhelmsfeld in the Odenwald hills not far from Heidelberg.

The Mendezes then motored to Wilhelmsfeld. All they accomplished on their first visit was a lunch of wieners and sauerkraut at a small inn. The language barrier prevented them from asking the other guests if they had heard of a certain Filipino named Jose Rizal.

But they remembered the name of the inn, and back in Paris, Mrs. Mendez wrote a letter of inquiry to the innkeeper, with the aid of a German translator. It was almost like writing a letter to Santa Claus. The innkeeper referred her letter to Pfarrer (Pastor) Gottlob Weber, who, after some time, wrote Mrs. Mendez the astounding news that he was occupying the vicarage where a Filipino had stayed as a guest of Pastor Karl Ullmer in 1886. He also informed her that the great-grandsons of the Pastor, Hans and Fritz Hack, aged 22 and 23, had inherited a box of precious memorabilia dating from Rizal's vacation in Wilhelmsfeld.

At dawn of New Year's Day, 1960, the Mendezes left Paris by train, the Minister clutching a heavy black marble plaque destined for the Wilhelmsfeld vicarage. They reached the village in the evening, after a rainy ten-hour journey. They were welcomed as dinner guests by the jolly Weber family in the historic vicarage where Rizal had put the finishing touches to the *Noli Me Tangere*.

The following day Pastor Weber drove them to Heidelberg to visit the Hack family. Hans and Fritz brought out their great-grandfather's old wooden chest and showed them what no other Filipino, except Rizal, had ever seen: several letters and postcards in German from Rizal to the Ullmers; an original copy of the first edition of the *Noli,* with the author's dedication to Karl Ullmer; some sketches, cartoons, and comic strips drawn by Rizal for the Ullmer children; a newspaper clipping about Rizal's death, and a letter from the German consul in Manila, confirming to the Pastor that it was indeed his friend who had been executed by the Spaniards. The box also contained newspaper articles and an unpublished poem that Karl Ullmer had written about Rizal. Appended to the poem was a quotation from Rizal's "Song of Maria Clara": "How sweet to die for one's native land."

It was the Rizaliana revelation of the decade.

The next afternoon Pfarrer Weber drove the Mendezes back to the Hack residence for tea. Mendez chose this opportunity to talk about acquiring the Ullmer collection. In her report of the event, serialized by the *Manila Times,* Mrs. Mendez told of how her husband had brought up the subject:

Our experience in such matters being zero, we did not know how to begin. Then my husband broached the subject diplomatically. He could understand, he said, the great sentimental value of the collection to the Hacks, and he hoped they appreciated its equally great value to the Philippines. Those relics were part and parcel of our nation's history. The Hack family would see our legitimate interest in acquiring them, which was to perpetuate the memory of our hero. It was a happy circumstance that the Ullmer name went inextricably with that memory, and should the collection find its fitting place—as we hoped it would—in the Jose Rizal Memorial Museum, the Ullmer stamp would be there indelibly. Nothing really would be lost to the Hacks, for photostatic copies could be made available. Would they perhaps take a price?

The answer was gentle: they would not. They would rather present the collection to the Filipino people in person, as a gift of the family. And they recalled how in one of his letters Rizal had asked Pastor Ullmer to come to the Philippines as his guest. We said we thoroughly approved of the idea and in fact had it in mind. We would certainly recommend it to the Commission in Manila. What a relief it was not to have to bargain over a matter that should be above commercialism![16]

In March 1960, Hans and Fritz Hack arrived in Manila to donate the family heirlooms to President Carlos P. Garcia. Their trip was publicized in an Associated Press story sent from Paris and featured in German newspapers. The story was exactly as reporter Mendez had written it on the typewriter at the A.P. office in Paris.

The celebrated brothers spent their Philippine vacation at the home of Dr. Leoncio Lopez-Rizal, the hero's nephew. Thus, after 74 years, did the Rizal-Ullmer relationship come full circle.

Minister and Mrs. Mendez were the first Filipinos after Jose Rizal to step on Wilhelmsfeld soil. After their discovery, hundreds of Filipinos journeyed to Wilhelmsfeld, turning the sleepy hamlet into a tourist spot and national shrine combined. Articles about Rizal by both Germans and Filipinos multiplied in German newspapers and periodicals. Pastor Weber became a full-fledged Rizal scholar and visited the Philippines several times. Every year, on Rizal's birthday anniversary, he would don a *barong tagalog* and hang Rizal's framed photograph under the plaque. Among the villagers who attended the 1961 Rizal centenary in Wilhelmsfeld was Adam Reibold, 86, a shoemaker's son. As a boy of eleven, he had delivered the shoes that Rizal had ordered from his father in 1886.[17]

On December 30, 1964, the German government donated to the Philippines the Wilhelmsfeld sandstone fountain from which Rizal used to scoop a refreshing drink or two. Arrangements for the donation were made by newsman Gene Cabrera and Minister Pura Santillan-Castrence of the Department of Foreign Affairs. Appropriately enough, it was Mauro Mendez, then Foreign Secretary, who received the fountain from German Ambassador Johann Karl Von Stechow at the rites held in Rizal Park.

Perhaps it can be truthfully said that no other event has brought Germany and the Philippines so close to each other as the discovery of the so-called "*Noli* Village."

The Philippine press acclaimed the Mendez achievement in editorials and columns. A *Manila Times* editorial by Jose Luna Castro paid the Mendezes this tribute:

> The performance of Minister-Counselor Mauro Mendez and his talented wife further reinforces our claim that our foreign service is second to none in those factors that make for the complete rounded diplomat—for men who yield to none in the culture, the intellectual achievements without which the diplomat is only a high-grade clerk-messenger, possibly capable of doing one job well, but lacking the imagination and the intellectual daring to strike out for himself in the absence of specific orders.
>
> The fine and devoted research carried out by Minister and Mrs. Mendez in a field so strange that it may as well be described as impossible for any but natives to explore, has operated to bridge a wide gap in our history. It will restore to the possession of his countrymen articles of inestimable value, the property of Jose Rizal; and will at the same time cast light on an era in the hero's life that has long been in darkness.
>
> For all this the nation owes a debt of lasting gratitude to Minister and Mrs. Mendez. But their claim on the nation's appreciation rests on the more stable basis of having demonstrated, to their own people and to the world, that culture and intellectual capacity distinguish the Philippine diplomat, and contribute to making him a representative abroad of whom his government and people have real reason to be proud.[18]

Alejandro R. Roces, in his column, "Roses and Thorns," presented roses to Minister and Mrs. Mendez:

> The Mendezes prove what we have maintained all along: that the best foreign officials are those who have a wide cultural

background. We know many people in our foreign service who will not cross a street to discover something new about Rizal's life unless there is some money in it. The Mendezes have succeeded in their quest because, first of all, they have great interest in Rizal. And there is no substitute for that.[19]

Paraluman Aspillera, in her "Tagalog Corner," praised the Mendezes as "tunay na kinatawan" (true representatives):

> Ang mga Mendez... ay tunay na karangalan ng Pilipinas. Sila ang mga dapat na kinatawan ng ating bansa sa ibang bayan. Mayroon silang talinong ginagamit sa mabuti. ... Ang pinayayaman ng mga Mendez ay ang Pilipinas.[20]
>
> (The Mendezes... are truly an honor to the Philippines. They are the kind of representatives that our country needs abroad. They use their intelligence for a good cause. ... The Mendezes have enriched the Philippines.)

"Monkey Business in Laos"

In July of 1960 Mr. and Mrs. Mendez left Paris for New York to spend a vacation with their children and to await the birth of their son Manuel's third child. Mendez also attended the U.N. General Assembly as Alternate Representative of the Philippine Mission.

In December of that year, he received word from the home office that he was being appointed Ambassador to Laos and Cambodia. He immediately began delving into the historical, cultural, and political backgrounds of the two countries so that he could approach his new task intelligently.

Unfortunately, he had no military training to go with his intelligence. Laos was in the midst of a raging civil war between the Pathet Lao Communist forces and the royal Laotian government. Mendez was saddened to learn that neutralist Prime Minister Souvanna Phouma had fled to Cambodia. He had met the Prince when the latter was Laos' Ambassador to France, and they had smoked many a Corona cigar together.

Minister Mendez called at the Laos Mission to the United Nations for a briefing, and the personnel were most pleased that the Philippines was interested in the welfare of their war-torn country.

However, Cambodia's Deputy Permanent Representative to the U.N. was surprised that Mendez was going to be stationed in Laos, where, according to the Cambodian, the troubled situation did not warrant the presence of a nonfighting man. With Vientiane reduced to a pile of rubble, he wondered where the Philippines would house its legation. Even worse, it was not easy to say where the next bullets would come from. It was rather strange, he concluded, that when most people were rushing out of Laos, the Filipinos were rushing in.

The Cambodian representative's opinion was that the Philippines would be wiser to establish its mission in Phnom Penh, where some seventeen diplomatic missions were thriving. Mendez agreed with him and communicated his recommendation to the Department of Foreign Affairs. Phnom Penh was an excellent listening post, he wrote, and "both shades of opinion may be observed to the advantage of our policy makers. While we are committed to the free world it does not mean that we are to neglect what the so-called slave world is doing and thinking. Indeed, it would be to our advantage to keep ourselves posted on the trends and developments on the other side." Foreign Secretary Felixberto Serrano, however, preferred to open the legation in Laos to demonstrate Philippine support for the struggling young nation.

For the next few months Mendez kept in touch with the Laotian and Cambodian Missions in New York and with the Laotian desk at the State Department in Washington. In weekly letters to the Department of Foreign Affairs, he communicated his findings on what he called "monkey business in Laos." "The State Department's view," he wrote in January 1961, "is that Laos' priority in Soviet Russia's attention rests on the fact that the landlocked kingdom separates the Communist bloc from the rest of Southeast Asia. Ultimately, by the same token, the Philippines, which separates Communism from the free world, must also be crushed in the interest of Communist hegemony." In a remark characteristic of his prewar editorials, he added, "No country outside of the Soviet orbit is free from this diabolic scheme aimed at the enslavement of all mankind."

The situation in Laos worsened with the build-up in arms by the Communists through their continuous supply from North Vietnam. The Philippine government then decided not to risk the lives of Minister and Mrs. Mendez and their Filipino staff. The opening of the

Philippine legation to Laos and Cambodia was deferred for better times, and Mendez returned his plane tickets to the airlines.

It was just as well that his Laotian mission was not accomplished, for he was to turn 65 in November and was preparing to retire. In December 1961, the Mendezes were back in Manila for the second time since they had left for New York in 1948. They had hardly begun to uncrate their household goods when President-elect Diosdado Macapagal announced Mendez's appointment as Ambassador to Japan.

Cherry-Blossom Country

On April 5, 1962, Mendez donned his ambassadorial ensemble—top hat, striped pants, and swallowtail coat—for his first formal audience at the Imperial Palace. As he handed his credentials to the Emperor, he thought to himself, "It's a small world after all."

Over thirty years before, as *Tribune* editor and later as *Herald* editor, he had written annual congratulatory editorials on the Emperor's birthday. On April 29, 1935, the 34th birthday of his Imperial Majesty, Mendez wrote that the Emperor deserved national homage not only because of his position as supreme ruler of the Empire but also because under his regime Japan had reached "the full zenith of its power, the rays of the Rising Sun shining in full splendor...and reaching the remotest corners of the globe."

While he was against Japanese military aggression, Mendez saw much to admire in the Japanese:

> We admire the Japanese nation and are anxious to emulate certain Japanese traits as a people that have made Nippon the power that she is in the world today. To our children we point to Japanese patriotism and that intense nationalism that have made the Japanese people a socially-disciplined nation, as virtues that we must cultivate to achieve national greatness.[21]

When Emperor Hirohito turned 35 the following year, Mendez composed another editorial, fittingly entitled, "Banzai":

> The line of Japan's progress has always been straight and inflexible; it runs through the tangled destinies of this nervous world with the force of a formidable portent. The West has stood agape, has gone into bewilderment rapidly, before the

unparalleled demonstration of Japan's ascendant power in the last fifty years.[22]

Thus, Mendez was not surprised at Japan's miraculous recovery after the twin tragedies of Hiroshima and Nagasaki. He recalled his first trip to Japan as a young man, when he had toured Nagasaki in a rickshaw in early autumn. Who ever dreamed that he would return 42 years later in a Cadillac!

By a pleasant coincidence, his ambassadorial term in Tokyo was marked by the first trip to the Philippines of a member of the Imperial household. In November 1962, Crown Prince Akihito and his wife, Crown Princess Michiko, arrived in Manila and stayed for five days. Ambassador and Mrs. Mendez were on hand for the visit. At first it was feared that their royal highnesses would encounter a cold reception; it was a relief to see that the Filipinos were charmed by the youthful couple.

China-Watching in Tokyo

To Mendez, the supreme advantage of Tokyo as a foreign assignment was that it was the most prestigious in the Far East. It was also the contact point for foreign missions with which the Philippines had friendly relations but which had no diplomatic offices in Manila. Mendez's position gave him an excellent opportunity to feel the pulse of a large and bustling diplomatic body.

After France opened ties with the People's Republic of China, the question in ambassadorial circles was, "Can Japan be far behind?" Reporting to Padre Faura in January 1964, Mendez wrote: "It is clearly in the cards that Japan's recognition of Communist China is only a question of time. After that, how to handle an angry Chiang Kai-shek will be a most pressing political issue in Japan in the months ahead."

Japan's policymakers constantly reassured the Ambassador that like the Philippines, they would stand by Taipei. Nonetheless, Mendez could smell Peking duck in the air. In March of 1964, Communist China announced plans to stage a million-dollar trade fair in Tokyo, to occupy 100,000 square feet of ground, and to be handled by a staff of 70 people. At that time Japan's official policy toward mainland China was "Trade yes; diplomacy no." However, Mao Tse-tung sent a representative to Tokyo with word from the Chairman that his government would not separate trade from politics in considering future relations with Japan. Observed Mendez dryly: "The comrade is now in Tokyo to supervise the preparations for the coming trade fair."

U.S. Ambassador Edwin O. Reischauer tried to comfort Ambassador Mendez with his own (perhaps) wishful thinking that Japan would not recognize Peking. But the Tokyo press praised Senator William Fulbright for having issued a statement calling the American people's attention to the reality of Red China. Mendez's assessment of Taiwan's situation was dispassionate despite the metaphors: "There is no denying the fact that the rainbow in Taiwan's sky has been considerably clouded.... Mr. Fulbright has dimmed the landscape for the Generalissimo."

The following month Mendez received the biggest surprise of his diplomatic career—a cable from Malacañang offering him the position of Foreign Secretary. His first impulse was to decline it because of the difficulties it entailed. His only desire was to retire in the near future. He sat at his desk, his pen poised to draft his reply—"I humbly decline"—but his wife and two of his daughters surrounded him, exclaiming, "Accept! Accept!" Outnumbered, he changed his mind.

The news of his appointment appeared in the Tokyo papers on April 29, 1964, the Emperor's birthday. Later that morning he attended his Imperial Majesty's reception at the Palace, where he received almost as many congratulations as the Emperor himself.

XIII

THE PREMIER POST

When Mendez was chosen for the premier Cabinet post, he had no inkling that his appointment had anything to do with a speech that his predecessor, Salvador P. Lopez, had delivered only two days before. In his April 27 speech before the Rotary Club of Quezon City, Lopez called for a more flexible attitude toward Russia. It was his belief that the Philippines' traditional hard line was no longer tenable in view of the Sino-Soviet rift. The world was undergoing a "sea-change," said Lopez, and the enemy of Philippine security was no longer "a movement in the ideological guise of international communism, but a certain region of the world where the communist dogma has assumed a particular shape and found a local habitation and a name." He identified the enemy as Communist China and added that "any enemy of the common enemy is, if not necessarily a friend, at least a potential ally."[1]

A day after Lopez's speech was quoted in the press, Malacañang announced the details of an ambassadorial *rigodon:* Mauro Mendez had been appointed Foreign Secretary to replace Lopez, who was to replace U.N. Ambassador Jacinto Borja, who was to replace Mendez in Japan.

The *Daily Mirror* made this editorial comment regarding "Deviationism at Faura":

> ...the Administration has been quick to see the need for coming to terms with neutralist countries, especially a big neighbor like Indonesia. ... But beyond this the Administration is as yet unprepared to go. Mr. Lopez's attempt to formulate a new guideline—if such was indeed the purpose of his speech—placed the President in a position where he had no recourse but to replace his

foreign secretary. This is not to say that Lopez's assessment of the situation lacks validity, it is simply that it is opposed to the country's foreign policy as defined or implemented by the President.[2]

Interviewed about his reaction to the Lopez speech, Macapagal declared, "Our firm policy against Communism stands. It remains unimpaired. We are not softening up on the Communists." However, he denied that there was any disagreement between him and his Foreign Secretary. He described Lopez's speech as "just an academic and general dissertation on foreign affairs." To prove that there were no hard feelings on his part, Macapagal explained that Lopez's reassignment to the U.N. was a fulfillment of a promise he had made the latter in December 1963.[3]

On May 6, 1964, Mendez arrived in Manila to take his oath of office as the ninth Foreign Secretary since Philippine independence. He was greeted at the airport by his old friend, Undersecretary Librado D. Cayco, and a platoon of curious newspapermen and photographers.

The Philippine press was then going through what Teodoro Valencia has described as a "rambunctious stage, when the press was run like a contest to see who could make the most noise."[4] Alfonso Policarpio, *Herald* feature writer, compared Mendez's situation to that of an "aging lion...suddenly thrust in a den of clawing wolves."[5]

As the news gatherers surrounded Mendez at the airport's VIP Lounge, he confessed to them that his appointment had taken him by surprise. "It's a thankless and sensitive post and I may make mistakes," he said cautiously. "But President Macapagal is my pilot, and I am only one of those asked to carry out his policies."[6]

An interviewer who asked him about Communism received this reply, an opinion he had held long before the President became his "pilot": "Under our laws Communism is out, no matter what the stripes, Russian or Chinese. They are all tailored to infiltrate or down our people."[7]

Some of his answers to his interviewers' questions evoked laughter from the large crowd of people in the room. One columnist observed that "Mr. Mendez displayed a refreshing quality of wit and humor so unexpected of one whom certain people had prematurely branded an 'old man.' "[8] Another journalist noted that the new Secretary had "a very sharp mind, as sharp as the blue pencil he wielded years ago as an editor."[9]

On May 8 Ambassador Lopez turned over the Department of Foreign Affairs to Secretary Mendez at a simple ceremony attended by D.F.A. officials and employees. The turnover, according to a newspaper account, "sparkled with the exchange by the two men of witty remarks and slogans as they stood in the shadow of Juan Luna's grim canvas, the 'Spoliarium' at the foreign office on Padre Faura."[10]

Referring to his U.N. appointment as a "homecoming," Lopez said, "I'm going back to my first post with a sense of deep joy and a feeling of fulfillment." To which Mendez added that S.P. was returning to his "first love."[11]

Before Mendez could warm Lopez's chair at Padre Faura, it was time to return to Tokyo for his diplomatic good-byes. He received the Order of the Rising Sun, First Class, from Japan's Foreign Minister, Masayoshi Ohira, for his contribution to the promotion of Filipino-Japanese friendship.

The Maphilindo Summit

Mendez's stay in Tokyo was extended until June because of the tripartite summit conference of the short-lived Maphilindo association composed of Malaysia (formerly Malaya), the Philippines, and Indonesia. The purpose of the conference, organized by Ambassador Lopez as the President's special envoy, was to seek a peaceful solution to the dispute between Indonesia and Malaysia over the presence of Indonesian guerrilla troops in Malaysian Borneo.

Before proceeding to Tokyo, President Sukarno celebrated his 63rd birthday with Filipino friends in Manila, perhaps adding credence to Malaysian suspicion that the Philippines was on his side. Both the Philippines and Indonesia were smarting over the recent formation of the Federation of Malaysia, which Sukarno looked on as a neo-colonial invention. His current slogan was "Crush Malaysia."

The Philippines, in the meantime, had a pending claim to Sabah, or North Borneo, which Malaysia had incorporated into its Federation. In Tokyo, Secretary Mendez presented a fully-documented memorandum on the Sabah claim to Malaysian Deputy Premier Tun Abdul Razak, with the assurance that the Philippines would recognize Malaysia if the question of Sabah ownership were to be elevated to the International Court of Justice.

President Macapagal undertook the difficult role of referee between President Sukarno and Prime Minister Tunku Abdul Rahman, even as the two glared at each other on the first day of the summit meeting. Secretary Mendez presided over the ministerial meeting attended by Indonesian Foreign Minister Subandrio and Deputy Premier Razak.

Amando E. Doronila of the *Daily Mirror* was among the Philippine correspondents who covered the tripartite conference. In his report on what went on "Behind the Summit" he wrote:

> Foreign Minister Mauro Mendez had an impressive performance at the first round of ministerial talks yesterday. He was presiding officer and moderator of the conference. It was his first plunge into active mediation...in Maphilindo diplomacy with all its twists and turns. Mendez steered the proceedings skillfully and tactfully especially when tempers began to flare between the Malaysians and the Indonesians. The Malaysians, who had some thoughts in the back of their minds that the Philippines was inclined to the Indonesians, were impressed by his fairness and objectivity.[12]

The Philippines' objectivity was also noted by the Malaysian national newspaper, *Straits Times:*

> The Philippines...is out to use the summit platform to erase world suspicion that she is aiding President Soekarno in his confrontation tactics. In this direction she has made considerable headway.
> Observers here were full of praise today for the impartial manner in which the Philippine Foreign Secretary, Mr. Mauro Mendez, handled the Foreign Ministers' deliberations yesterday and this afternoon.[13]

Whether the Tokyo summit was a success or a failure was a topic that newspapermen debated among themselves. The mere fact that the Philippines had succeeded in bringing Malaysia and Indonesia eyeball to eyeball at the conference table was considered an optimistic sign in itself. Mr. Mendez, when interviewed, assessed the situation with what a *Chronicle* reporter described as a "puckish sense of humor." "It was rather warm in Tokyo," said Mendez, "but up at the summit there was a lot of wind.... It was slippery, muddy.... But we will build a road to climb it."[14]

In any case, the only definite conclusion reached by mischievous Philippine correspondents was that a good time was had by all except President Macapagal. Maximo Soliven of the *Manila Times* implied that the dapper Sukarno had tried to lure Macapagal to the Latin Quarter for some "midnight diplomacy" but that the Philippine President had chosen to live a life of "monastic circumspection" at the embassy residence "presided over by the President's ninang in marriage, Mrs. Paz Policarpio Mendez."[15]

Little Brown Americans Vs. Little Bung Karnos

After winding up his affairs as Ambassador to Japan, Mendez returned to Manila to a desk piled high with cablegrams and letters congratulating him on his appointment. A few of his well-wishers were thoughtful enough to commiserate with him. One of them was Leon Ma. Guerrero, Jr., then Ambassador to Spain. "You have inherited a rather difficult situation," wrote "Leoni" to "dear Mauro." "I am relieved that so far, you have not yet become a political target, something to be expected on the eve of a presidential election."

Another sympathetic letter came from Marcial P. Lichauco, Ambassador to London:

> Because of the serious world tensions prevailing today the position to which you have recently been appointed is perhaps the most important among those on whom the President relies. As a personal friend of yours I do not know whether to congratulate you or condole with you because of the great burdens you will have to assume. You may be assured that you can count on my fullest co-operation.

Condolences were in order. The Vietnam war had escalated to new heights, and Saigon was beaming SOS signals to all her allies. Filipino critics of America's Vietnam policy feared that the R.P. would answer the call, since the Philippine attitude toward the United States was reputed to be "Whither thou goest I will go."

At Mendez's first weekly press conference, a reporter asked for his opinion of the latest maneuvers of the U.S. troops against the Viet Cong guerrillas. He replied that he welcomed the moves because if South Vietnam were to fall to the Communists, Laos and Thailand would surely follow. When another reporter asked him whether he thought the war should be extended to the north, he said, "Why not? If I had the power, I would attack North Vietnam." The powerless Foreign Minister quickly added that he was expressing his "personal opinion." [16]

His statements caused alarm among opposition lawmakers, who assailed him for "seeking to fight the war of the big powers with Filipino lives."[17] A *Sunday Times* cartoon showed him mounting the rocky hill to Hanoi, armed with a cane. "Out of the blue came Field Marshall Mendez's full-throated cry to rip into Hanoi," jeered J.V. Cruz of the *Times*. Cruz advised Mendez to take a lesson from S.P. Lopez by keeping his personal opinions to himself.[18]

The "Field Marshal's" utterances were by no means alarming to everyone. Apolonio Batalla of the *Bulletin* was impressed with his initial rapport with the diplomatic press corps:

> Newsmen covering Padre Faura got a jolt from new Secretary of Foreign Affairs Mauro Mendez. At his first weekly press conference yesterday he gave them policy statements free from diplomatic double-talk. He did not evade questions, answered them forthrightly. It was an auspicious start.[19]

To J.V. Cruz, however, it was an "unfortunate start." [20] It was also the beginning of Cruz's relentless attacks on the new Foreign Secretary in his *Times* column, "Here and There."

The response to Mendez's first press conference revealed that even before his appearance on the Padre Faura scene, the nation's foreign policy had already polarized certain journalists into two camps, known to each other as "Little Brown Americans" and "Little Bung Karnos." The "LBAs" were militant anti-Communists and favored the American presence in Southeast Asia. The "LBKs" were anti-Americans and espoused a neutralist foreign policy patterned after that of President Sukarno. The fact that Indonesia was then veering toward Peking made Bung Karnoism synonymous with leftist leanings.

Belonging to Mendez's ideological persuasion, the "Little Brown Americans" took it upon themselves to defend him gallantly whenever he was attacked. Nestor Mata, the *Herald*'s Chief of Foreign Correspondents and the most outspoken of the "Little Brown" ones, described Mendez as "intellectually vibrant," "frank and forthright," "a man to watch." [21] Oscar Villadolid of the *Bulletin* was pleased that the President had appointed a Foreign Secretary "of firm and unshifting ideological convictions." [22] Villadolid noted that although the Secretary was "vilified and ridiculed at every turn by those who sought a swing toward neutralism, Mendez adamantly stood his ground, refusing to compromise the national interest for favorable publicity." [23]

J.V. Cruz, on the other hand, lambasted Mendez week after week for such things as allegedly setting back "the cause and ideal of an independent Philippine foreign policy at least 50 years" [24] and for "cluttering the air with his quaint—if they were not so sinister—views... consistent with Mr. Mendez's unblemished reputation as the most faithful spokesman of the American line in our country." [25]

Jose Ma. Hernandez, a prominent Catholic lay leader, was apparently so exasperated by Cruz's columns that he wrote an article reminding Cruz of his contribution to the Philippine recognition of South Vietnam in 1955, when he was press secretary to President Magsaysay. Chiding Cruz for hurling "insults" at "Filipinos who, like him, might have convictions for which they would like to fight," Hernandez said:

> The present Secretary of Foreign Affairs has expressed a personal opinion that if it were up to him he would carry on the fight to North Vietnam. For this he has been pilloried and ridiculed by the ex-press secretary of the late Ramon Magsaysay—one of the greatest anti-Communist fighters of all time.[26]

Luis D. Beltran of the *Evening News,* self-appointed Chief of what he called the "Non-Aligned Newsmen's Association," expressed regret that Mendez was caught in the cross fire between two press factions:

> Mendez is caught right in the middle—if he supports one group he is mud to the other and vice versa. This is most unfortunate for the Secretary, who is certainly one of the best friends newspapermen ever had, giving out legitimate news and adequate background information on an informal basis.
>
> The little brown brothers and those opposed to the white and Western press should not allow their tiresome squabbles to interfere with the work of the newsmen who consider Padre Faura a beat, and not an ideological battleground.[27]

The Secforaf (his telegraphic title) took the altercation in journalistic stride. In fact, he barely had time to read the numerous daily papers. However, he did wonder how he fared in the news reports of

Francisco Tatad, a young correspondent for Agence France Presse. Mendez was reminded of his son, Ruben, every time he looked at Tatad's boyish face. Little did he know that Tatad would become his "heir," so to speak, as Secretary of Public Information in the 1970s.

As for Luis Beltran, he loved to take potshots at the Secretary even while he acquired an education in the latter's company. Over a year later, he was to recall his association with Mendez:

> It was when Mendez doffed the heavy trappings of his office... that the newsmen who covered Padre Faura grew to like and respect the man they were duty bound to criticize. In informal discussions over lunch—preceded with a sharp "Off the Record, huh?" admonition from the former editor—Mendez would begin talking of Philippine journalistic history and the foibles of past Presidents and government officials.
>
> For the newsmen covering the diplomatic beat, these were instructive periods where they gained an insight into their profession as well as the public officials whose personal quirks often were significant in forming future governments. It was also during these periods when Mendez would display his one serious vice: his love for that "lowest form of humor," the pun. (Sample: "Columnist So and So is so biased, he should be better dead than read.") A pun on the standard diplomatic phrase "better dead than Red," of course.[28]

Peeking into Peking

Because of the Mendez hard line against Communism, reporters were astonished when he said that he had no personal objections to Filipinos going to Red China. Max Soliven, one of the first journalists to make such a trip, said it was "surprising that such a high-ranking official as the secretary of foreign affairs should view with such tolerance all possibility of Filipino newspapermen crashing through the curtain into China." The official government policy, according to Soliven, had always been "so stern, unbending, even sanctimonious—as if it had been decreed by revelation—against allowing Filipinos to travel to Communist countries."[29]

Mendez's opinion, as expressed to reporters, was this: "As long as the government cannot be said to be behind such a trip, it is all right. This is part of their freedom, but I hope that they will not be encouraged because there is too much risk."[30]

He had in mind the difficulties that the government had gone through in trying to extricate Filipinos from the clutches of the Viet Cong, with whom the R.P. had no diplomatic relations. The People's Republic of China was still a no-man's land for Filipinos, and every Philippine passport was stamped with the warning that it was not valid for travel to Communist countries.

But the journalist in Mendez made him sympathetic to reporters who were curious about what went on behind the bamboo curtain. He suspected, of course, that the Peking tours would be confined to the primrose path. But he still adhered to the opinion he had expressed three years before, that it would be to the advantage of the free world to know what the "so-called slave world" was doing and thinking.

Following the President's orders, Undersecretary Cayco confiscated and cancelled the passports of newsmen who had traveled to mainland China. This happened when Mendez was abroad on an official trip. When he returned, he found himself the defendant in a lawsuit filed by the irate newsmen. Max Soliven was moved to pity: "Poor Don Mauro, a nice understanding man, a symbol of the best in Philippine journalism in his day, is now being taken to task by the postwar journalists!" [31]

The problem was solved in a "very Filipino way," said Soliven sometime later. When he and other journalists decided to travel again, Mendez simply ordered the issuance of new passports.[32]

The Futility of Neutralism

It was not so much Mendez's anti-Communism as his anti-neutralism that made some journalists fume over their typewriters. He saw no reason why he should abandon his opinion that a policy of neutralism was futile insofar as the conflict between Communism and the free world was concerned. The Philippines' geographical location was simply too strategic for combatant nations to ignore in case of a global war. From the experience of Laos and Tibet, it was easy to predict that a Philippine shift to neutralism would be a prelude to another Communist "war of liberation," this time on the shores of the archipelago.[33]

This notion was, however, becoming both unpopular and unfashionable, coming as it did when outspoken neutralists in the R.P.

were in a "Go home, Yankee" mood. With mainland China flexing her nuclear muscles in the vicinity, her neighbors found themselves at an ideological crossroads. Nowhere was the confusion more apparent than in the words of Cambodia's then head of state, Prince Norodom Sihanouk, when he declared in July 1964 that his "dream" was to see "a neutralized Southeast Asia, with the U.S. remaining nearby.... What would please me would be to see the Americans accept the neutrality of Cambodia, but not to remain too far away, that is, in Thailand and the Philippines."[34]

President Macapagal was not given to such equivocations, and neither was his Foreign Secretary. At a time when neutralists loudly protested Philippine aid to South Vietnam for fear of involvement in an "American war," Mendez explained that the R.P. was merely discharging its obligation as a friendly nation whose duty was to relieve a neighbor in distress. Australia, Thailand, and New Zealand had already responded to Saigon's cry for help. As a member of the Southeast Asia Treaty Organization (SEATO), the Philippines was morally committed to help her co-members against Communist aggression, even if the aid came only in the form of medical and technical assistance.[35]

This was consistent with the stand Mendez had taken ten years before, as a delegate to the U.N. General Assembly: "A government like my own does not enter into an international obligation with closed eyes and with no sense of responsibility. The people of my country honor their international commitments in the observance and not in the breach, and they do not have to be reminded of their duty in every case where their word is pledged."[36]

An Indonesian Affair

In any conflict where the security of the Philippines was not at stake, or where Communism was not an issue, the government could afford to maintain a neutral stand. During the 1965 India-Pakistan dispute over Kashmir, the Pakistani ambassador paid an official visit to Padre Faura to request aid from the Philippines, but Mendez told him that the Indians and the Pakistanis were both friends of the Filipino people, and that the warring parties could still come to terms through the intercession of the United Nations.[37]

The Philippines also maintained its neutrality on the Indonesian-Malaysian skirmish. However, when Indonesian immigrants threatened to make Mindanao a second home, neutrality was out of the question. Mendez's problem was how to repatriate the "wetbacks" without straining Indonesian-Philippine relations to the breaking point.

The infiltration had been going on for over a decade and had the makings of another "Davaokuo." Thousands of illegal immigrants were scattered all over Davao, Lanao, Cotabato, Zamboanga, and Sulu. Some of them had even become chieftains of their communities and owned extensive landholdings in Southern Mindanao, especially on Sarangani and Balut Islands. During a public hearing of the House Committee on National Defense, the story was told of a Filipino businessman who had been obliged to get a permit from the Indonesian consulate in Davao so that he could build a house in a village on Sarangani Island.[38]

The Indonesian embassy was naturally on the defensive. A spokesman said that the immigrants were "good and harmless," unlike Harry Stonehill and Peter Lim, alien businessmen who had been deported by President Macapagal. Mendez's reply to the embassy was that regardless of ideology or nationality, anyone who had violated Philippine immigration laws would have to leave.[39] When a newsman remarked that perhaps the poor wetbacks had no rice to eat in Indonesia, Mendez quipped, "Let them eat camote."

Seriously speaking, however, Mendez was just as concerned over the Indonesian problem as the Philippine Army and the Constabulary. Looking very much like their Filipino neighbors, the Indonesians posed a threat not only to local labor but also to national security, in view of President Sukarno's growing affection for the Partai Kommunis Indonesia (P.K.I.), his *entente cordiale* with Peking, and his withdrawal from the United Nations. Narciso G. Reyes, then Ambassador to Jakarta, disclosed in an official report that Indonesia was marching toward Marxist socialism. "Lefter and lefter" was how Mendez viewed the political situation in Jakarta.[40]

The illegal immigrants were rounded up with some difficulty and finally prepared for repatriation. It was discovered that about 1,500 of them had previously been sent home to Indonesia but had sneaked back into the Land of Opportunity. This was probably why Mendez, during his talks with the Indonesian ambassador on the border-crossing problem, once made a Freudian slip of the tongue and called it "double-crossing."

Philippine relations with Jakarta were strained even further by the arrest of an Indonesian "professional student" named Iljas Bakri, who had been studying in the Philippines for eight years, in violation of immigration rules on the stay of foreign students. A high-ranking official of a Filipino-Indonesian society, Bakri was accused by the N.B.I. of subversive activities, especially with radical student groups. He was declared *persona non grata* by then Secretary Lopez in 1963, but before he could be expelled, his embassy transformed him into a junior diplomat overnight.

The Bakri episode was reminiscent of the Tan Malaka case in the 1920s. Posing as an ardent Indonesian nationalist persecuted by the Dutch, Tan Malaka came to Manila in 1935 and made many friends among nationalists in high places, such as Quezon, Recto, Aguinaldo, and Jose Abad Santos. In 1927 he was arrested for illegal entry and deported to China, but not before he had successfully played his deceptive game. Unknown to his famous friends, Malaka was among the founders of the P.K.I. While in the Philippines he was in secret contact with leftist labor leaders, helping them sow the seeds of international Communism in the Far East.[41]

It was almost as if Iljas Bakri was a reincarnation of Tan Malaka, bent on finishing his earthly mission in the R.P. He was eventually deported, or rather repatriated, as part of an amicable arrangement between the Indonesian embassy and the Department of Foreign Affairs. Mendez was reluctant to subject Bakri to a court trial which would further strain Philippine relations with Jakarta.

Meanwhile, Secretary Mendez, assisted by Consul General Leon T. Garcia, continued to meet with the Indonesian ambassador, Nazir Pamontjak, in an effort to come to terms over the location of border-crossing checkpoints in the South. While they negotiated, the authorities in Jakarta went through bureaucratic procedures that delayed the entry of Philippine vessels ferrying the overstaying Indonesians to their proper home.

When reporters expressed anxiety over the delay, Mendez replied that the Indonesian ambassador had assured him of the "good intentions" of his government, and that the delay was one of procedure and not of policy. "Jakarta is entitled to consider all precautions consistent with its best national interest," he explained discreetly.[42]

The "Little Bung Karnos" remained strangely silent.

Caution and patience finally produced results in August 1965, when the last batch of 1,400 Indonesians bade good-bye to Mindanao for good. In September Secretary Mendez and the new Indonesian ambassador, Abdul Karim Rasjid, exchanged notes for the immediate implementation of the 1956 border-crossing agreement between the two countries. The exchange of notes plugged all the loopholes in the border pact and provided that thereafter, all illegal immigrants would be immediately repatriated without much ado. The inauguration of checkpoints in Indonesian Celebes and Balut Islands marked the end of the double-crossing affair.

Death in Crow Valley

The greatest challenge to Mendez's stamina as Secforaf occurred during a diplomatic crisis that involved the American military bases and William McCormick Blair, Jr., United States ambassador to the Philippines.

It all began on November 25, 1964, when Airman First Class Larry Cole fired at four Filipinos whom he took for intruders at the Crow Valley bombing range in Tarlac, an extension of Clark Air Base, Pampanga. The next day he learned that he had killed Rogelio Balagtas, a teen-age Negrito on a harmless scavenging mission.

Cole confessed his guilt, and the Clark authorities paid the boy's father ₱3,000. Balagtas signed an affidavit waiving any future claim for damages. The case would probably have ended with Cole comfortably ensconced on a plane headed for the U.S.A. if the local press had not gotten wind of it. After the furious publicity, there was no way Cole could leave the country without facing a court-martial.

Although he was off-duty at the time of the shooting, Cole was subject to the jurisdiction of the U.S. military court, in accordance with the 1947 Military Bases Agreement. Article XIII of the agreement provided that the U.S. had jurisdiction over all offenses committed within the bases, except when both offender and offended parties were Filipinos, or when the crimes were against the security of the Philippines.

Three months later a weeping Cole was convicted of unpremeditated murder and sentenced to two years at hard labor. Chief State

Prosecutor Emilio Gancayco, the first official Philippine observer to attend an American court-martial, pronounced the trial "fair."[43]

On December 13, less than a week after the Cole story broke into print, another shooting occurred, this time in the restricted waters bordering a highly sensitive ammunition dump in Subic Bay, Olongapo. Ricardo Villedo related that he and his brother, Gonzalo, were spear-fishing at night when they were fired upon. Gonzalo dropped dead in the water. The accused marines—Corporal Jesse A. Edwards and Lance Corporal James B. Thomas—testified that they had fired warning shots up in the air and down into the water. Like Cole, they learned only the following day that warning shots could kill. Both were acquitted by the court-martial. Villedo's widow fared much better than Balagtas' father—she received ₱10,000 from the base authorities and used it to build a new house.[44]

Investigations reported in the newspapers disclosed that over the past 17 years, more than 30 Filipinos had been killed by U.S. servicemen for alleged trespassing, pilfering, and other offenses. None of the Americans had been tried by a Philippine court.

Nick Joaquin, writing for the *Philippines Free Press* under the pseudonym Quijano de Manila, viewed the deaths of Balagtas and Villedo as symbols of two cultures suffering from a communication gap. The Subic shooting was a case of a stone-age spear-fishing culture colliding with a nuclear culture. To the residents of Angeles City, Clark Air Base was not a "bastion of democracy" but, at best, a treasure house for looters and scavengers, and at worst, "an alien camp squatting aloofly in the midst of uninformed folk who, because they didn't feel involved in it, couldn't identify themselves with it, had no qualms about despoiling it."

In his thoroughly objective coverage of the Clark court-martial, Joaquin depicted Larry D. Cole as a "victim of history": "It was his bad luck to suffer one moment of stupidity at a time when Philippine public opinion demands scapegoats for all the stupidities of the American military establishment in the Philippines."[45]

Bombshell from Blair

It was under this tense atmosphere that President Macapagal decided to renegotiate the bases treaty so that the Philippines would have jurisdiction over all the Larry Coles of the future. There was general agreement that in matters of jurisdiction, the Philippines was on the losing end, compared with other countries which had bases treaties with the United States.

During the previous administration, Secretary Felixberto Serrano and Ambassador Charles Bohlen had held talks and exchanged notes on the revision of the 1947 Military Bases Agreement. Their talks had ended in 1961 in a deadlock over the question of criminal jurisdiction. A few days after the Crow Valley tragedy, President Macapagal instructed Secretary Mendez to resume the long-delayed negotiations with Ambassador William McCormick Blair, continuing where Serrano and Bohlen had left off. Other members of the Mendez panel were Undersecretary Librado D. Cayco and Minister Gauttier Bisnar, assistant officer for legal affairs.

Shortly after the opening of the Mendez-Blair diplomatic talks, the Ambassador invited Filipino newsmen to a background briefing at the American embassy to discuss the security problems of U.S. bases in the Philippines. In the course of the briefing, Blair mentioned a report he had received from Clark Field only a few hours before, to the effect that two unidentified male Filipinos had thrown a 57-mm. mortar shell into the premises of a grammar school then occupied by 750 American children. The children were evacuated, and a bomb disposal unit detonated the shell. Blair told the newsmen that the report had not yet been confirmed.

Confirmed or unconfirmed, the explosive story was all over the papers the next day. If the embassy briefing had been held to soften the impact of the Cole shooting, it certainly achieved the opposite effect. Philippine society was in a rage over the doubtful report. Manila Mayor Antonio Villegas declared that Filipinos had "no history of violence against children."[46]

Justice Secretary Salvador Mariño, together with the Pampanga constabulary and Clark personnel, conducted a thorough investigation of the reported bomb throwing. The tale turned out to be an invention of a Filipino security guard who wanted to ingratiate himself with base authorities.

Ambassador Blair was the first to suffer the consequences of having passed on the fictitious tale. Angeles City officials and the Quezon City Bar Association wanted him declared *persona non grata*. In Angeles 2,000 people burned an effigy of the Ambassador straddling a bomb. Some of the placards read, "GO HOME YANKEE DOGS" and "STOP FOOLING US YANKEE!" Jose Ma. Sison, member of the radical Kabataang Makabayan (K.M.) and former instructor in English at the U.P., was one of the speakers at the Angeles rally.

The Angeles bonfire was followed by a series of anti-American demonstrations by labor and student groups in Manila. The moderate groups were peaceful and merely called for an end to economic exploitation and the killing of Filipinos by Americans. The ultra-leftists, such as the K.M., demanded the outright abrogation of the Military Bases Agreement. "Filipinos, unite, you have nothing to lose but the Americans!" shouted Jose Ma. Sison, who was destined to become head of the Communist Party of the Philippines.

More bases irritants were dragged into the open, prompting President Macapagal to warn the people that inflammatory public statements would only strain relations between the Philippines and her ally. Ex-Secretary Serrano deplored the fact that some Filipinos wanted the bases "scrapped" every time an unpleasant Fil-American incident occurred. He said that such reactions were "understandable but unwise and should not be permitted to exert their perverse influence in the policy councils of the nation."[47]

But it was precisely the purpose of the radical groups to strain relations, as *Free Press* editor Teodoro M. Locsin pointed out:

> It is to the communist interest that Philippine-American relations remain as they are, making more anti-American demonstrations inevitable. Nothing would suit the communists better than if the American government were to show no understanding of the Philippine position. What's anti-Filipino is grist for the communist mill.[48]

The *Weekly Graphic* noted that "expert planning and a good deal of expense" had gone into the demonstrations in Angeles City and those in front of Congress and the U.S. embassy:

> The appearance of the Hammer and Sickle symbol, splashed in red paint on a wall at the Agrifina Circle, and printed on leaflets that urged the people to join the Jan. 25th parade, as well as the use of vulgarities on placards and in speeches, give good ground for concern. ... Communist agitators, known by name to the military and other intelligence agencies of the government... have been at work in recent weeks, and have robbed our

demonstrations of the significance that they had, or the validity of legitimate grievances that they sought to sponsor.[49]

The anti-Blair reverberations reached a climax when outspoken public figures and legislators from both political parties demanded that the Ambassador apologize to the Filipino nation for his role in the bomb story—"for blackening the honor of Filipinos," as Senator Estanislao Fernandez put it.[50] But Mendez took a less simplistic view of the situation. "Apologies are offered, not extracted," he told his family at the dinner table.

There was also a fact of international diplomacy apparently unknown to the Blair detractors. No ambassador apologizes without authority from the head of state whom he represents. An apology from Blair would, in effect, be an apology from President Lyndon Johnson. Who could tell if President Johnson was of a mind to say "I'm sorry" for having repeated a Filipino security guard's fairy tale? And if Johnson were to answer the Philippine demand with silence, what would the Republic do next?

Mendez then announced the government position: the Philippines was not going to demand an apology from Blair because such a demand might provoke a "serious crisis" between the two countries.[51]

Now it was Mendez's turn to receive the backlash. Newsmen heaped their wrath on him, and opposition lawmakers demanded that he resign for refusing to squeeze an apology out of Blair. Cloaked with legislative immunity, the lawmakers accused the Secretary of being "craven," "cowardly," "anti-Filipino," and "unfit to represent the Filipino people."[52]

Fortunately, some legislators, such as Senator Jovito Salonga and Representatives Manuel T. Cases, Joaquin Roces, and Godofredo Ramos, took the nonpartisan view that it was pointless to magnify the Blair issue to the detriment of good relations between the United States and the Philippines. Ramos, Chairman of the House Foreign Affairs Committee, told his angry colleagues that "international comity demands courtesy.... Ambassador Blair is an extension of the sovereignty of the United States in the country for the same reason that Ambassador Oscar Ledesma to Washington is an extension of Philippine sovereignty in the United States. He is entitled to certain immunities."[53] Ramos also appealed for "sobriety and restraint" to prevent the Mendez-Blair negotiations from being dragged into political partisan

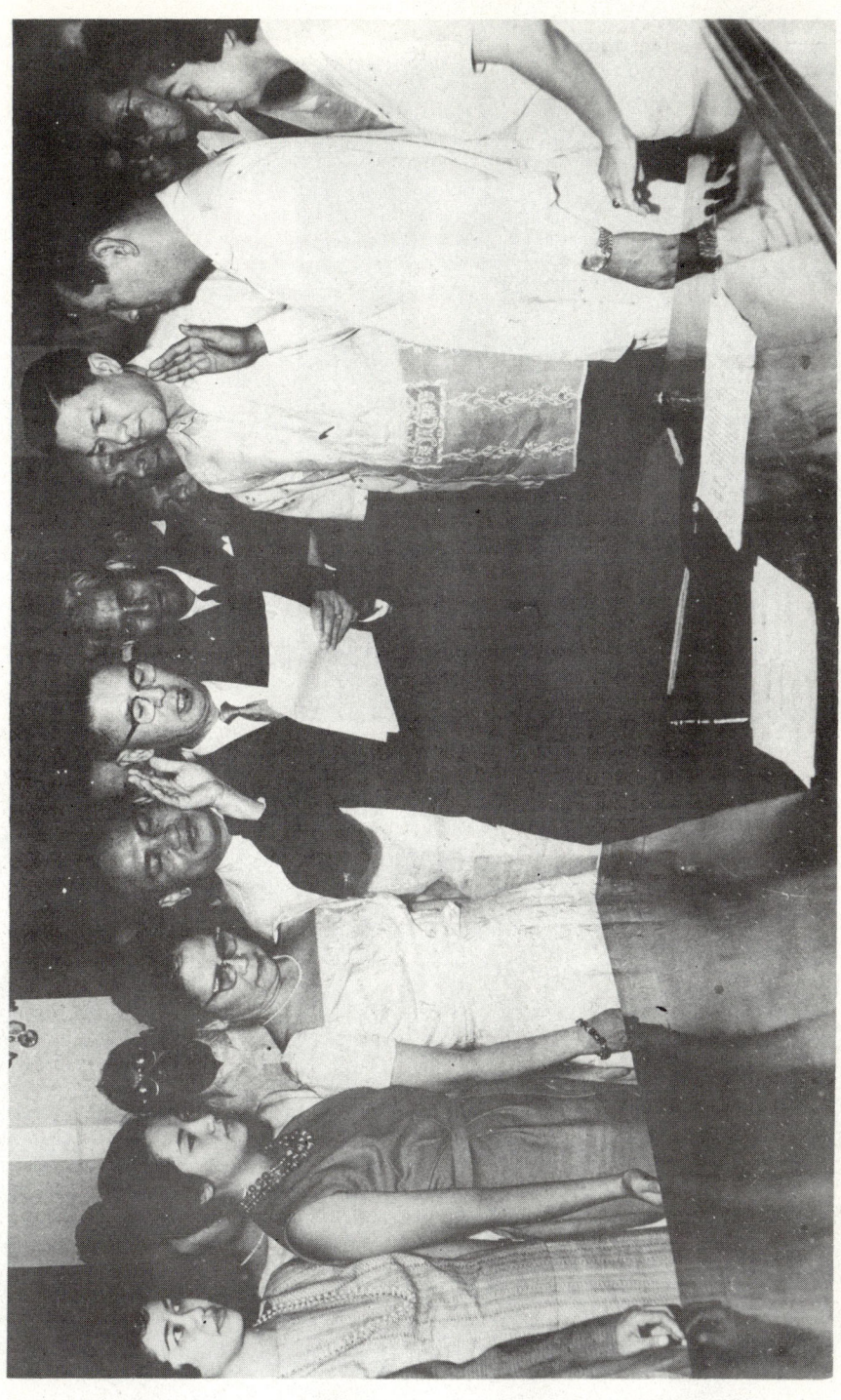

Mendez taking his oath of office as Ambassador to Japan before President Diosdado Macapagal in Malacañang. Looking on are, from left: daughters Sylvia and Nina, Mrs. Mendez, Ambassador S.P. Lopez, Ambassador Roberto Regala, Vice President Emmanuel Pelaez, and Mrs. Eva Macapagal. Behind Mrs. Mendez is Hilarion Henares, Sr. (1962)

*Ambassador Mendez leaving the Imperial Palace in Tokyo after presenting his credentials to Emperor **Hirohito**. At his right is the Palace master of ceremonies. (1962)*

Senator Jovito Salonga, Foreign Secretary Mendez, President Macapagal, and Ambassador S.P. Lopez discuss Philippine claim to Sabah during Maphilindo summit meeting in Tokyo in 1964.

Mendez receives Order of the Rising Sun from Japanese Foreign Minister Masayoshi Ohira in May 1964 upon Mendez's departure from Japan to become Philippine Foreign Secretary.

Secretary Mendez with President and Mrs. Diosdado Macapagal during their visit to the Department of Foreign Affairs in 1964. Behind Mendez is Ambassador Eduardo Rosal, Chief of Protocol.

U.S. President Lyndon B. Johnson welcomes President Diosdado Macapagal during the latter's state visit. Also on the platform are Mrs. Eva Macapagal, Mrs. Lady Bird Johnson, Secretary Mendez, and Oscar Ledesma, Philippine Ambassador to Washington. Behind Mrs. Macapagal is Finance Secretary Rufino Hechanova. (1964)

Secretary Mendez with President Johnson in Washington D.C. (1964)

Mendez with U.N. Secretary General U Thant and Ambassador Privado Jimenez. (New York, 1964)

The German government donates to the Philippines the Wilhelmsfeld sandstone fountain from which Rizal used to drink in 1886. Pictured above during the unveiling ceremonies are German Ambassador Karl von Stechow and Mrs. Stechow, Secretary Mendez and Mrs. Mendez. (1964)

It Takes Two To Tango: Secretary Mendez and Spain's Marquesa de Villaverde. (1965)

Secretary Mendez and Ambassador William McCormick Blair, Jr., sign revised Article XIII (Jurisdiction) of the Military Bases Agreement between the Philippines and the United States. Behind is Rizal Adorable, D.F.A. press officer.

Pope Paul VI greets Secretary and Mrs. Mendez at the U.N. (1965)

The late Secretary Mendez's casket is carried down the stairs of the Foreign Office after necrological services on January 5, 1966. At extreme left is Foreign Secretary Narciso Ramos; behind him is Ambassador Narciso G. Reyes. In front, right, is Minister Mariano Ruiz; behind him are General Carlos P. Romulo, Ambassador Tomas Benitez, Undersecretary Librado D. Cayco, and other members of the diplomatic corps.

Manila Memorial Park funeral of Secretary Mendez. Pallbearers at left are Carlo Mendez, Luis D. Beltran, and Benigno Aquino, Jr. On the right, behind undertaker, are Nestor Mata (partly hidden), Dick Pascual, unidentified Foreign Affairs employee, Oscar Villadolid, Alberto Alfaro, and Ruben Mendez.

quarrels. "Name-calling," said the Congressman, "serves no useful purpose and merely hampers diplomatic work."[54]

The *Graphic* also asked the public to keep cool: ". . . there is no reason as yet under the sun why a man with a long diplomatic background like Mr. Mendez should be assailed. Those who would make the unsensational Mr. Mendez act in haste, or engage in dramatics, are doing themselves and their country a great disservice."[55]

A *Bulletin* editorial squib made this terse comment: "Solons now want Foreign Secretary Mauro Mendez to resign because the U.S. Ambassador has not apologized over the Clark incident—off with Peter's head because Paul's head is beyond reach."[56]

Morale-boosting messages reached Mendez from sympathetic friends, strangers, and commentators in media. Jose E. Romero, onetime Secretary of Education and former Ambassador to London, wrote him this encouraging letter:

> Allow me to congratulate you for your courageous stand on the matter of the "apology" from the U.S. Ambassador which some people would demand. It takes courage and wisdom not to be carried by hysteria, and we want you to feel that there are many thoughtful people who are behind you and President Macapagal on your stand.
>
> Differences with the American government and officials we will always have, but there is no reason why such differences cannot be settled in an atmosphere of calmness and reason. There is no reason to exaggerate our differences while minimizing our many points of cooperation and mutual helpfulness. The free world has tremendous challenges to face which it cannot meet effectively if we emphasize elements of differences rather than of cooperation.

The Mendez-Blair Agreement

Another reason for the outcry against Mendez was that he refused to ask the U.S. to waive criminal jurisdiction over Larry Cole. On this point he had the support of former Secretary Serrano, who stated that an imprudent demand for a waiver of jurisdiction before all the facts had been gathered could be embarrassing to the government. Certain conditions and circumstances had to be fulfilled before a waiver of jurisdiction could be requested.[57]

Mendez chose to proceed with the negotiations and to obtain the best terms for the Philippines, leaving the Cole case to pass like so much water under the bridge. As columnist Oscar Villadolid pointed out, "If Mendez did not publicly debate with the Americans with an eye toward self-glory, it was because he knew he could promote more the national interest through quiet negotiations and under an atmosphere of friendliness."[58]

The Mendez-Blair meetings were conducted in a spirit of goodwill, despite the merciless efforts of hostile quarters to cast a gloom on the proceedings. Even before the talks began, the critics had arrived at the conclusion that the Philippine panel was doomed. Their knowledge of the subject matter was presumed to be "zero" while the American panel was "well prepared."[59] J.V. Cruz alleged that it was impossible for Mendez, "with his congenital subservience to the U.S.," to deal with Blair "on a serious level."[60] It was "all give and no take on the bases parley."[61] The talks might yet turn out to be an "exercise in futility."[62] Mendez was "giving in inch by inch" to the Americans. Let's "suspend the bases talks."[63]

Even former Secretary Serrano was doubtful when Mendez told inquiring reporters that he had made "substantial gains" in the talks. Serrano thought his successor had expressed "undue optimism." Said the ex-Secretary:

> The question of criminal jurisdiction had, for months, defied the combined talents of the Philippine and American panels in 1956 to the extent that their brave and constant labors had abruptly tapered to a dead-end in the autumn of that year.
> With the advantage of mutual confidence achieved and a large area of agreement already reached on profoundly delicate issues, Bohlen and I nevertheless failed to gain any appreciable headway when the sensitive question of criminal jurisdiction came next for our deliberation.[64]

It may have come as a surprise to many when Mendez and Blair finally signed a new executive agreement successfully revising the most sensitive provision—Article XIII—of the 1947 Military Bases Agreement. The exchange of notes, performed at a simple Padre Faura ceremony on August 10, 1965, made the new arrangements effective immediately with no need for ratification by the Senate.

Among other provisions, the agreement gave the Philippines considerably wider jurisdiction over offenses involving American bases personnel. It ended the concept of on-base and off-base offenses and made the act itself, rather than the location, the factor that was to determine jurisdiction. The primary jurisdiction of the United States was reduced to two types of cases:

(1) Offenses solely against the property or security of the United States, or offenses solely against the person or property of a member of the United States Armed Forces or civilian component or dependent.

(2) Offenses arising out of any act or omission done in performance of official duty.

In all other cases, including those occurring within the bases, the Philippines acquired the primary right to exercise jurisdiction. Any repetition of the Cole case would henceforth be handled by Philippine courts. (See "Postmortem on Mendez-Blair Agreement.")

The agreement also removed from the U.S. the right to exercise jurisdiction over Philippine citizens involved in offenses within the bases. The U.S., however, had never exercised this right.[65]

Contrary to the expectations of critics who assumed that Mauro Mendez would cower before William McCormick Blair, the Secforaf made it clear that the Philippines would settle for nothing less than a broadening of her jurisdiction over U.S. bases personnel. Blair, for his part, was prepared to offer a choice among types of jurisdiction provided for in similar agreements between the United States and other defense partners, including the NATO countries. The Philippine panel settled for a NATO-type agreement, with improvements, or what Mendez called "a Filipino-type treaty."

Mendez anticipated difficulties over the interpretation of the term "official duty," while Blair thought that the meaning was clear enough in the NATO treaty. Mendez reminded him that the Philippines was not a NATO country but a former colony. "There must be a precise definition to leave no room for doubt," he said.

Ambassador Blair obliged by writing him a note of clarification: "I would like to clarify the definition of official duty set forth in Agreed Official Minute No. 2 as follows: A substantial departure from the acts which an individual is required or authorized to perform in a particular duty will usually indicate an act outside of official duty."

Acknowledging receipt of Blair's note, Mendez added his own clarification: "As defined in the Agreement, the term 'official duty' is limited to those acts which are required or authorized to be done as a function of that duty which he is performing. It does not include every act while on duty." [66]

Within the limits of this definition, it would be difficult for an American serviceman to prove that killing a scavenger or manhandling an unwitting trespasser was a necessary outcome of his official duty. The new agreement would thus minimize any possible attempts on the part of bases authorities to abuse the "duty certificate" clause.

The Mendez-Blair Agreement was acclaimed in newspaper editorials and columns, while the habitual Mendez-Blair detractors were at a loss for words. Luis D. Beltran expressed these benevolent thoughts "Straight from the Shoulder":

> As a man occupying the frontline post in the conduct of this country's foreign policy, Foreign Affairs Secretary Mauro Mendez is a natural object of criticism. However, the spate and nature of criticism in some quarters has tended to portray a picture of Mendez as either senile or incompetent—or if it is an aberration, slightly pro-American. This is far from the case. Mendez, in the course of his short period of incumbency as foreign secretary, has accomplished the solution of two major problems which had frustrated the supposedly best diplomatic brains in this and other administrations before him. First, he has at last succeeded in negotiating the revision of Article 13 of the RP-US military bases agreement affecting criminal jurisdiction. This article alone has been the object of diplomatic failure of other secretaries in the past. Secondly, Mendez has succeeded in ironing out the problem of what to do about the Indonesian illegal entrants—who are now being repatriated to Indonesia as a result of the work of the Padre Faura team headed by Mendez. These accomplishments are not those of anyone [who should be] accused of senility or incompetence.
>
> As for his being pro-American, it is difficult to say. For one thing, he seems more pro-democracy in the matter of ideological orientation than either pro-communist or pro-neutralist. Besides which, in a country where both parties vie for American support, being pro-American is not essentially a vice in the same way that being anti-American is not essentially a virtue.[67]

In December of the same year the Mendez-Blair Agreement was extended to include other provisions beneficial to the Philippines. The

American government relinquished seventeen bases reserved for the U.S. Army, including 10,000 hectares of land at Clark Air Base which were not covered in the Serrano-Bohlen exchange of notes. The two countries also agreed to cooperate in consecrating Corregidor Island as a memorial site. The U.S. government promised to build a memorial consisting of a battlefield park with historical markers and relics of the Second World War, twin flagpoles at a high point to fly the American and Philippine flags, and a building to house an auditorium and tourist center.

"No Twisting, Please"

Even as the embattled Foreign Secretary was busy worrying about overstaying Indonesians and trigger-happy Americans, he was beset by other matters relative to policies both foreign and domestic. His hectic agenda often made him inaccessible to the newspapermen who haunted Padre Faura day in and day out.

Popsy, his daughter-secretary, would peer into his office and say, "There's a reporter here to see you." And he would answer, "Padalhan mo na lang ng retrato ko." ("Just send him my picture.")

The Secretary's vanishing acts caused Beltran and Amando Doronila to gnash their teeth. First they accused him of playing favorites by entertaining only his "apologists." Then Beltran complained that the attendance at the Mendez press conferences was growing too large for comfort. "As it is, anyone, including alleged journalists passing through, just drop in and get treated at times to off-the-record statements on Philippine foreign policy." [68]

Mr. Mendez was like a sheik surrounded by a harem of jealous wives. What upset the reporters most was his decision in July 1965 to end his weekly face-to-face press conference and replace it with a written question-and-answer system, a mode of communication which, reporters claimed, took up too much of their precious time. They were required to type out their questions in the anteroom of Mendez's office. The press counselor would bring the questions to the Secretary's inner sanctum and return a few minutes later with the handwritten answers.

The reporters could not understand how a former newspaperman could do such a thing to them. Doronila bewailed what he regarded as Mendez's failure to appreciate "the hard-grind of a reporter digging out facts daily to keep his editor happy and his paper alive with news."[69] "News management and suppression!" protested Beltran.[70]

From Mr. Mendez's standpoint, however, keeping editors happy was not the primary function of a foreign minister. He was too busy to think of generating publicity. Furthermore, his journalistic background was no reason why he should accept the hazards of a Cabinet position without attempting to minimize them. One reason for requiring that questions and answers be spelled out in black and white was that he had been misquoted or misunderstood on the basis of his verbal answers, to the possible detriment of the country's foreign relations. It appeared that if he was not dragging his foot on one issue or another, he was putting it in his mouth.

For instance, before he left for the second Afro-Asian Conference in Algiers in June 1965, he was asked whether the Philippines would vote for Russia's participation in the conference. His reply was that the Philippines would oppose Russia for geographical reasons. He added, in passing, that Israel was closer to Asia than the Soviet Union. A correspondent picked up the casual remark and announced the following day that the Philippines was planning to sponsor Israel's admission to the Afro-Asian summit.

The fact, however, was that the R.P. had no intention of sponsoring Israel for the simple reason that Israel was not interested in the Algiers conference. But President Sukarno, godfather of the summit meeting, reacted to Mendez's alleged statement by telling the world belligerently that all countries in favor of admitting Malaysia, South Korea, and Israel should keep away from Algiers.[71] Echoing Sukarno, J.V. Cruz used up much column space berating the Secretary for his "bombast and illusion of grandeur" in antagonizing the Arab world with his supposed Jewish sponsorship.[72]

Shuttling to and from Algiers via Bangkok and Paris was one of the most nerve-wracking experiences in Mendez's tenure as occupant of the premier post. First, he flew to Bangkok to meet with an all-star cast of Philippine ambassadors who were also en route to the summit meeting. Vice-President Emmanuel Pelaez, the delegation chairman, preceded them to Paris. Vice-Chairman Mendez left Manila in the company of then Tarlac Governor Benigno Aquino, Jr., official spokesman of the Philippine delegation. A crew of newspapermen completed the entourage.

Mendez had barely arrived in Bangkok when the Afro-Asian world was jolted by news of a coup d'etat against Algerian President Ahmed Ben Bella. Nobody knew what position the Philippines would take under the circumstances. On the advice of his colleagues, Mendez flew back to Manila to complete what one writer described as "the fastest diplomatic round trip on record."[73]

After receiving new instructions from President Macapagal, Mendez boarded the hateful jet once more, landed in Algiers after a back-breaking flight, and walked right into a political and diplomatic maze. After several days of factional intrigues and widening communication gaps, the proposed Afro-Asian summit fell apart. Disagreements between conflicting ideological blocs over who should run the show, assuming that the show could even get underway, culminated in the explosion of a bomb at the conference hall. The all-star ambassadorial cast returned to their respective posts, there to ponder over the improbability of another Afro-Asian get-together in the near future.

Mendez flew back to Padre Faura to resume his negotiations on the Indonesian question and the bases agreement. He was also busy with Commerce Secretary Cornelio Balmaceda, strengthening Manila's bid—a successful one—to become the site of the Asian Development Bank. Surprisingly, he softened a bit on Russia, telling inquiring reporters that the Soviets would be allowed to enter the Philippines if they were to become members of the A.D.B.[74]

It was at this time that Mendez instituted the much-criticized question-and-answer press conference.

Reporter: "Mr. Secretary, is it true an Indonesian high official assaulted a Filipino singer at the Hotel Indonesia for doing the Twist, and our embassy did nothing about it?"

Mendez: "Twisting is bad and not advisable. For example, twisting the news. I have no official report on this. Therefore, no comment. On with the dance, but no Twisting, please!"

Chuckling over this "flowing immortal prose," Luis Beltran remarked, "Secretary Mendez does it all the time, effortlessly. . . . It is a pity that not all cabinet members have such talent." [75]

On such occasions Mendez could not resist the temptation to be "as corny as Kansas in August" (to quote his favorite line from the musical, *South Pacific*). In the first place, he was a born humorist. In the second place, it was not always easy to give serious answers to the types of questions the press corps loved to spring on him.

For example, a reporter asked this ticklish question: "Does the Philippines contemplate taking any official action on the matter of President Sukarno's announcements that Indonesia will explode an atomic bomb off Indon waters by Christmas?"

Mendez pondered for a moment. Bombs always put him in a spot—atom bombs, Afro-Asian bombs, Blair bombs. So he simply wrote what he felt at the moment: "We hope to be able to enjoy Christmas in the usual traditional way. Please do not dangle any atomic bomb before my eyes when the 'simbang gabi' * starts. Let's all have a Merry Christmas." [76]

The Changing of the Guard

In November 1965, Ferdinand E. Marcos was elected President of the Philippines, defeating re-electionist candidate Diosdado Macapagal. For the post of foreign secretary, President-elect Marcos appointed Narciso Ramos, veteran diplomat and Ambassador to Taipei.

In December Ambassador Ramos paid a courtesy call on Mendez at the foreign office, and the two reminisced about their past association in the Philippine press. Ramos was the fifth ex-newspaperman to become head of the D.F.A., inspiring diplomatic observers to quip, "Old newspapermen do not fade away. They become foreign secretaries." [77]

A few days later Mendez hosted an *au revoir* luncheon for the diplomatic press corps. He told the reporters that Ambassador Ramos had gone to see him for "advice on what to do about you boys.... Ramos, an old friend, now knows what to expect from you all." [78]

Loud laughter emanated from Ramos' future tormentors.

The "guided press conference" was now just a memory, and Mendez bantered jovially with the boys. None of them suspected that he was seriously ill and that they would be his pallbearers within a fortnight.

They took turns responding to his farewell speech. Mike Marabut, the Reuters correspondent, said, "I'd like to thank Secretary Mendez for all his choice quips and quotes which gave spice to my copies."

Amando Doronila, one of the Secretary's most bitter critics, concluded his unusually sentimental response with a tribute to "Don

---
* Midnight mass

Mauro"—"an honorable man, a conscientious official, truly a public servant." [79]

Recalling the luncheon a few weeks later, Luis Beltran had this to say:

> Of his many achievements in life, Mendez was proudest of the fact that he was a newspaperman. His one affectation and one concession to vanity was to carry a pin denoting his membership in an international journalists' society. Yet, he also said that his fellow newsmen were the "cross I have to bear" in his work as Padre Faura Chief. For him, it was a conflict of where Mendez, the secretary, ended, and where Mendez, the newspaperman, began. At his farewell luncheon for diplomatic reporters, Mendez expressed his affection for his "colleagues" and his lack of resentment over their "mischief." The response, delivered by several newsmen, carried such tributes as "affection, respect, admiration," and closed the chapter on a relationship that was rich and fruitful on both sides.[80]

XIV

THE LAST DEADLINE

Preparations were under way during the Christmas season for the coming inauguration of President-elect Ferdinand Marcos. Mendez was named co-chairman (with his friend, Senator Gil Puyat) of the bipartisan inaugural committee. The outgoing Foreign Secretary was also assigned to escort the incoming President to the grandstand for his oath-taking.

It would have been the crowning touch to Mendez's own career, for he was ready to retire from the government service on January 1, 1966. But he was unable to perform his last official function. He was then lying in a hospital bed, suffering from the pain of a diabetic complication.

Despite his condition, he continued to sign papers and to remind the people around him to make sure that his desk was cleared for Secretary Ramos. He instructed his daughter to send the official car to Ramos early enough so that he could reach the inaugural ceremonies on time. One of his last questions, asked almost in a state of unconsciousness, was "When does my term end?"

It ended at dawn on New Year's Day, 1966. Strangely enough, while he was breathing his last, he seemed to be in a state of exhilaration. "I feel like a new man," he told his wife. Finally, before he passed away, he murmured, "It is finished."

The press and the diplomatic community could hardly believe that he was gone, for he had been very much in the news only recently. President Marcos was receiving well-wishers in Malacañang when he was informed of Mendez's passing, and his guests noted the momentary look of sadness that crossed his face.[1] The President immediately issued a statement to the newspapers, summing up Mendez's contribution to the Filipino nation:

The nation has lost one of our pioneers, for the late Secretary Mendez was one of our gifted men who blazed the trail for others in journalism, in liberal thought, and international diplomacy, a career which he finally entered at the height of his maturity and which, fortunately, reached its highest crest before he retired and before his sudden passing. The foreign service will be therefore the poorer for having lost him forever, but he made deep marks on our national consciousness and left many valuable friendships here and abroad. I knew him personally as a man who believed in dignity, in the dignity of free men and free nations. I will remember him always for that.

Former President Macapagal and his family were in Hong Kong when the sad news reached them. He cabled his condolences to Mrs. Mendez:

> We and the children were grieved beyond words to hear of dear Mauro's demise. He was one of our true friends and one of the best persons we had the privilege to know.
>
> He had a most distinguished career of which his posterity and our people will always be proud. And it is part of our own happiness that our lives and career were associated with his.

Ambassador Blair, Mendez's co-sufferer in the bombshell affair, praised the late Foreign Secretary for his "quiet courage, uncompromising principles, and unlimited patience." British Ambassador John Mansfield Addis, in a personal handwritten letter to Mrs. Mendez, extolled her late husband in these words:

> I think the quality I admired most in Secretary Mendez was his uncompromising integrity. He was always the devoted servant of the best interests of his country, and there were no secondary considerations in his mind. We have all watched with admiration the courage with which his indomitable spirit held him to the line of duty despite his visibly increasing frailty in recent months.
>
> In his dealings with us Ambassadors, he was always sincere, open, and frank, so that it was a pleasure to do business with him, and there were never any ambiguities. During the year that I have had the pleasure of being associated with him, I have had the satisfaction of feeling a real bond of sympathy and under-

standing grow between us, so that it is now a personal friend whose loss I mourn.

Newspaper editors and columnists who eulogized Mendez were unanimous in their praise of his honesty, his integrity, and his humility. In the words of Teodoro Valencia, "he never had the feel of greatness that some people assume even from humbler positions than Mendez had." [2]

A *Daily Mirror* editorial showed glimpses of Mendez in the milieu where he had first made a name for himself:

> Mr. Mendez was not only one of the country's leading editors in his time but also helped to raise the big crop of journalists who took their places in the newspaper world after the war. They remember him affectionately for his sound advice and warm personality, which the hard-boiled front he assumed during working hours could not quite conceal.
>
> The reporters who covered Mr. Mendez...at Padre Faura knew him by the same signs. Highly controversial he and some of his views certainly were. But...be the criticism of his policies ever so hard, Mr. Mendez always had a smile for them at the next confrontation.[3]

Necrological services were held in Juan Luna Hall at the Department of Foreign Affairs, with Mendez's flag-draped coffin set at the foot of Luna's giant canvas, *The Spoliarium*. His lifelong friend and associate, General Carlos P. Romulo, delivered the principal speech, "Farewell to Mauro Mendez." The other speakers were Secretary Narciso Ramos, former Secretary of Commerce Cornelio Balmaceda, representing the outgoing Cabinet, and Msgr. Carlo Martini, Apostolic Nuncio and dean of the diplomatic corps. Secretary Ramos later announced that he was donating to Mrs. Mendez the swivel chair that her late husband had occupied while in office.

Balmaceda recalled that Mendez was class poet at the Manila High School and that "he possessed to a high degree what Christopher Morley described as 'a secret nerve in every man's heart that answers to the vibration of beauty.'" Balmaceda concluded his eulogy by reciting from memory Mendez's short ode, "To the Filipino Flag." It was the first time the late Secretary's family learned of the poem that the young Mendez had written for his friend in 1918.

THE LAST DEADLINE 157

Msgr. Martini's tribute to the late Foreign Secretary dwelt on the significance of Mendez's parting words:

> His final words, "It is finished," remind us of the last words of Christ: "Consummatum est."... These words of Christ meant the accomplishment of a sublime mission of sacrifice and love .... the late Hon. Mauro Mendez also repeated his "Consummatum est" at the conclusion of a life entirely consecrated to the good of his family, his country, and the community of nations.

Mendez's pallbearers were his own colleagues—members of the diplomatic press corps and a galaxy of Philippine ministers and ambassadors—symbolizing the highlights of a career that had led him from journalism to diplomacy.

POSTMORTEM ON THE MENDEZ-BLAIR AGREEMENT

As of this writing (November 1977), the Philippines and the United States governments have resumed high-level negotiations on the future of Clark Air Base and Subic Bay Naval Base, the two most important military bases in the country. Although the final outcome of the talks may render all previous bases agreements academic, it might be enlightening to see how the Philippine government has handled cases of offending U.S. servicemen who fall under the terms of the Mendez-Blair Agreement.

At one time, the validity of the Agreement itself was called into question, with the result that in two sensational and embarrassing cases, the offending GIs literally "got away." The first case began on July 26, 1968, when Marine Corporal Kenneth Smith shot and killed a Filipino, Rogelio Gonzales, at Sangley Point, Cavite. The Philippines was entitled to jurisdiction over Smith, in accordance with the 1965 amendment, but in November of that year, Justice Secretary Claudio Teehankee ruled that the Mendez-Blair Agreement was not valid because it had not been ratified by the Senate. The Department of Foreign Affairs yielded to the Department of Justice. The United States then assumed jurisdiction over Smith and found him not guilty, whereupon the Filipino people expressed righteous indignation.

The following year a similar incident occurred. On July 10, 1969, Sgt. Michael Moomey shot and killed Glicerio Amor at the naval base in Subic, after mistaking him for a wild boar. Again the base authorities recognized the Philippines' right to exercise jurisdiction over the case. However, Justice Secretary Juan Ponce Enrile sustained Teehankee's opinion that the Mendez-Blair Agreement was invalid. Enrile also expressed his opinion that the 1947 agreement was "better" than the amended version of 1965 because the latter "widened" U.S. jurisdiction over American servicemen.[1]

Thus, on September 2, 1969, the Philippine government gave up its jurisdiction over Michael Moomey. The Navy Court-Martial tried the accused and acquitted him. He was later discharged from the U.S. Navy and returned home, his tour of duty having ended.

This time Filipino reaction was downright fierce. Twenty students were hurt when demonstrators hurled rocks at the U.S. embassy in protest against the acquittal of Seaman Moomey. The Department of Foreign Affairs charged that the trial was a "gross miscarriage of justice" and requested the U.S. government to return Moomey to the Philippines to face another trial.

U.S. Ambassador Henry Byroade replied, in a diplomatic note to Padre Faura, that his government had acknowledged the right of the Philippines to try the accused, but that the Philippines had waived that right. Byroade added that "the request to return Michael Moomey to the Philippines would subject him to a second trial for the same offense. The principle of double jeopardy is embodied in the law of both of our countries. . . ."[2]

A *Manila Times* editorial blamed the Philippine government for its repudiation of the Mendez-Blair Agreement:

> As the US reply yesterday showed, the Philippine government had all the chance to act on the Moomey case before it was brought before a US military court. And even after the Philippine government yielded its jurisdiction over the case, a justice department representative sat in during the whole trial proceedings and eventually pronounced it "fair and impartial."[3]

A *Bulletin* editorial remarked that local agitation to have a Philippine court trial for the acquitted Moomey made "as much sense as crying over spilt milk." Citing double jeopardy and the absence of an extradition treaty with the U.S., the *Bulletin* concluded that it was "unrealistic to expect the U.S., considering Philippine and American laws on the case, to humor us on the matter."[4]

Herald columnist Emil Jurado volunteered this opinion:

> It becomes clear, then, that the foreign affairs office and the justice department had no reason not to assume jurisdiction over the Moomey case, granting even that there were no precedents that could guide them to do so. The non-ratification of the Mendez-Blair Agreement was no excuse, either, because both governments agreed to its immediate implementation. To be sure, it was unkind to the memory of the late foreign secretary for the administration to claim that it was doubtful if the agreement was advantageous to us.[5]

Former President Macapagal, in one of his weekly television programs, deplored the repudiation of the 1965 amendment, and declared that if it needed Senate ratification, it should have been sent to the Senate to protect Philippine rights within the military bases.[6]

The validity of the Mendez-Blair Agreement was defended by a number of legal authorities, such as Senators Jovito Salonga and Salvador H. Laurel, as well as by officials of the Department of Foreign Affairs. Then Vice-Consul Nelson Laviña and Minister Pacifico Castro (current Ambassador to Algeria) cited a 1961 ruling of the Supreme Court: "Treaties are formal documents which require ratification with the approval of 2/3 of the Senate. Executive agreements become binding through executive action without the need of a vote by the Senate or by Congress."[7]

It has also been pointed out that to go by the ruling of Teehankee would be to invalidate other agreements signed by Secretary Felixberto Serrano and Ambassador Charles Bohlen, and by Secretary Narciso Ramos and Secretary of State Dean Rusk. For instance, the lease of the U.S. bases in the Philippines would be re-extended to the original 99 years instead of the reduced 25-year period, and all the land returned by the U.S. to the Philippines would revert to their former status as military reservations of the United States.

In March 1970, the Department of Foreign Affairs finally announced its official stand declaring the Mendez-Blair Agreement valid and effective on the date of signature. The Foreign Office instructed the Justice Department to notify fiscals and trial judges about the reversal of the Philippine government's position on the matter. This indicated that President Marcos had sustained the stand of Padre Faura.

Jose D. Ingles, Undersecretary of Foreign Affairs, has cited the advantages of the Agreement:

> The principal advantage to the Philippines of the Mendez-Blair Agreement lies in the fact that the Philippines acquired jurisdiction over "off-duty" offenses committed inside a U.S. military bases. . . .
>
> Another advantage. . .was the fact that it deprived the United States of jurisdiction over Filipino citizens unless they are in the U.S. military service.

x x x x x x x

Moreover, the Mendez-Blair Agreement follows the standard form of Status-of-Forces (SOFA) Agreements entered into by the U.S. not only with NATO countries but also with Asian countries, like Japan and South Korea. The Mendez-Blair Agreement is also an improvement on the Japanese Agreement. On the whole, therefore, the Mendez-Blair Agreement satisfies the desire of the Philippines to have a NATO-type SOFA agreement on par with other allies of the U.S.[9]

The Duty Certificate

Unfortunately, some misunderstanding has also arisen over the so-called duty certificate issued by a base commander on behalf of a serviceman who commits an offense while on official duty. It has been argued by certain quarters that the Mendez-Blair Agreement is "onerous" because it removed the right of the provincial fiscal to determine whether an offense was committed in the performance of a specific official duty. In the 1947 agreement this right was supposedly vested in the fiscal.

However, a careful reading of the 1947 agreement discloses that the fiscal's right to determine the duty status of an American offender was limited only to offenses committed *outside* the bases. The fiscal never had the right to determine the duty status of a G.I. who had committed an offense *within* the bases, for the simple reason that such an offense was under the jurisdiction of the United States. Therefore, it is inaccurate to conclude that the 1965 amendment deprived the fiscal of all his previous rights.

Another point overlooked by uninformed critics is that in the Agreed Official Minutes of the Mendez-Blair Agreement, the term "official duty" is defined precisely as "any duty or service required or authorized to be done by statute, regulation, the order of a superior, or military usage. *Official duty is not meant to include all acts by an individual during the period while he is on duty, but is meant to apply only to acts which are required or authorized to be done as a function of that duty which the individual is performing.*" (Italics supplied)

The Department of Justice, and city and municipal judges, often cite this definition in reply to servicemen who attempt to use the duty certificate as a shield.[10] It is misleading, to say the least, for critics to assert that with the Mendez-Blair Agreement, "we practically surrendered, abdicated, and/or gave up our sovereign rights to try in our courts American servicemen (offenders) *no matter what infraction of the law they commit.*"[11] (Italics supplied)

Furthermore, in case of a controversy over the circumstances attending the performance of an official duty, the 1965 amendment provides that "it shall be made the subject of review through discussions between appropriate officials" of the Philippine government and the American embassy. "Along the corridors of diplomacy" is how Undersecretary Manuel Collantes puts it.[12]

The Philippine government, however, has the right to reject diplomatic overtures in cases which it does not consider meritorious. For instance, in May 1977, a Filipino scavenger, Fernando Nuguid, was attacked by military dogs at Clark Field allegedly on orders of Sgt. Joseph Gaines. Claiming that he had already surrendered when the attack order was given, Nuguid filed charges against Gaines, who, forthwith, secured a duty certificate. The Angeles City Court, nevertheless, issued summonses to Gaines and to the chief of the base security police and the base commander. The officials rejected the summonses and suggested that they be coursed through diplomatic channels. Justice Secretary Vicente Abad Santos replied firmly: "To suggest that service of summonses on American servicemen should pass through diplomatic channels is not only to stretch overly thin the fabric of legal authority, but also to adopt an attitude bordering on flippancy, on a matter which merits the utmost graveness."[13]

A duty certificate, therefore, is no guarantee of immunity from prosecution by Philippine courts.[14] And yet some critics would go so far as to condemn the Mendez-Blair Agreement in its entirety on account of this one "onerous" provision on the duty certificate. To repudiate the entire agreement on this ground would be tantamount to throwing out the baby with the bath water.

PART TWO

SELECTED ESSAYS, ARTICLES, EDITORIALS, AND POEMS

by

Mauro Mendez

PART TWO

SELECTED ESSAYS, ARTICLES,
EDITORIALS, AND POEMS

by

Mauro Mendes

ESSAYS, ARTICLES, AND EDITORIALS

RIZAL IN THE NATION'S LIBRARY

Yesterday, birthday of Jose Rizal, ushered in Book Week in the Philippines. This is a plan wisely conceived, for if there is a figure in our national history who could inspire us to more reading, that figure is Rizal.

Rizal's *Noli Me Tangere* and *El Filibusterismo,* introduced into the Islands in spite of the vigilance of the Spanish authorities, provoked more intellectual curiosity among the Filipinos than any book had ever done before.

To our people, that was the beginning of the great fermentation of ideas which was to culminate in the Cry of 1896. A widespread epidemic of reading followed. Rizal's works were read secretly, and were read more often as the prohibition against them was increased.

Not that the Filipinos did not read other books, for there was Bonifacio, whose mind was steeped in the lore of the French Revolution, and there was Mabini, with his keen understanding of the philosophy of government acquired through reading, and Emilio Jacinto, whose literary abilities and profound humanitarian convictions were the products of conscientious study.

These were a few of the many who were already reading when Rizal published his novels, but they did not mark the intellectual level of their time; rather, they were reading far in advance of their countrymen, were preparing to lead them for the great debacle that was to follow.

Rizal's books for the first time presented a concrete picture of Filipino life and were the cause for a great stir among the people.

With them the Filipinos had two novels at last in whose chapters they could see their own selves, recognize their own faults and virtues, and live their own ideals.

Rizal gave his countrymen something to read, not for the mere sake of reading, but for their improvement and the attainment of their supreme ambitions. He gave them the opportunity to read, not idly, but profitably. He stimulated their reading habit and developed that habit into an attitude of self-analysis.

How did Rizal do it? By being a novelist, by proving himself a master of the art which has maintained its predominance in literature through the last two centuries.

Rizal has, as a first requisite, the ability of sustaining the narrative thread of his story without boring his reader. He is never monotonous, he seldom exaggerates.

He has Dickens' discursive power, and the interpretative specialty of Thackeray and Carlyle. His studies of the manners of men and women of his time are subtle and full of humor, but humor of the finest kind and of universal appeal.

His caricatures live to this day, and there is no reason to believe that they will fade. We remember Doña Victorina and cannot resist the pleasure of seeing her in the person of this or that respectable lady. So grotesque and yet so real, she cannot be missed every now and then.

There are Doña Victorinas moving about in our society today and there will be Doña Victorinas in the future as long as the fabric of our society remains essentially as it is. Rizal created their prototype to live forever as a realistic picture of the affectations of some of our women.

But if Rizal's caricatures live, more so do the serious characters of his novels. How many of us can forget Elias, the far-seeing youth of reckless bravery and yet of the disciplined mind and deep sense of righteousness? How many of us can forget his profound disappointments which embittered his mood and yet did not rob him of the virtue of self-control?

Elias' spirit of sacrifice constitutes one of the most edifying passages in *Noli Me Tangere*. How he helped Crisostomo Ibarra escape by hiding him in his banca and taking him out of the reach of the authorities, and how when they were found out and pursued, he jumped into the bay and swam ashore, under fire, pretending that he was Ibarra, who was safely concealed in the banca—this incident presents human loyalty in as thrilling a manner as any we have read.

Ibarra, too, will linger long in the memory of all of us. As the exemplary young man in *Noli Me Tangere,* thinking of nothing but the improvement of his countrymen, loving his Maria Clara nobly and truly, and preaching tolerance to his people; and then, as Simoun in *El Filibusterismo,* sinister, vindictive, and seeking the destruction of those who had desecrated his father's tomb and robbed him of his only love—the picture of Ibarra persists as a warning against the futility of human embitterment and violence.

"Pure and stainless must the victim be if the holocaust is to be acceptable!" exclaims Father Florentino, in the concluding chapter of *El Filibusterismo,* as the disappointed avenger of his father's loss and Maria Clara's disgrace breathes his last. And he adds, "God forgive those who have distorted his path."

But Elias and Ibarra alone are not the characters that show Rizal's creative genius as a novelist. Other figures less important but truthful fill the pages of his novels with their thoughts and actions ably interpreting the mental attitudes of his time. Such characters as Isagani, Basilio, Señor Pasta, and Placido Penitente, in *El Filibusterismo*; and Sisa, Capitan Tiago, Tia Isabel, and Filosofo Tasio, in the *Noli,* are more than merely passing incidents in the intense drama which Rizal develops with consummate skill for the benefit of his people.

Each of these characters has his or her appointed part in the progress of Rizal's purpose. With them he cannot, as the French novelists of the last century might have wished, be "politely impersonal" as a requirement of the art; he has to be passionately devoted to each of them because each has something to accomplish in the far-reaching scheme of his dramatization.

Rizal was a propagandist and his novels perhaps will not escape the stigma of propaganda. It is expected that the novelist will be an artist first and an interpreter, if need be, afterwards. But Rizal was both with equal power. He knew his art because he was by soul an artist, and he interpreted because he also knew his history.

He wrote at a time of political stress, when foreign hands were bleeding his people white, when there was one justice for the white man and another for the brown. Before that situation, he could not have been less than a propagandist—he had to be a crusader.

Rizal had to destroy the fabric of established tyrannies, had to break bounds without fear or favor. A mere story teller he could not be, with so much distress in his country. He had to take the sword, as it were, and fight his way through in that darkest of hours in his people's fate.

It was no time for contemplation alone. There were things to do and they were great things. Rizal knew the melody and beauty of poetry, but that was not needed in the tremendous task for which he was destined. His scholastic erudition was conceded, but even that could not have sufficed.

It was the great fire of his spirit, the challenge of his mind that was needed, to lend sincerity and power to the cause which he had espoused. None other than a crusader could have accomplished the task which he had chosen for himself. Rizal proved the crusader that knew no fear.

We cannot desire more than that *Noli Me Tangere* and *El Filibusterismo* be read by every son and daughter of this land. This is Book Week and therefore a most propitious time to reiterate this desire.

No Filipino has a right to call himself educated without having read both novels of Rizal. For here, indeed, is not a mere refuge for the mind that is not anxious to think, but something to challenge the civic spirit of every native of this land.

His portrayal of our customs and traditions is truthful. In those customs and traditions we find the good and the bad. In some of them we find ineffable beauty, in others there is but shame for us. Our duty is to cultivate those that are useful and destroy those that are pernicious.

Let Book Week be a rededication of Rizal's two immortal novels on the destiny of this race. Let there be emphasis on the duty that these novels be read more seriously by young and old alike. For Rizal, be it stated, remains not only the aesthetic god, but the moral god, of our national conscience.

Indeed, it would avail us little to steep our minds in the lore of exotic literature unless we know that which is ours first. True, knowledge is universal and ideas admit of no barriers. But there is nothing like understanding our soul first as the foundation of knowledge useful and practical.

Rizal, through his *Noli* and *El Filibusterismo,* enlarged our intellectual as well as our moral vision. Through them he taught us to snap out of our lethargy of ages and direct our steps towards wider horizons.

If our Revolution was an epic of our common achievement, it was because the *Noli* and *El Filibusterismo* prepared the ground for it. And we are where we are today—on the threshold of a new life of greater freedom—because the seeds Rizal planted have germinated and the harvest of his free ideas is here.

Philippines Herald
June 20, 1934

* * * * *

THE LESSON OF BALINTAWAK

Today, for the twenty-first time, the people will gather at the foot of the monument in Balintawak to consecrate the event known as the "First Cry" in the libertarian struggles of the Filipinos. Nothing will impede the expression of the popular regard for the decisive hour which this day recalls, when the anonymous son of his country resolved to throw off the yoke that had kept him down in ignominy.

No one can deny that the cry of freedom was uttered by the oppressed of this land, and that thenceforth subservience to Spanish rule was to cease forever. From those dark and quiet evenings back in the year 1892, when Bonifacio and his counsellors used to meet secretly in Trozo to plan out the organization of the "Association of the Sons of the Country," otherwise known as the Katipunan, the revolt against foreign subjugation took concrete form.

Those meetings under cover contained the rumblings of the first cry of battle. They marked the conception of great ideals and the formulation of a code of human dignity and human freedom, which were to play such a formidable role in the struggles that were to follow. They set the bases for rules of conduct which flowered into the noble teachings of Emilio Jacinto's "Kartilla" and the unassailable precepts of the Katipunan's internal government.

The country was in ferment and the spirit of Balintawak was already hovering over town and city. Very soon it became clear that no human obstacle was to stand in the path of that gathering maelstrom of revolt against the imposition of an alien power. And thus the cry came to be uttered. And whether the cry was given in Balintawak or in Pugad-Lawin really does not matter. What concerns us is the symbolism of that cry, of that supreme resolve of a people struggling for the light of day from the odious shadows of the dungeon into which they had been forced to crawl. What is important is the memory of the supreme action launched by the Great Plebeian and his men.

It is such reminders as these which a celebration like today's brings to us, inviting the spirit to rise from sordid materialism to peaks of patriotic contemplation. In the larger interests of our love of country, the people will commune with the soul of the event which this day commemorates, seeing in the message of the occasion the mandate that we of the present live more in the abnegation and the self-effacement of that interlude in Filipino history glorified by the blood of the Katipunan.

Tribune
August 28, 1932

* * * * *

THE PRINCE OF TAGALOG LETTERS

One hundred and forty-six years ago on Monday, April 2 last, there was born in a barrio of the Municipality of Bigaa, Province of Bulacan, a man by the name of Francisco Balagtas. It is the memory of this man whom our Tagalog writers are honoring this week, the commemoration ending next Sunday with a grand literary festival under the auspices of various societies of Tagalog letters.

Balagtas represented the florescence of Tagalog literature which the Spaniards, curiously enough, helped much to cultivate. It was fixed policy on the part of the conquerors of the Philippine Islands to communicate with the islanders in their own dialects. Possibly, it was to convert them more rapidly, or possibly it was for political ends;

but the fact was that the translation into Tagalog of the literature of the church served to stimulate Tagalog letters far and wide.

With this literary renaissance it became impossible to stem the consequent tide of intellectual awakening, and the political stresses of the time but served to accentuate the mental curiosity of common men. The works of theologists were read and the people saw the light of divine justice, saw how that justice compared with the justice dispensed in their daily life.

Balagtas came into public prominence on the crest of this literary tide to add impetus to the growing intellectual impulses of his time. He wrote voluminously; it was even said of him that at times he used to dictate dramas right on the spot with notable success. His resourcefulness for creating characters was inexhaustible; his power of versification was beyond compare. He wrote more than a hundred plays which were staged throughout the Tagalog provinces, many times, it is said, anonymously.

His dramas invariably drew large audiences which always applauded them because they saw in their characters their own selves with their sorrows and joys, their hopes and fears. Something perhaps like Cervantes' freedom was what Balagtas introduced into the moods of his time. The fabric of current absurdities he destroyed by the power of his sarcasm, and yet he was able to make laughter a permanent relieving feature of otherwise monotonous themes.

None of these dramas, according to the late Epifanio de los Santos Cristobal—that foremost of Filipino scholars—was printed by Balagtas. Thus, time has deprived us forever of their charms, their subtleties and their wisdom. But whatever we have lost of that unrecorded outbreak of Tagalog Letters we have gained in the undying literary beauty of Balagtas' *Florante at Laura*.

The *Florante* is a narrative poem based on a story of love and struggle, virtue and perfidy, and the final triumph of faith and friendship. Florante is seen tied to a tree in a fantastic forest, there to pine for his love Laura, his father's affection, and weep over the misfortunes of his country. Two fierce lions rush to him to devour him, but Aladin, swift as lightning, slays the beasts and saves him. Florante and Aladin then recount their experiences to each other. Meantime, Flerida, in search of Aladin, surprises Adolfo in the act of attacking Florante's love, Laura, in another part of the forest. She kills the villain, and Florante and Aladin are attracted to the scene of the killing. Menandro then enters the scene after having restored order in Albania, which had revolted at the instigation of the perfidious Adolfo, who wanted to usurp the crown from King Linceo and marry Laura. Florante and Laura are finally proclaimed sovereigns of Albania.

The names of the characters in the poem are foreign, and foreign also is the setting of the story, but the theme is Filipino and represents conditions of Balagtas' time in an allegorical manner. It was one way of escaping the censorship of those days, as in fact the *Florante* escaped the censors and became the literature of every Tagalog home.

It is impossible not to read in the laments of Florante the profound sufferings of the country of Balagtas. The very atmosphere of the fantastic forest, in spite of its two lions, is inescapably native. The Beata and Hilom rivers in Pandacan mentioned in the dedicatory verses to Celia seem to murmur softly through the rhythm of the poem. Laura, besides, is no other than Celia herself, the divinity of the poet's dreams.

Rizal was a faithful reader of *Florante,* and here and there in his *Noli Me Tangere* he quotes from the poem passages in which the poet's wisdom is revealed at its best. During Ibarra's thrilling escape, Elias, his savior, recalls that their banca is to enter the Beata river which Francisco Baltazar sang in his *Florante*. In fact, Rizal was able to interest Ferdinand Blumentritt in the beauty of *Florante* so much that it is said the Austrian Rizalist tried to learn Tagalog in order to be able to appreciate the work in the original.

Epifanio de los Santos Cristobal considers *Florante* a constant inspiration of Dr. Jose Rizal and draws excellent parallels between the characters in the poem and in the *Noli*. In both works, indeed, it is hard to miss the soul of the Filipino race in the words of the principal figures, with the only difference that while in *Florante* something of the serene vision of Tennyson pervades the poet's lines, in *Noli Me Tangere* the patriotic ideas assume a fuller and more vigorous force, the very force of Rizal's life and demonstrated sacrifice.

Balagtas' position in Filipino culture is that of a poet who sought expression for the heroic longings of his race even in his verses of incomparable melody rather than of epic force. His *Florante* with its ineffable sweetness, which is the sweetness of his own mind in spite of the poet's private reverses, is not a mere song as the Troubadors of Provence wrote their songs during the fifteenth century. Nor might one read in it the merely decorative poetry, for instance, of Spenser's *Fairie Queene*.

Balagtas combined emotion and wisdom in perfect harmony. The suffering will find in his *Florante* innumerable lines to appeal to their hearts; those not inclined to poetry will read in those lines the persuasion of unalterable principles and the wisdom of our rich ancestral traditions. Poet and philosopher alike will find in his allegory on patriotism a safe anchorage for the spirit.

Although Balagtas was a Tagalog, it is impossible to place a barrier to the influence of his literary activity upon Filipino life. Ideas admit of no sectional limitations, and Balagtas was not a mere singer but an intellectual genius with a profound understanding of human nature, rich in the wisdom of experience and a keen interpreter of the moods of his time.

His precepts are not forgotten. They live in every Filipino household, unnoticed perhaps in some cases, but they live. Mere differences in dialects cannot affect the influence of such precepts. Wisdom is universal and anywhere a thing of beauty is a joy forever.

Balagtas in writing for his native land transcended all sectional boundary posts with the magic of his style and the prophecy of his word. He is not the Prince of Tagalog Letters alone, but the Prince of all Native Letters, for by showing the great possibilities of the Tagalog tongue as a force for human expression he has revealed how that tongue might serve as a unifying force in his people's life.

No other work, except Rizal's *Noli Me Tangere*, has been able to excel the great uplifting influence of Balagtas' *Florante* on the character of his people. In the Tagalog provinces, at least, most of the sayings in the poem persist with the force of a moral code. Nothing, in fact, can replace the beauty and importance of this monumental work in the architecture of Filipino culture.

Philippines Herald
April 4, 1934

* * * * *

MR. AVERAGE MAN

There is a character in this endless, ever-recurring drama we call life, who is as essential in its general scheme as the stage on which it is played, and as insignificant in its peculiar phases as a nail in the planking.

This paradox has been known by various names. Cartoonists have been fond of labeling him the Ultimate Consumer, the Average Citizen, The Man in the Street, and the Common People. We have recently heard him alluded to by no less an authority than our present Governor-General—who, it appears, would pull him out of his obscurity and give him a place in the sun—as the Average Man.

What is meant by the Average Man in this connection is the man who has never aspired to political or professional preferment; has never sought the emoluments or honors of public office; has never conceived the notion of forcing his way into what we are pleased to call the "higher" circles, either of society or of business.

The Average Man, for our present purpose, is the man, wherever he may be found, whether standing knee-deep in the ooze of a rice-paddy, or bending over a ledger, or selling stockings or cigarettes over a counter in Manila, or tossing boulders into a ditch on a government highway in Cagayan—the man engaged in any of these occupations, who has no other aspirations than to live at peace with the world, to provide for his family and for himself, and to insure his children an opportunity to be something more than himself.

He has no "protection," no political influence. From newspapers, if he reads them, he recognizes the names of the great, of the public officials, vaguely as names of beings far beyond and above his ken. He is the Mass—the Mob Scene in the photoplay of our political life.

Politicians and orators recognize his existence. They not only recognize it, but they make of him the motif for their best forensic symphonies. Largely and generously, they speak of his rights. Vaguely, they allude to him collectively as The Public, which "demands" this or "clamors" for that. But always collectively. Always in the mass. When they speak of ameliorating his hardships, they speak of relieving the burdens of the People. To them the People is a distinct entity, a whole, a unit. Seldom, if ever, does it occur to them that the People is but a conglomeration of many millions of average men, each with his own desires, his own feelings, his own modest aspirations, his own yearnings.

Our present chief executive has proclaimed it to be the foundation of his policy of government to break up this collectivism and to bring the Average Man—the man who pays the taxes, who puts the money into circulation, who, by his own personal labor, produces wealth, who in rearing his family adds to the uncountable yet intrinsically sound benefits of the state—to bring this man into his own.

He would open to the Average Man a road along which he could travel, by dint of his own efforts, to that felicity which every human craves. The farm-hand in the rice field and the white-collar wage-slave in the trading house would be able to consider themselves as objects of the government's attention. The State, to the support of which Mr. Average Man is the chief contributor, would fulfill its functions by serving him in all respects, in all ways compatible with an enlightened conception of the duties of the State of the Citizen.

This is the present Governor-General's intention. The sincere good wishes of all of us are with him in his undertaking. No one will watch the progress of his endeavors with keener interest than that same Average Man, who at last sees, emerging from the ruck of officialdom, one man with the purpose, the determination, and the ability to help him.

In gauging the measure of his success, it might be well to consider the conditions which he will encounter, or rather, the conditions which beset this Average Man of ours, in this depressed year of grace, 1932.

First, there is the Average Man of the farm lands, by far the predominating factor in our social scheme, because he is, in fact, its foundation.

Usually, he is a farm laborer or a poor tenant, holding his land from a wealthy proprietor, in a vassalage which a system of debt makes all but eternal. We say "eternal" advisedly. The average farm-hand is in debt to the local magnate. Not only that; he was in debt before he was born, as the obligation was his inheritance from his father. And it will probably be the only inheritance he will leave his son.

What privileges, what rights has this Average Man of the farm?

The closest examination will reveal nothing more than the inalienable right to take whatever comes, and like it.

From the government he gets little and expects less. He may be given police protection of life and property. But he never sees a policeman in his outlying barrio. The municipal police stick pretty close to the poblacion. And the work of the insular police force, in its larger aspects, laudable though it is, is wholly unknown to him. As far as he is concerned, it does not exist.

He has a barrio school. But as depression strikes the town, the space in the school shrinks, and year by year, more and more of the children of the Average Man find that there is no room for them.

He is supposed to have the benefit of a health service—but when a health officer does tear himself away from the poblacion on an infrequent inspection of his barrio, he comes, not as a public servant eager to help, but as a pro-consul, clothed in all the dignity and puissance of a great government, demanding and receiving, from the unlettered Average Man, the homage that he feels is his due.

Then there is the question of the debt. The cacique of the town is his creditor. The original debt, by an ingenious system of interest charges, has doubled or trebled. The time comes when the debtor, after much scratching of his head, decides that something is wrong. He goes to the law and complains to the justice of the peace. The latter is usually a creature of the cacique, who had recommended him to the district senator. He informs the Average Man that patience, humility, and submission to his betters are the cardinal virtues. Besides, the Average Man in this case has always been poor, always in debt. That is his lot, and, the justice of the peace implies, it would be flying in the face of Providence to fight against it.

By means of his wealth, and through his children who are at school, or in government positions in Manila, the cacique establishes valuable connections in the capital. These connections are useful in "grinding his axes," and, incidentally, in keeping those over whom he holds the whip-hand in due subjection.

Let us say that the Average Man in this case, gifted, perhaps, with more than his share of aggressiveness and perseverance, goes to Manila to present his case. In the first place, he has to contend with the influence his cacique wields in the capital. But even if that does not exist, what are his prospects for a square deal?

He presents himself with his complaint, be it usury or anything else, at the proper government office. The messenger in the director's outer office stares at him condescendingly. In that outer office he sits all morning, watching others more favored pass through the sacred portal into the director's or secretary's office. He is armed with a letter from his representative, it is true, a perfunctory note—for the representative cannot waste his time on a man of no influence—but he waits, until the director decides it is time to go to lunch.

Late that afternoon the director returns, finding the Average Man waiting for him. Disposing of him in short order, he refers him to the chief clerk, who would attend to him were it not for the fact that he has to hurry to the golf links, or to the class in the private college where he is teaching "after office hours." The man's complaint finds its way into a pigeon-hole...and stays there.

Weeks pass. The Average Man decides that perhaps the Governor-General can do something about it. In his innocence, he finds someone to write his letter to the chief executive, believing that it will go direct to that official. He does not know that it will be endorsed to a secretary of a department, who will, in turn, endorse it to our friend, the bureau director, who, incensed at the temerity of the petitioner in going over his, the bureau director's head, makes it his business to find the tiniest loophole through which he can crawl, to turn down the petitioner.

And all this, even without invoking the influence of the cacique against whom the plaint is usually made.

We take the instance of the Average Man of the city. Is he in a better position? Scarcely. His difficulties are not those of the farm laborer, the common tao. His perceptions of the value of government and its services are keener, because he is in daily contact with them.

But what does he see all about him as he goes his daily way? What if not the seemingly impregnable position, the limitless power of the smallest bureaucrat? If occasion should ever take him to a government office on his own business, does he, by any chance, dream of going there without first arming himself with the proper "protection" of some powerful individual, of an important citizen? Or does he go confident in the sense of his own importance as a citizen of the Philippines, secure in the knowledge that in calling on the government for a service, he is only calling for something that is his due?

It all boils down to the same thing. City man or country man, "protection"—pull—influence—connections—anything to carry him past the scornful petty clerks in the director's outer office, into the director's presence; and there, to help him get what is, after all, his due, but what in our benevolent "padrino" system is made to appear as the largess of a monarch, bestowed only at the monarch's pleasure.

We cannot here give in detail the hindrance and the obstacles which face the Average Man in his dealings with the government. They are reflected and summarized in the Average Man's outlook on the government: the state of mind with which he approaches it—a state of mind which dictates that he must be provided with something more than his rights as a citizen before he can get what we know is his due.

To this Average Man of ours—which means you and the rest of us—the government is not the structure which he himself has built to dwell in, to be sheltered by, but something strange and apart from himself. Something for which he must have a pass, countersigned by someone with the requisite "pull," to enter.

It is to divest the Average Man of this conception of government, to impress on him that the government is his servant, to call on at lawful need, and not the Government, something sacred and untouchable—that is one of the tasks of our present Governor-General in his laudable endeavor to champion the cause of the Average Man.

The country is unanimous—the Average Man of the country—in praying that the Governor-General will achieve his object.

Tribune
July 22, 1932

* * * * *

THE REDEMPTION OF LABOR

The eight-hour law, as proposed in the Legislature, only needs the agreement of the conference committee of the senate and the house before going to the Chief Executive for final action. It is almost a foregone conclusion that the legislative approval will be completed without a hitch.

Should the Governor-General sign the bill, the Philippines will have gone on record as the first country in the Far East to have the eight-hour labor law in its statute books. And thus we will have set the pace for progressive labor legislation in this part of the globe.

Eight hours a day devoted to their work by wage earners represent an adequate measure of mutual benefit for labor and capital. Five hours in the morning and three in the afternoon can hardly be stretched in a tropical country like the Philippines without jeopardizing the workingman's health and ultimately impairing the productive capacity of an industrial plant, for from whatever angle we look at it, the employer's interest goes with the failure of the laborer's health.

The legislation in its present form provides for reasonable exceptions which the government may allow with the proper explanations by the employer, as when it is shown that an industrial establishment must have the labor or go to the wall. Such a provision indicates that due recognition will be given urgent cases where the larger interest of the public demands a variation in the application of the law.

The day has come for our government to do justice to labor without doing violence to the interests of capital. There are many of those who are making all the money in this country, who have been virtual dictators to their laborers and employees. To many of such capitalists the only measure of the workingman's loyalty is his ability to work himself to exhaustion and, maybe, sickness. And when sickness comes, he is often forgotten.

When Karl Marx lamented that capital was fattening its purse at labor's expense, he foresaw what is happening in the world today on a larger scale. Men who have no claim to the respect of society except their wealth, ill-gotten or inherited, exploit the physical strength of their laborers and the brains of their employees to increase their hoards and justify their lordly squanders—these men who feel that they are entitled to draw for their losses on the energy and mental resources of their underdogs, these are the men who constitute the vulnerable tendon of the capitalistic Achilles.

Against conscienceless capital, the only safeguard for labor is enlightened legislation. No government on earth can afford to be apathetic in this respect, in the light of recent tendencies which the great economic dislocation has brought about. Widespread unemployment, the heavy slump in currencies, the rotting of crops in the fields and of goods in warehouses in the midst of a starving world, have shown up the capitalistic system in its lack of regimentation and have embittered the mind of the common man.

And while all this was taking place, a Soviet Russia was all absorbed in a Ten-Year Plan with human labor as the central force of a new economic religion. Undoubtedly a lot can be said about the weak spots of the communistic system, but a despairing capitalistic world has witnessed in the last few years a labor government move ahead without Teapot Dome and banking scandals and such tragedies as Ivar Krueger's and the Insulls' rise and fall.

The bitterness of the great discrepancies in the social system of capitalism has been poisoning the common man's mind, and there has always been the danger that the Red Flag may be hailed as the banner of mankind's ultimate salvation. It is to avert the catastrophe which a violent upset in the established order would necessarily cause, that governments now are turning their attention to the welfare of the masses.

The eight-hour labor plan is nothing new in the history of proletarian progress. It dates back to more than fifty years, when the first sacrifice was paid by labor in the city of Chicago and the eight-hour idea was consecrated as one of the goals of labor. May Day has since been observed the world over as the universal reiteration of labor's demand for justice, one principle of which is the regulation of the wage-earner's working hours.

It is to the credit of the present men who compose our Legislature that they have seen the wisdom of enacting the very measure which has been one of the cardinal premises of Filipino labor movements. In Cuba, one of the first things done after the declaration of the revolution against the regime of President Machado was the enactment of the eight-hour labor law.

Fortunately in the Philippines, labor need not be restive in its demand for redress of its grievances. We have a government that is becoming increasingly more committed to the uplift of the proletariat. A plan is being considered to establish a separate department of labor. An inspector-general of labor has just been appointed. And now the eight-hour labor bill is almost ready for the Chief Executive. Considering the progressive attitude of our present Governor-General toward labor welfare, there is every reason to believe that the law will be approved.

Philippines Herald
Oct. 31, 1933

* * * * *

OUR NATIONAL DEFENSE

The story of war is an old, old story, dating back to the primordial dweller of the cave, long before the dawn of written tradition.

Since the day man was able to carve the implements of his food-hunt from stone, the spirit of war has never died.

The wandering food hunter of the dim beginnings of human evolution had the fighting spirit already burning in him. He had to fight with beasts, had to do his best to subdue them in his struggle for existence. Then, his rivals for the dominance of the earth were only the beasts.

When nomadic man began to settle down and saw the possibilities of the soil on which he stood, a new world opened to him. He had reached a higher scale in civilization. The good earth yielded him crops, the earth was generous. He was upon a new basis of human existence.

An imperceptible idea of the necessity of stability was dawning upon his mind and he began to seek the company of his equal. That was the remote beginning of human association. The tribe was formed and man divided his loyalty between himself and the group into which he had graduated from the desolateness of his solitude.

The tribe became a ferocious tribe at times, when its common interest was menaced. Then it was necessary perhaps to attack: that was aggression, the beginning of the art of making war. Sometimes it was necessary only to defend itself, and that was the beginning of the science of self-defense.

As man developed in the course of thousands of years, he began to be dissatisfied with his meager surroundings and so looked for other domains to conquer. The tribal idea had grown into the empire idea and the first empires of the world were founded. But the jealousy and ferocity of the tribesman were not dead: indeed, they had merely expanded into the terrorism of armies.

The doctrine of militarism is not new. It was the first obsession of the earliest empires of men. How to make war on a systematic scale and how to obtain the most spoils out of it, were already in the thoughts of man as early as 3,000 years before Christ.

It is probably right to say that the swagger of the militarist is bound to pass out of the picture of human affairs, but how soon that will be is something which we can only guess. The plain fact is that the conquests of Alexander the Great, of Charlemagne, of Julius Caesar, of Napoleon are still of the world's inheritance of hero-worship.

Mankind still takes its orders more or less from unscrupulous military men who are drunk with dreams of personal glory. Conceited national gangsters and mailed-fist dictators continue to enjoy a predominance not given to men of peace. It is a fact that the masses turn to where there is the most noise made by the arrogant demagogue.

As long as such a state of affairs exists, war will remain a danger. Before this danger no nation on earth can escape the duty of preparing its citizens for the exigencies of war. Weak nations, especially, cannot dodge this duty, unless they prefer to receive insults to their dignity and are satisfied with being dictated upon.

This is not a plea for militarism, but it is a plea for military preparedness. We don't believe in war, but if war comes to us we will have to fight. We have fought in the past and fought without flinching under staggering handicaps. Our Revolutions were led by men who were trained in no war colleges, but they led honorably and well. It is not beyond the range of possibility that we may have to fight again.

Therefore, we have to prepare. Let the enemy be an imaginary enemy, but the absolute truth is that we are a weak people and so long as there are ambitious peoples around us we are not safe. We cannot sleep at the switch, so to speak, and be caught unawares. These, as we all know, are days of penetrations. Let us get ready for the dangers of such penetrations.

We believe that the time to prepare for the military exigencies of the future Philippine Republic is now. The Commonwealth period will comprise ten years. During those ten years it is our duty to develop the nucleus of our armed forces indispensable to our independent existence.

The first step our government should take is the arrangement for facilities for the sending of Filipino young men to West Point and other military academies in the United States. Money should be appropriated to pay the expenses of these scholarships, which should include not only army training, but training for a navy and training for a flying corps.

If it is possible to arrange for 20 Filipino scholarships at West Point, the government should do it. At least ten Filipinos should be sent to Annapolis and an equal number to the United States Army's Primary Flying School at Randolph Field.

Other flying schools in America should not be forgotten. There should be additional pensionados sent to the Pensacola school of naval flying, to the Air Corps Tactical School.

By the end of the Commonwealth regime, these Filipino students will have formed the officer nucleus of the national defense of the Philippine Republic. This officer nucleus is the major premise of all our military planning.

General MacArthur, chief of staff of the United States army, reporting to the department of war, calls the officer "the foundation of the Regular Army." To his mind the officers constitute "the mainspring of the whole mechanism" of the army. He adds: "Each one of them would be worth a thousand men at the beginning of a war. They are the only ones who can take the heterogeneous mass of citizens and make them a homogeneous fighting group."

We will probably not be able to afford a big standing army in the future and will therefore have to depend on a conscript army in which the soldier serves only for a short term. This makes the officer personnel indispensable to the continuity and progress of military principles and methods as well as the use of weapons.

Our future army reserve will be made up largely of men who have graduated from our public schools. The schools, therefore, should be made to do their part efficiently in our scheme of military preparedness.

Citizenship training should receive an increasing emphasis in the classroom as well as on the campus. Patriotism and nationalism should be stressed in the lessons of every school child, and drills calculated to develop the body and inculcate discipline should be a regular requirement.

When these children grow up to manhood they will know what social discipline is. In that way they will have the fundamentals of military training and their development to combat efficiency should follow as a matter of course.

But it is essential that the task of moulding this raw material into a dependable army be commended to expert hands. Upon the shoulders of the officers whom we will train in American military academies will fall the burden of inculcating in our citizens military discipline and the ideal of service.

A national defense bureau is indispensable to all this organization work. This bureau should be charged with the duty of prescribing graduated military instruction in our schools, colleges, and universities. Private educational institutions should be included in the program.

Every citizen of every country in Europe, with the exception of England, is liable to military service. It would not be amiss to consider such a proposition for the Philippines. Let us at any rate be prepared, and begin the preparation now by taking the steps necessary towards the organization of the technical command, the nucleus, of our future national defense.

Philippines Herald
September 12, 1934

* * * * *

RECTO TO THE BENCH

President Claro M. Recto of the Constitutional Convention takes his place in the highest tribunal of justice of the land, upon the testimony of a brilliant record of public service hard to parallel. He comes to this reward with the universal recognition of his merits by his countrymen.

Senator Recto is one of those men who give the thought of their age the distinguished stamp of their minds. In the relief map of the ideas of their generation, they are the altitudes that overshadow the puerilities of their fellowmen and give the common level its peaks of idealism.

In politics President Recto has shown himself above the mark of the vulgar demagogue. To be in the graces of his constituencies he has not had to abet their faults: those with whom he has labored have looked up to him with respect rather than with the feeling that he is necessarily their accomplice in unholy acts.

Doubting Thomases seriously questioned his selection for the presidency of the Constitutional Assembly, but it did not take them long to recognize the power of his leadership. His natural ability for conciliating the views of his fellowmen, and his quick grasp of the facts of any situation, saved the Assembly from many a crisis that threatened to disrupt it.

When there was confusion, he had a mind always ready to see the rectilinear course; to the garrulous demagogue he had an irresistible logic, an irony that routed his worst foe. During the long days that he wielded the gavel, his intelligence served as a commanding force in a camp of cross-purposes and conflicts.

There is nothing hollow in his reputation as a juridical thinker, as he steps up to his new high place in his public career. His eminence in the law is an established fact. It will never be said of him that he has been promoted on the strength of vociferated but not demonstrated mastery of this or that branch of his subject, or worse still, that he had to struggle his way into political security because in legal practice he had been colorless and a failure.

Recto as attorney-at-law has commanded an undisputed name for ability and clear thinking. His practice has not consisted in the hanging out of shingles now and the disappearance of those shingles tomorrow. Others have done just such a thing and finally have had to seek the security of the public payroll. Then, kicked upstairs, they leave a big question mark below—the question whether, if they had not pushed their way politically, they could have landed anywhere.

President Recto leaves no such question mark below as he steps up to the Supreme Court. His appointment by President Roosevelt is, by common consent, fully deserved. There is not the least doubt about his ability as a lawyer, and his perception and natural talent as an interpreter of the law. He honors not only the bench but his whole profession in this country.

Philippines Herald
March 25, 1935

* * * * *

JOSE ABAD SANTOS

As it must to all war criminals, the long arm of justice came to the Japanese who ordered the execution of our Jose Abad Santos. Perhaps the lieutenant general, who has just been arrested and delivered up at Sugamo Prison, thought that he had gotten away with it; perhaps he believed that he would never be noticed. It brings abundant credit to the investigators of the United States Army that they never abandoned their search for their man and that at last the criminal is in the toils of the law.

Within a short time the curtain will have been drawn back on the episode that most excited the imagination of our people during the early days of the occupation. The news of Abad Santos' death reached Manila as a confirmation of the common fear that the Japanese were here to liquidate all opposition by the swift expedient of the sword. It now only remains to be seen how the patriot preferred the sword to the ignominy of treasonable collaboration with the enemy.

They will soon be unfolding the drama of simple fidelity to duty and of undivided loyalty to the country of one's birth. In that drama we shall have occasion to see for ourselves the only way to respect an oath, which is that one must stand up manfully on it and refuse to take another incompatible with its mandate. Our generations will long remember that Jose Abad Santos died upon his oath of loyalty to the country of his birth and to the government that had invested him with its trust.

Others chose to live. There were more men who believed in being live cowards than dead heroes, than there were men like Abad Santos who knew only the courage of their convictions. The eminent quality of mortals in those days was self-preservation, manifested in a various language. Standing apart by himself, Jose Abad Santos spoke only one language, that of duty and loyalty to trust.

There were many expedients available to the great jurist. He could easily have regaled his compatriots with tales of Japan's infinite magnanimity in having come to redeem us from the talons of the American eagle. He could have joined the chorus of our own Wang Ching-weis and pleaded to our men in Bataan to give up the futile fight.

Jose Abad Santos could have gone to Capas after the fighting was over and blamed his countrymen for having made common cause with MacArthur's men. He could have chosen to be the Henri Petain of that regime and, by entrenching himself in power, saved his life. And how easily he could have chosen to surround himself with the comforts in Tokyo while the rest of his people starved on kangkong and linugao.

Yes, Jose Abad Santos could have done many things not only to save his own life but also to enrich himself in the soft lap of Co-Prosperity. Who knows if at this moment, guilty as he would have been had he chosen the line of least resistance, he also might not be enjoying the company of the less guilty and basking in the reflection of their popularity and considering himself also as the object of a popular clamor for amnesty?

Soon we shall be reconstructing the story of a martyrdom as glorious as that of Rizal 50 years ago, one in which the tyrant proved as impotent in suppressing the mind by the sword as in the Rizal case, and as in every other case where free men preferred death to slavery. It is an excellent story to reconstruct in this resplendent era of sham and shameless pretense.

Morning Sun
August 21, 1946

* * * * *

WELCOME TO ROMULO

We welcome Carlos P. Romulo. We welcome the servant of his people from his laurels abroad. There has never been one like him to us, none so distinguished, and none so effective.

The Commissioner has his critics, no doubt. Many would like to see him less embarrassed by so many personal glories, perhaps by so many possessions. But Romulo comes from a land prodigal of its glories for the deserving, and lavish in its rewards for the hard worker.

The point that matters is that Romulo has been very effective in dramatizing our cause, and in bringing to the attention of a confused world the heroic role of his people in the dark days of awful jeopardy to human liberty. Without his dash, and without his verve, none so poor would do us reverence today.

Let us give credit where credit is due, and that means to Romulo, still the inimitable Filipino citizen of the world and worthy spokesman of our ideals and aspirations.

Morning Sun
July 2, 1946

* * * * *

THE TORCH OF LIBERTY

It has been hundreds of years since the Magna Charta began to shed its light from England. At least seven centuries have elapsed since the English barons, tired of the oppressions of their king, revolted to give their country its present legal foundation, and the world its first charter of human rights.

What were those rights? They were contained in one word: liberty. The liberty to have and to hold one's property without interference from a self-seeking monarch, liberty of person as befits a human being created in the image of his God—such was the essence of the demands of men still fettered to the doctrine of the divine right of kings.

Four hundred years thereafter, the great issue was joined. Inspired by the same Magna Charta, the English Parliament, through the historic Petition of Right, demanded due process of law before the king could imprison or tax a man, or quarter his soldiers on the people.

It is at least 700 years from Runnymede to Kawit, where President Roxas relighted the Torch of Liberty the other day. Without a single faltering step, our President was still walking the noblest traditions which gave the human race its Grand Charter and the Petition of Right.

We have no more kings with divine rights. We have no more rulers to tax our pockets in order to make war on other rulers, or to combine with them in the quest for power. No one may now be imprisoned for debt or for non-payment of a poll tax, and with the Japanese fadeout, soldiers are no longer quartered on the people.

Undeniably, there is liberty in the land today. There is freedom of speech, which is vital, and there are these freedoms, besides: of conscience, of domicile, of association, of assembly. In short, there are life, liberty, and the pursuit of happiness for every person, whether natural or juridical.

But while our individual rights are safe, they will profit us little if we should find one day that our sovereign rights have been impaired. The preservation of these rights is the important thing now. Probably it will be more important than anything else in the next twenty years or so.

In Runnymede, as it was, too, in the interregnum of the rump Parliament, purely individual rights were at stake. The question of sovereignty was not involved for the simple reason that it was not threatened. Today, in the Philippines, while our personal rights are secure, our sovereignty, which is still to come, may not be as indivisible as it ought to be.

President Roxas' liberty speech the other day should be heard in every barrio in the land. The banner of liberty, according to him, will fly proudly over us. The only way it can fly proudly over us is when we are sovereign citizens of our country, not free hewers of wood and carriers of water.

Morning Sun
June 14, 1946

* * * * *

SPAIN'S HOLIDAY

The people of Spain observe today their national holiday, and we in the Philippines who lived under Spanish tutelage for three centuries cannot but claim our modest share in the rejoicing of this moment.

The Philippines once figured in the clustering glories of the Castilian crown, in the days when the sun truly never set on the Spanish domain. And we came into those glories because Spain had her Magellan to brave the inscrutable seas and die as a gallant soldier on the island of Mactan, and because another intrepid adventurer, Legaspi, followed Magellan's trail later to plant, with Father Urdaneta, the Cross on Philippine soil.

Legaspi's blood compact with Sicatuna on the island of Bohol signalized the annexation of these islands to the empire of Philip II. In the beauty of that symbolic act two races pledged mutual friendship, and our country may be said to have won its place in the sun.

The details of Spanish misrule in the Philippines are written clear upon the page of history, but they are not our concern today. We cannot, in the pleasure of remembrance, dwell on irrational policies and blunders of foresight which were the acts of buccaneers rather than the wish of a courageous race forever rising toward nobility.

All the bitterness is past. How adventurers, in their unchecked greed, blundered with the situation in the Philippines will be remembered as the experience of fallible men who must be fools first before they will be wise. History is full of blunders, but man has risen to sublime heights in spite of them.

The circumstances of opportunity come and go without waiting for nations and men to arrest them for their own benefit. Spain was undoubtedly quick at seeing her chance to annex the Philippines, but after her conquest of these islands, she merely drifted as mankind has always preferred to drift in the easier currents of life.

For three centuries Spain wasted her opportunity in the Philippines, but so did we. However, those were centuries of difficulties for the whole world. For the greater part of that period, only galleons crossed the seas to carry on trading with the colonies, and very little intellectual interest animated mankind to bring peoples closer together. Governments were beset with imperialistic intrigues and diplomacies, and individual adventurers merely dreamed of their El Dorados.

But a formidable instrument was then already in the hands of a man, and that was the Cross. No matter what they say, Spain delivered that Cross here as the symbol of a new dispensation. When Magellan brought the image of the Christ Child, he did not bring it to an inhospitable land; when Legaspi and Urdaneta planted the Cross on Philippine soil, a people already Christian at heart was quick to comprehend its meaning. It is a tribute to the race of Sicatuna and Soliman that it accepted the Christian gospel without demurring, that the establishment of the Church here was not accompanied by sword and fire as in other heathen lands.

We want especially on this day to remember the great beauty that Spain's religion has brought to our life. That beauty has been our sustaining inspiration. It has taught us to worship on a level above the vulgar, to see the divine objects of our adoration vividly rather than to get lost in abstractions that are beyond the apprehension of our minds. If anything, this faith has been to us a unifying force, and Spain, all honor to her, was the nation that bestowed this force on us as an enduring legacy of her cultural grandeur.

Philippines Herald
July 24, 1934

* * * * *

BASTILLE DAY

Today is Bastille Day in French history, but well may the day be a day of celebration for the whole world, to mark the triumph of ideals common to all mankind.

This day, whose glory is written large across the book of France's destiny, signalized the vindication of common men against the autocracy of wealth.

On this day, 145 years ago, the French people took a leaf from the American Declaration of Independence, and declared themselves free from the greed of predominant nobles.

That grim bulwark in Paris, called the Bastille, where innocent men had suffered torture and indignities at the hands of Tyranny's myrmidons, fell, and its fall was the signal for the deluge after the oppressors of the people.

This deluge was accompanied by a widespread burning of the chateaux of the wealthy nobles and the declaration of all the private wealth of these nobles as property of the state. It was perhaps the first case on record of the ideal of communism translated into action.

It could not have been otherwise. In the States General which had convened at Versailles for the purpose of working out some way of meeting the bankruptcy of the kingdom, the rights of the common people were being ignored, and an unscrupulous monarchy was trying to back out of its word to respect those rights.

For a time before the deluge came with its terrific force, the monarchy had been raising money with no apparent difficulty to finance the extravagances of the reigning court. Then one day the realization came like a jolt that there was no more money, that no more money could be manufactured out of air or borrowed, and that the government was at the end of its resources.

Then the proposal was made to levy new taxes for the purpose of raising funds for the state. The common people maintained that no taxes could be levied without their consent; in short, that the taxation power rested solely in the hands of their representatives in the States General.

That was the fundamental issue upon which the French people revolted against the aristocracy of the nobles, the issue whether for the benefit of the extravagant proprietary class the state should saddle common men with taxes beyond their means to pay.

It was the same grievance of the British colonies against the crown of England, which saw in the plantations in America an excellent opportunity to replenish its coffers. And it was the same grievance which drove the British Parliament to desperation against Charles I, resulting in the latter's decapitation.

The significant fact is that the revolt of the tax-paying common men of France ushered in the beginning of their actual participation in the affairs of the state. The principle was laid down unmistakably that there was to be no taxation without representation, that there was to be, in fact, no decision by the government without the consent of the governed.

Subsequent events in French history tell of attempts to brush aside this principle of the sovereignty of the people, but the seeds of democracy sown by the revolution which the capture of the Bastille on July 14, 1789, signalized, did not fall on infertile ground. They germinated and, watered with the blood of patriots, yielded their abundant harvest to France and the world.

The French people paid dearly for their present liberties. They paid for them with the atrocities of the Reign of Terror, creator of the Guillotine. For them they suffered humiliation at the hands of Machiavellian militarists. For them they were betrayed at Sedan and at Versailles.

But they did not surrender their spirit, did not lose honor when they lost their great battles on account of the blundering of adventurers whom they trusted. The disasters of history have distressed but not downed the people of France, and now, as in the days of the glorious liberation of the Bastille, their country remains the militant champion of Man's ideal of equality and liberty.

Philippines Herald
July 14, 1934

* * * * *

HANDS ACROSS THE SEA

Two hands have joined across the sea, in a tight clasp—symbol of a new friendship. America and Russia, after sixteen years of enmity, have renewed diplomatic relations which the installation of the Communist regime in the former Empire of the Czars in 1917 abruptly brought to a close.

This recognition of the Soviet Union by the most powerful republic on earth ushers in a new era in international affairs. It removes one more root of danger to the peace of mankind, and clears up a horizon for many years blurred by the clouds of misunderstanding.

As soon as an American ambassador is installed at Moscow, and a minister from Russia is officially received at Washington, the two nations will enter upon a new life of mutual benefits, not only politically but economically, and the world, then, will have seen the end of intolerance and the beginning of frank relations.

America, as the bulwark of Capitalism, has shown an intransigence toward Russia which has been pretty close to intolerance. Not only has she snubbed the Soviet Republic, but she has refused to give it credit for what it has done to prove that in many respects it has been more temperate and more solvent than the Wall Streets of the capitalist world.

If Soviet Russia has, in America's opinion, erred in placing the Proletariat on the highest pinnacle of human value; if Communism, in view of the established order, is fundamentally wrong in considering labor as the goal of human happiness, instead of merely the means to that happiness—still the Russians were entitled to American recognition.

That recognition was not only the mandate of America's tradition of freedom and every man's inalienable right to the pursuit of happiness, but it was also consistent with the American philosophy of giving a man the benefit of the doubt, of considering him not guilty until his guilt is proven.

It is sure that the Soviet regime was founded on violence, that it was installed upon the dead bodies of Russian men, women, and children in one of the bloodiest acts in the drama of history. But it was a revolution which culminated when Kerensky's power collapsed—a revolution which had been beating fiercely beneath the surface of Russian life. No power could have prevented the release of that mighty pent-up force. No messianic hand could have subdued the fury of that maelstrom into a semblance of peace.

The conspiracy which ended in the slaughter of the Czar and his family was the conspiracy of the common people, of the masses of the Russian population who had groaned under the lash of a profligate Aristocracy. It was a conspiracy which had been gathering momentum in every street corner of Moscow and St. Petersburg, in the prisons and the St. Helenas of political offenders, in the hives of the oppressed laborers where the Trotskys and the Lenins and the Stalins of Marx the Prophet preached their doctrines at the peril of their lives.

A nationwide system of espionage proved of no avail, and soon the maelstrom broke loose. Kerensky, swept by the onrush of the popular revolution, set up his republic—the first concrete institution of Russian democracy. But that proved insufficient to satiate the hunger of the masses. The masses wanted more after so many years of oppression and privation, wanted to see themselves installed in the Kremlin of the Czars and avenge the wrongs of ages.

Few people have been so oppressed as the Russian people. Few people have suffered the humiliation that they have suffered, the pains that they have endured. When, therefore, the day of their redemption was proclaimed, they went beyond bounds and the sentimental Russian soul profoundly affected by its centuries of servitude turned callous.

The Spirit is no more—only Matter remains. Every symbol, every relic of the odious past was crushed under the feet of the emancipated masses. A new religion was installed—the religion of Necessity. Priests were hounded out of their retreats, all manifestations of divine worship were obliterated, and the money changers were admitted anew into the temples of a repudiated God.

These are not the things that America has necessarily recognized. They are not the doctrines which have been exalted for the edification of the world. Neither is there sanction for the Communist postulate of destruction for the established order of things as an imperative means to the attainment of human happiness.

The American recognition implies renewal of diplomatic relations and the mutual enjoyment of economic benefits. But at the same time there will be an end to the subversive propaganda to which Russia has been forced to resort by a policy of repression. Henceforth there will be an open deal between the two nations, and tolerance will be the rule. More wrongs can be righted under a policy of tolerance than under a system of persecution.

Herald
November 20, 1933

* * * * *

THE FICTION OF RED PROPAGANDA

Last week, in this column, we had occasion to point to the fallacy of the professional agitator's deliberate misinformation that the man of the barrio in this country is being oppressed by his

Government. We took up, as a specific instance, the case of the Cedula Tax, and showed how this tax is the only contribution of the barrio man to the treasury of his nation.

Two pesos a year, or five thousandth of a centavo a day—this and nothing more is the obligation of the man of the barrio to his Government. In exchange for this infinitesimal burden on his shoulder, if it can at all be called a burden, he gets police and health services, free education for his children, and the chance to avail himself of the advantages of our commercial progress made possible by a stable government.

The discrepancy between what the Government is doing for the barrio man and what the barrio man is doing for his Government, is so manifestly against the latter that it cannot be conceived how the professional agitator can so distort the facts as to make the barrio man refuse to pay his Cedula Tax, and on top of this, to incite him to take up arms against constituted authority in these islands.

This brings us to the point of this article, which is this: Is there reason for our common people to consider sedition against our Government as the agitator would want them to do? Do the conditions in this country warrant the adoption of a violent attitude by our masses against those in authority? Is the professional agitator preaching things that are consistent with reality as we know it, or is he not rather saying things fantastic to our mind, repulsive to our conscience?

The Communist, for instance, who is the most uncompromising enemy of our established order, would demolish our national edifice stone by stone and leave no vestige of private ownership in this country. Why? Because the Bolsheviks of Russia did exactly that in 1917. But why did they do it? What were the circumstances that drove them into the greatest but most horrid of revolutions in the annals of modern time? What impelled them to massacre the Tsar and his entire hierarchy of Grand Dukes?

The Russian peasants' hatred for Tsardom did not begin in 1917 but many, many years before. It dated back to the odious days of serfdom in Russia. Tsar Alexander II emancipated the serfs in 1861 but only to throw them at the mercy of money-lending landlords. The immediate result of Alexander's decree was the rise in rents by ten times what they used to be before the serfs were proclaimed free. Taxes rose proportionately and prices fell to the utter distress of the peasantry's agricultural industry.

The peasants were deprived of their animals and work in the fields was paralyzed. This was followed by a wholesale migration from the countryside to the towns, and thousands of what used to be self-sustaining tillers of the soil had to beg in the streets. The peasant machinery of production collapsed and in 1891 a most unheard-of famine struck the country.

The emancipator of the serfs in the meantime had been assassinated and what followed that assassination was the most brutal chapter in the dynastic history of the Romanoffs. Practically all freedoms were suppressed and bloody executions of suspected revolutionaries became the order of the day.

The peasantry was converted into a huge army of proletarian workers. These workers did not know what their wages were, their employers being perfectly free to pay their laborers as they pleased. There were no decent homes for the proletariat; there were only prison-like houses for them, the houses that nurtured the Bolshevik revolution which later was to exact its harvest of terror and carnage.

Lenin, the father of the Soviet revolution, had lost his elder brother during the brutal repression that followed an unsuccessful conspiracy against the Tsar in 1887. They hanged him. That rankled in Lenin's breast. Later on he himself was arrested and exiled. He would not even be allowed to educate himself. To the Government, he was suspect, and that ended his chance of enjoying any personal liberty under the Tsarist regime.

Nobody in fact enjoyed any personal liberty in Russia during those days, with the rigid system of censorship and espionage that was in force, and this is the point we would like to bring out for the enlightenment of our people. The least suspicion virtually doomed a man forever, landing him if not in prison, in Siberia, and if not in Siberia, in the hangman's noose. In the Philippines, the Communist who insults the Government and preaches subversion against it, enjoys his freedom of speech and receives money, besides, from his backers in Moscow.

Our point is this: The Bolshevik revolution was the result of a slow process of bleeding the Russian people white, a process which culminated in the betrayal of the masses who, in their grey suits, had to lay down their lives or sacrifice their health on the battlefronts of a senseless war.

That revolution was the handwriting on the wall. It was the inevitable outcome of a saturnalia of terrorism, of enrichment at the expense of the peasant and the laborer, of dishonesty in the management of the public finances, of the squandering of the people's money for the wine and women of corrupt Grand Dukes. A desperate situation called for a desperate remedy, and the Bolshevik revolution was the result.

Now, what is the desperate situation in the Philippines that can call for such a desperate remedy as the taking up of arms against the Government which the Filipino Communist advocates? Whose right to speak here was suppressed? Who was arrested and hanged for being a suspect? Who is the laborer who was not paid his wages and did not have recourse to our bureau of labor? What workingman suffered a physical injury while at work and did not get redress for his grievance under our labor compensation law?

Let us not lose our sense of proportion. Let our people maintain their levelheadedness. We have tried to bring out certain facts of Russian history to point to the logic of the Bolshevik revolution of 1917, but in so doing our purpose is to show how absolutely nothing in common exists between us and the Russians who destroyed Tsardom and established their dictatorship of the proletariat.

The Bolshevik soul, steeped in the doctrines of Marxism, had to deal the deathblow to capitalism because the "kulak" of the Russian village had taught the peasant to dread his insatiable greed, while the industrial capitalist of the city had absolutely no sympathy for his starving laborer. No such condition exists in the Philippines, and we have no cause to develop class feeling against another class. This is not Russia but the Philippines, and other gods than Marx hold the secret of our happiness.

Philippines Herald
March 23, 1935

* * * * *

THE WARNING OF DEMOCRACY

Acting Governor-General Ralston Hayden chose a timely subject for his address to the University read by Mr. Horace B. Pond at the commencement exercises on the campus yesterday morning. His discussion of "the reaction of the world to the concept of political democracy" was indeed most illuminating.

He cited the cases of Sweden, Norway, and Denmark, "perhaps the best governed nations in the world today"; of the Netherlands and Switzerland, which "have passed through the storms of the past two decades on even keels"; of Britain, which now is "more completely and securely democratic than ever before"; of France, which "has survived the post-war debacle with her democratic institutions unimpaired, almost unchanged"; and of the United States, which is "laying the foundations for a purer democracy in which the rights and welfare of every citizen will be more zealously guarded than ever before."

"Thus," he went on, "the epic events of the past twenty years have left the genuinely democratic states of the world still democratic, still sound and still pressing onward towards the perfection of popular government. . . . The ancient principle that the will of the sovereign people should prevail still stands as the soundest and most satisfactory foundation for that institution called the state." Of modern dictatorships he had this to say: that they are "the products of national desperation and are only made possible by the national will to survive in the face of overwhelming peril."

This, then, is clear: democracy has weathered the storm on an even keel, whereas modern dictatorships, which are nothing but a reversion to the days of crowned autocrats, are at best merely tentative. The voting masses in those countries that are the bulwark of democracy today continue to have their voice in the affairs of their governments; those who have consented to renounce the ballot in favor of a salute, more or less ridiculous, to a sabre-rattling dictator, are in a state of experimentation.

It is a fact clearly established by the post-war debacle that the existing dictatorships are the outcome of distress and demoralization. Appalling misery called for any semblance of relief, the suffering masses were ready to cling to anything to save themselves from sinking. A small minority of men saw their opportunity and entered the scene. They were magnetic men, managers of men, and they were able to stem the popular desperation. More than this, they were able to inflame the imagination of the crowds.

In all fairness, it must be said of these men that they have succeeded in cleaning up their governments of the frivolities of their predecessors. They have brought about a noteworthy simplification in the businesses of their states and have eliminated the personal enrichment of crowned autocrats at the expense of the common people. But in uncrowning the autocrats, and in some cases putting them to death, they did not cast away the crowns: they wore the crowns themselves.

Thus, it can be said, they merely reinforced the old system of autocracy and have given it another name. The swagger of the militarist—that evil genius of a previous age—did not disappear. In fact, the militarist has been rattling his sabre all along, and the war cloud is ominously thick on the European horizon. The masses appear satisfied because they see more bread around, but they do not see more liberties for themselves. And since it is not by bread alone that men live, when the pangs of hunger are appeased, it is logical to expect them to demand their political rights.

This is the weakness of the tactical, not fundamental, triumph of the newly-dressed autocracy of Europe today, this wrong diagnosis, so to speak, of the popular ailment. The apparent calm of the masses after they have been given more bread is being interpreted as the plenitude of spiritual satisfaction. The doctors have diagnosed tuberculosis as a cold, and they are satisfied with their pronouncement, or at least appear satisfied with it. Heads will continue to roll in the public square, suspects will be put on mock-trials without benefit of defense counsel, when an omniscient State orders it in the name of its supremacy.

There is something unnatural in all this set-up of minority rule, something that tells us the lesson of History has not been learned. We have in Marxist Russia, for instance, an insistence on class rule—the rule of the proletariat—by force, but a greater mind than Marx had thought, before the latter's prophecy began to disturb our social harmony, that while labor must rule as a class, it must rule by more than its hatreds and prejudices. There are also those dictators who would ape the magnificent Caesar, but would not understand that Caesar foresaw the power of democracy and created enemies, and died at their hands, because he wanted a wider popular representation in a republican government.

The idea of the dignification of the masses does not enter the head of the dictator today. It is the idea of the supremacy of the State over all private rights that preoccupies him and directs all his acts. The philosophy of that State is force, and its symbol is the steel bayonet. The vitality of the masses—the vitality that in the nature of things will not be restrained—is subordinated to the instrumental power.

The futility of such a formula of sovereignty is written clear upon the page of History. The Greek aristocracy upheld the principle that they rule who have arms, and that aristocracy failed. The Roman concept of liberty was the liberty not of the masses but of the established institutions of supremacy over those masses. Rome died in decadence. All down the ages this has been the case: small minorities trying to arrogate unto themselves omniscient powers to control the social majorities. But all through the political mutations of the world the point is clear that the natural position of man is to enjoy his private rights, and that the less interference there is with those rights by the State, the happier he is.

The warning of Democracy is that it is open to the usurper's opportunism if its chief instrumentality—the ballot—is not assured its place in a republican community. The warning is for the masses to use this ballot as the incorruptible medium for the expression of their sovereign will. There is nothing utopian in this and we must consecrate our efforts to its achievement. The ballot is the core of democracy, and its security is the death of all dictatorships. Let us not make the mistake of substituting it with a salute.

Philippines Herald
March 27, 1935

* * * * *

HISTORY AND DEMOCRACY

"Let us never forget," said Governor-General Murphy last night, addressing the members of the Rotary Club all over the Islands, "that there are innumerable humble creatures about whom history is silent, whose numbers and strength and spirit lend power to the mighty—they are the people, and a democracy closing its eyes to this fact is headed toward an inglorious end."

Two simple truths appear in that statement—a truth of history and a truth of democracy. Let us endeavor to examine their meaning and draw from them a lesson for our present life. For never as on this day, when we are on the threshold of a historic era, did we need more of the emphasis of such truths.

The simple truth of history is that it is not the story of human paroxysms but of the silent labors of the multitude; these labors supply the basic stratum; their sum and substance is history itself. This has been, and always will be, the process of all historic realizations.

All through the ages the multitude has labored to cement the groundwork of civilization. When under the lash of the Pharaohs, Egypt gave the world her pyramids, nothing was said of the prodigious industry that built them. That industry was of the multitude, and the multitude made Egyptian history.

These pyramids, these stupendous monuments of human vanity, are a fair example of what the masses can do. The patience and the strength given to the task of constructing them may never be calculated. But all in all, what are they? Sterile wonders, and nothing more.

Looking down upon this age, and doomed to look down, perhaps eternally, upon the future, these pyramids are constant reminders of the vast human energy wasted for the benefit of a few mummies that are now the simple objects of idle curiosity.

These pyramids show how the multitude can perform its feats prodigiously; these pyramids are a perfect example of what team work can do, and has done, to make history. What that history is, is another matter; it may be resplendent history, and again it may be stupid history. It may be like the history of Greece, full of glory; it may be like the history of Rome, full of grandeur; it may be like the history of France, full of light. And again, it may be like the history of Babylon's civilization, of which nothing is left today.

But it has always depended on the multitude, working in cooperation with a ruling class. This class supplies what Governor-General Murphy calls the "great men in the life of every country." They furnish the ideas, and the "innumerable humble creatures" about whom history is unusually silent, transmute those ideas into living realities.

When, therefore, the ideas are vain or sterile, what the multitude accomplishes cannot be more than the pyramids—gigantic monuments condemned to the corrosions of time and incapable of giving flesh and blood to the ideals of mankind. Here is where it should be clear to us that democracy is the logic of history itself.

It is futile to hope that the mighty can move the world without the collaboration of the people, and this collaboration, therefore, is the principal motor of human progress. When the mighty are the slavers, when those at the top are the lash-wielding masters, and not the creatures of the people, all work is futile and civilization is doomed.

The only permanent formula is understanding between the multitude and the ruling class; when both meet in a common parliament of the intellect, when one receives the loyalty and the obedience of the other without the use of force, that is democracy. Deviations from this line of understanding have always met "an inglorious end."

The great paroxysms of history are nothing more than the inevitable collision of democracy with the force of divine rights. In the days of the Pharaohs there was no democracy, but only slaves building pyramids under the overseer's lash. The multitude obeyed, and there were no revolts. What happened to the civilization of Egypt? Nobody cares to know.

But when man began to rebel against his fetters, there was democracy. When the subjects of Rome began to see eye to eye with Julius Caesar, under whose genius the Roman senate assumed its historic majesty, the end came for the forces of divine rights that had sapped the vitality of the people.

Rome passed the torch to France, and France kept it aglow. From that torch was diffused the light that was to penetrate the galleys of injustice and redeem the people from their sewers of misery. Social reform assumed its meaning, and democracy began its great crusade.

The French Revolution—that act of God, as Victor Hugo calls it—sounded the death knell for divine rights. For Europe it was the beginning of a new history—the history of parliaments, and of the right of the rabble to build its own barricade against the armies of the mighty.

Then history began, the kind of history to which we turn for inspiration when our lives are oppressed. The mighty do not make this history; the people make it—the people rising from the depths of misery to the light of social reform, the people achieving the level of its national destiny.

Such is the spirit of democracy that constitutes the very soul of permanent history. The historic mission of every nation, the historic mission of this country of ours, is the elevation of the multitude to a sense of their part in the drama of the human race. It is the people who will make our history; it is they, or it is nothing.

Philippines Herald
September 20, 1935

* * * * *

THE PRICE OF MAN'S FRIVOLITY

Our electorate are almost on the eve of choosing their standard-bearers for the elections of the Philippine Commonwealth. This act of choosing will be for them part of the monumental task of building a new nation. The kind of men they will choose will more or less determine the physiognomy of their government.

Let us bypass those men who have arbitrarily foisted themselves on us as "candidates of the people." Let us bypass them who are megalomaniac enough to think that they have a great following, who fool themselves by harking to the phantom clamour of our populace. Let us bypass such men as inconsequential to the determination of the format of our new national existence.

Let us talk of the men whom our large existing groups will nominate, the men who will be chosen through the normal processes of our political system. Let us consider only the cases of those who are not personal adventurers, but candidates who will "accept" because their parties will nominate them and not because a coterie of office-seekers would use them for vindictive purposes.

Let us demand of such candidates the moral nerve and the intellectual poise that will make them deserving of our common respect. Let us exact of them adherence to the moral code of the race and loyalty to the fundamental principles of the national decency. Let us, in other words, insist from now on that our public men be responsible, not vain; sober, not frivolous.

We are not asking that the platforms of our parties include a plank specifying the kind of morality that their candidates shall observe. We are not asking such a thing, for the simple reason that the moral conduct of no public man can be guaranteed by words, and that rather than make our elective officials *promise* to live straight, we would have them *actually* live straight.

It is a fact of historic veracity that if the lives of great men whom we remember today were to be judged by their frivolities, many of them would not be great. This is not said as an apology for the frivolities of our own living great but to show that only angels can be faultless.

Our public men will have their faults, naturally enough; still it is not unreasonable to demand that frivolity, of all human faults, should not be theirs by their own will, by their own acts of commission. Frivolous tendencies can be controlled; for the public man there is only one course open, and that is, to control them.

We are reminded of the public life of the great Pericles of Athens, the builder of the most beautiful city of ancient times. He was a most noble man, and of a distinguished elevation of mind which made the minds of his envious contemporaries look small and vulgar. But he committed a grave error which made him suspect in the rabble's eyes.

Pericles had caused a law to be passed which had the effect of restricting the so-called democracy of the city state into a narrow oligarchy of Athenian blood. Slaves, freed men, and foreigners were excluded from the collective management of the government. The citizen had to prove Athenian descent on both sides to be considered a member of the state.

There was one woman of high education, Aspasia, whom Pericles took as his mate but whom he could not marry, thanks to his own strict law of citizenship, the woman being from Miletus and therefore a foreigner. This *affaire* with that woman proved to be the beginning of the end for the great builder of Athens. His critics abused him, humiliated him, until he lost his power. Then, when he had lost his power, his friends and associates were persecuted.

Pericles was hardly guilty of a moral outrage: he was merely the victim of his own narrow-minded law, a law of exclusion, a law eminently anti-cultural as we understand culture today. But within the moral code of his time, he committed a frivolous act and paid the price for it. Then, as now, the public had its own way of meting penalties for transgressions against its moral conventions.

Let us take two more emphatic cases of frivolousness which make the error of Pericles look like an insignificant detail, indeed, in the history of the human race. Let us take the cases of Alexander the Great and of Julius Caesar, two of the greatest conquerors the world has ever produced.

Alexander, the first to have an idea of a world dominion in his head, was known to have been a most frivolous man who believed in the eternity not only of his power but of his personal charms. At the height of his career as a man of war, he never forgot his looks and took special care to represent them as perennially those of a handsome young man.

In the meantime, so the historian tells us, he gave himself to excesses and debauchery until one day, in the year 323 B.C., he collapsed from hard drinking in Babylon and died from a sudden attack of fever. With him the world empire he had once held in the hollow of his hand went down in pieces, and nothing but the legend of his personal life was left.

The case of Julius Caesar was even more tragic, because Caesar was far more advanced than Alexander in his idea of a world dominion, and, of all the warriors of ancient times, was nearest to the thought of these modern days. The Roman general, as all of us know, was assassinated by a group of his friends at the foot of the statue of his fallen rival, Pompey the Great.

Caesar, in all respects, eclipsed Alexander the Great. For the first time, under him, the world saw in the Roman republic the main lines of our present-day democracy developing into something substantial and tangible. There was the Popular Assembly and there was the Senate. In the deliberations of these two bodies the social conflicts of the great mass of the people and the clash of personalities were already clearly distinguishable.

The Roman people were becoming conscious of the need for some way of governing themselves to control their own destinies. The narrow city state of Grecian democracy had receded into the past. Caesar saw beyond the walls of Rome, stretched his mind out beyond the oligarchy of the ruling class and strove to save the people for the republic. It was he who first understood the value of enlightening the public on what their government was doing for them by causing the proceedings of the Senate to be published on bulletin boards.

That was as far as Caesar's statesmanship went; as far as his private life was concerned, his countrymen knew him as their leader who spent a year, when he was no longer young, in amorous carousals with Queen Cleopatra of Egypt, and not satisfied with that, brought her to Rome with him, to the bitter resentment of the Roman public. History also records his extravagance in fiscal matters and his public festivals staged on a most lavish scale.

Caesar's frivolity was the immediate cause of his downfall, and his downfall marked the complete collapse of the ruling minority of Rome. All that he had built was shattered to pieces with him, and all because he dared defy the Roman public in his pursuit of frivolous happiness.

The lesson of all these historical episodes for us of the present day is that our public men cannot be so sure of their success as long as they transgress our laws of morality. Men who wield power are apt to forget that the perdurability of no man's power on this earth is guaranteed.

These moments in the life of our people call for the most serious sense of responsibility on the part of our national leaders. We are about to turn the corner and advance into a new horizon. New and perplexing problems of state are before us. Our masses are restive, and the outlook for our economic existence as an independent country is certainly not bright.

In the midst of our difficult days our public men cannot even forget to dance and squander their time away in nightly pleasures. What example would thus be set for the great mass of our people? What incentive would our citizenry have to devote their attention soberly to the problems of their nation? What respect would our people have for their government when the leaders in that government are weak and frivolous?

There will come a time in the life of our people when they will forget to ask how "Miss Philippines" looked, what kind of a nose she had, and how gracefully she ascended the throne at the Carnival auditorium. Some day in the future people will cease to inquire how our debutantes dressed and danced and giggled, and how proud their parents looked when they were presented to society. What our leaders wore, how they tripped the light fantastic, in tango, in fox-trot, or rigodon, these too will be forgotten.

Then, the people will simply ask: "What constructive thing did they do?" "What did they think, and how did they think?" "Did they think of us today, or did they think of themselves alone?"

Then the physiognomy of this particular age of ours will be judged beyond mistaking. Needless to say, we are forming now the outlines of that physiognomy. Our present acts and preoccupations, our thoughts and desires, all are being drawn upon the page of this day in our history. It is impossible to escape the judgment of the Future. In the historic process of our race we are either benefactors or renegades. In History we shall be just what we are today, no more, no less.

Let there be the utmost sobriety then, at least in the deportment of our leaders, who will figure in the high spots of the present annals when they are written. Let these leaders forget the glamor of our social halls, let them turn their attention from our dainty debutantes to the more serious business of making our new nation stand on its feet. It is written in History that Athens, in its renaissance, wore the face of Pericles, and we know that Athens was beautiful and dignified. What we want our own leaders to do is to give this particular period in our history the stamp of their devotion and the noble elevation of their minds. This is the duty that Destiny imposes on them.

Philippines Herald
June 15, 1935

* * * * *

INTERVIEW WITH NEHRU

NEW DELHI, March 28—From this ancient land of marble palaces and mud-huts, from this India of immemorial sorrows—the captains and the kings are about to depart.

On the walls of the library of the Indian Congress the resplendent portraits of England's Viceroys, from Clive to Wavell, no longer hang, and within those walls the best minds of the land are at present engaged in framing the fundamental law of the Indian Republic that is to rise after June of 1948.

In the seething interim between the present and that promised day of India's manumission, a fair, handsome, slightly bent gentleman of about 57—Jawaharlal Nehru—has the unique satisfaction of being witness, on behalf of his exploited people, to the liquidation of an empire which began in the seventeenth century.

Exactly two years ago at this writing, this Indian patriot from Kashmir was stepping out of the Ahmadnagar Fort after an imprisonment of 1041 days, thus closing his ninth term of confinement extending over a period of ten years. A rich man, one of the richest in India, he could have lived on his estate without British molestation, by the simple expedient of co-operating with the invaders of his land. But, unlike in the Philippines, where love of freedom and love of America are not two disparate things, in India no one can love independence and love Mr. Kipling, too.

Nehru was one of those who had not forgotten. Impregnated with the long suffering of his countrymen, he had picked up the quarrel with the British as other Nehrus had done before him. He fought with a frenzy worthy of our own Andres Bonifacio. Hating injustice and mincing no words about it, he found the gates of British prisons always wide open for him.

That his anti-Nazi and anti-Fascist convictions should leap to the surface long before the war, was not strange. In 1936 he refused a pressing invitation from Mussolini, then a sort of darling boy to Downing Street. Another invitation, this time from Hitler, was extended and, again, he declined. To London's statesmen he made it clear that he feared the designs of those two gentlemen, but his admonitions fell on deaf ears.

Then, when the war against Hitler and Mussolini was in full swing, Nehru was arrested and thrown into jail, to save India from Nazism and Fascism!

Now, the wheel of Fate having turned, it becomes Nehru's special task as Premier of the interim Government to see that none of the Fascistic predilections are left behind in India.

British interests in India are definitely on the way out. Mr. Nehru told me that millions of pounds of British business have been transferred to Indian hands in a year's time, and that most of the stores and shops that still bear English signs are now Indian-owned. He referred to the *Times of India,* the British newspaper trust which for a hundred years had grown into a monstrous weapon of British wealth and power, recently acquired by Indians at a price of something like one million pounds.

"Should the British desire to invest again in India," said Mr. Nehru, "they will find themselves sadly in the minority."

The Pandit took pains to emphasize to me that under the Constitution of Free India economic control will be in Indian hands. Naturally, under the old colonial set-up no legislation prejudicial to

British interests has been possible, but the colonial set-up is broken, said Mr. Nehru, and from now on it is India first and India always.

At this juncture the Indian leader asked to be enlightened regarding the amendment to the Philippine Constitution about which he had heard so much. I assured him that the sovereign will of our people did that. We have given the Americans equal rights with us and such a concession, we appreciate, the Indians cannot grant to the British. I said that America does not inspire fear in us, whereas India's fears have been borne out by the fact of her almost static existence. In our own little way, I pointed out, we have advanced to political independence: that, I said, is the record on which America stands in the Philippines.

Nehru expressed the wish that Philippine-Indian relations be cemented. India, according to him, is very appreciative of the co-operation of the Philippine Ambassador to the UNO—General Carlos P. Romulo—who is a great friend of the Pandit's sister, the beautiful Madame Pandit. As a matter of fact, Romulo is the most popular Filipino in New Delhi and I remember that at least half a dozen journalists have interviewed me about him.

Pandit Nehru also recalled his congratulations to President Roxas upon the launching of the Philippine Republic, and asked that his best wishes be conveyed.

"I know your President's great abilities, and I have not the least doubt that his government will be a success," he said.

There is, according to him, a solution for every problem, when I asked him if India had Communists. The Indian Government, he assured me, has its own Communist problem. The Communists are well organized and count with very able leaders among them. It does seem, however, that by siding with the British during the war they committed the unpardonable sin and their cause has been discredited.

There was no tone of reproach in Nehru's reference to the comrades, and this was perhaps due to the fact that he has found much food for thought in both Marx and Lenin. In his monumental book, "The Discovery of India," of which he has presented me a copy, he writes of the Soviet Revolution as having "Advanced human society... and laid the foundations for the 'new civilization' towards which the world would advance."

Yet there is a wide difference between the truth and a supposition that Mr. Nehru is Communist. He is, to the exclusion of any other concept, a consummate nationalist. Thus he has not failed to note that in Russia, Fatherland now is more important than the International Proletariat; also, he points to the drift towards nationalism of all proletarian movements based on internationalism.

"The first and dominant urge is national freedom," said Nehru.

The Muslim Jinnah, chief stumbling block to a united India, is by common consent Nehru's principal headache. To Jinnah the current Inter-Asian Relations Conference is just another Co-Prosperity scheme designed to establish Hindu Big Business where the Japs failed. Jinnah's Pakistan (Divided India) is the very thing that can dash all of Nehru's hopes for an independent India on the rocks.

Jinnah, in the words of Mr. Nehru to me, is a Muslim without religion and a political fanatic. I had suggested that perhaps the Hindu-Muslim disagreement was more fundamental than it appeared to be, considering the religious stakes involved, but Mr. Nehru said that it was more political than anything else. By implication, the political agitator is Jinnah, and he is rocking the Indian boat.

What, then, could be the outcome of the current communal dispute that has so agitated India's internal life? Nehru gave the answer: "I cannot see how the Muslims can hold out for long. The nationalist movement is a tidal wave that must sweep all obstacles in its path."

It was typical of the wealthy nobleman to think in the simple terms of India's common man. Once upon a time, when he was young, moving among England's princes, including the Prince of Wales, he did live in astonishing magnificence. It is said of him that he used to send his suits to Paris to be cleaned, and no maharajah had ever done such a thing. Today, habited in the simple garb of an Indian gentleman, he moves about without the least ostentation, ever mindful of the hopeless misery of the millions of men, women and children whose lives are, to use his own words "a slow merging into non-existence."

Thus rationing in India today is absolute, with Nehru's government behind it. It is considered an offense to serve more than one course, and only soft drinks are allowed at any gathering of more than 24 persons. The Chief Justice here was once fined for having a cake at the wedding of his daughter because there were more than 24 at the party and cake was food! The size of sugar served at tea is microscopic, while sweets are a rare thing. There is no beer and, of course, no whiskey-soda. Frivolity is totally absent, and the common man does not smile.

"Of course you are entitled to exemptions from this rationing," I suggested. He had told me that his week's ration of sugar was all gone.

"Yes, that is true, I may ask for exemptions, but one does not really care for exemptions," was his reply.

That is India's Man of Destiny—Jawaharlal Nehru.

Special to the Manila Times
April 13, 1947

* * * * *

OUR OWN ABELARDO

The death of Professor Abelardo removes from our midst a composer of genuine Filipino music and an interpreter of the Filipino soul. The sweet melodies of his *kundiman* compositions will linger in his countrymen's hearts long after his name, perhaps, is forgotten by our generations to come.

Abelardo transmuted into music the glories of our morning hours, the languor of our siestas, the splendors of our tropic sunsets. The melancholy tenderness of his *kundiman* pieces haunts us like the memory of our own moonlights, with their romantic *haranas* and the perfume of *dama-de-noche*.

His native music will always charm our ears, but we know that the fountain source of that music is gone, and well might *Filipinas* sing at this hour of sorrow, "Na Saan Ka Irog?"

Philippines Herald
March 22, 1934

* * * * *

A GREAT MAN PASSES

Adolph S. Ochs, publisher of the New York Times, passes out of public life in America to leave a testament of journalistic integrity behind as his substantial contribution to the ethics of human culture. For to him journalism as a profession was nothing if it was a matter of dollars and cents alone, if it did not stand by its primordial duty of keeping faith with an organized, moral society.

It was his norm of conduct to print the news because it was fit to print, and not because it would excite the crowd in the street and boost his sales. He did not come into the journalism of America as an adventurer seeking money, or as one with inherited money that must be invested for profit. It will never be said of him that his reputation as a journalist was the reputation of a commercial opportunist.

Wealth came to him as the reward of his ability and dynamic passion as a newspaper man. It came to him because his views as a public benefactor inspired respect in his fellow man, and because he was an authentic journalist who spoke with the formidable authority of his intellect and experience.

That experience was not the experience of the investor solely interested in the figures in his ledger, but the experience of the printer's devil himself, of the compositor, of the foreman, of the reporter, of the editor-in-chief. Thus even as newspaper owner, he was intimate with the pulsation of the human element in his business, and he never failed to share the thoughts and feelings of his men.

He was never the absentee landlord of the newspaper profession, never the usufructuary of its benefits. He was respected not because of his money, but because of his keen intellect, his brains. In journalistic history, where his labors appear in their monumental lines, his personality is that of the newspaper man, not the commercial adventurer.

Philippines Herald
April 10, 1935

* * * * *

THE KING AND THE POET

Within five days England has lost her King and her most renowned poet laureate. George V, the most beloved monarch ever to preside over the destinies of the British Empire, is dead; and Rudyard Kipling, singer of England's imperial glories, also is no more. For these two, all the tumult and the shouting are over.

As the poet of British imperialism which rose to its tide towards the close of the nineteenth century, Kipling was largely responsible for the white man's supposed superiority over the other races of this earth.

He it was who gave contemporary literature the celebrated idea of "the White Man's burthen."

We think of Kipling when we think of the expansion of British financial and business interests beyond the borders of Merrie England; we remember him in connection with Europe's adventures across the seas, impelled by the needs of growing populations; the harsh notes of his poetry were in harmony with the rhythm of a new aggressive industrialism, and no people sang them with more gusto than the British military caste in India.

Kipling composed the music, and the industrial monopolists furnished the material support, for the sweep over palm and pine, the same triumph that sowed the seed of that harvest of hate and cruelty otherwise known as the Boxer Rebellion, the same triumph that swept over the frontiers of Africa, and, nearer home, was to blame for the recalcitrant Ireland of this century.

This is the Kipling that has just gone, the renowned poet laureate who has departed with the captains and the kings of his triumphant imperialism. Yet in the beloved monarch whose demise the whole British Empire mourns today, England has had the genuine model of the democratic ruler who was opposed to all the mailed fist and ostentatious lordship of the Kipling imperialism.

King George V was beloved of his subjects because he did not belong to that imperialistic caste of arrogant officials and military adventurers that was behind the foreign-office system of the present epoch. He was the monarch of the people, not the backer of Big Business, and never the tool of Machiavellis.

If imperialism, for the most part, was the creation of Monarchy, it was not so in England. The brand of imperialism that prospered on the European continent was the brand of kings. The Romanoffs and the Hohenzollerns were in the storm-center of the imperialistic battles early in the century; they provoked those battles; in shining armor they strutted across their scene.

When the prelude to the imperialistic drama was being played with Gladstone leading the Liberals, and all during the development of that drama which culminated in the grant of Home Rule to Ireland, King George did not show the least sign of approval of the acts of a ruling class who had all intentions of crushing the great traditions of free England.

This is the King whose death has just occurred to deprive the world of one of its best men who ever wore a crown; this is the King who ruled to the eternal credit of Monarchy as an institution of human government, because he was never, to use his most famous poet's own words, "drunk with sight of power," because he knew no "frantic boast and foolish word" and ruled only as the King of his subjects—the faithful custodian of their welfare.

Philippines Herald
January 21, 1936

* * * * *

THE LANGUAGE OPPORTUNITY

A week or so ago, there was introduced on the floor of the Constitutional Assembly a proposition to make the English language the official language of the Philippine Islands.

That action was entirely expected. Nobody for a moment could have imagined that anything else could be proposed. The English language has been cultivated in this country for the last 35 years, and it has brought us nothing but progress and enlightenment.

It has been the language in our schools, the medium whereby we have kept abreast of the times. It has been the instrument of our contact with the rest of the world. Through it we have understood other nations and new horizons of knowledge have been opened to our minds.

Not only have we gone so far with English that returning would be as tedious as going over the distance again, but the language is so generalized in the Philippines today that to eliminate it would be simply impossible.

We have planted here in 35 years the seeds of a language that have germinated into rich harvests of knowledge and understanding. This language has been to us the instrumentality of a more perfect unification. Under its universal influence our sectional ideas have receded into the farthest background of our life.

There are of course men among us of the sentimental persuasion who deplore the growing favor that English has found in this country, but indeed there is nothing at all to deplore when matters are viewed calmly in the light of present-day conditions in the whole world.

It is not correct, to begin with, to suppose that English can blur the stamp of our soul. We want to meet the English-speaking Filipino who is not a Filipino in the innermost recesses of his heart, and who can claim, without fear of successful contradiction, that his intimate conceptions of life are those of John Bull or Uncle Sam.

When we see countrymen of ours return from the United States to astound us with their American lingo spoken with much effort at the peculiar American pronunciation, when we laugh within us as we watch these men try their best to assume the American air in their ways and manners, we are simply witnessing a demonstration of what an impossible task is this of killing the native soul by the use of the English language.

The affectations which contact with Americans, and knowledge of American ways, have ingrafted on our manners, are but superficial, largely the product of emphasis on appearances, rather than on the intrinsic values of life. These are bound to pass as we mature into the responsibility of nationhood.

Nothing in the last analysis will remain but that which can stand the scrutiny of our moral conscience. Ideas are naturally assimilable, and so are customs and traditions. If the ideas and customs and traditions assimilated are good and beautiful, let us have them, if perhaps we cannot help but have them.

There is a possible formula of soul affinity for all the scattered fragments of the human family. This formula rests on the power of symbolism, on the persuasion of form. The Christmas tree is here with us, and so is Santa Claus. But who can say that our children have grown less Filipino by responding to the magic of that tree, the promise of that legendary old man?

The form is there, the form that is importable into any clime because of the prevalence of the common spirit of Christmas. If the form, perishable that it is, can persist, it is because the fundamental soul is also there to give it its sanction. But if the soul rejects it, it must go. That is the only test.

The soul dictates and forms are good only as contrivances of human convenience. Our moral and artistic conscience can stand for no monstrous appearances. Nothing, after all is said and done, can go against that conscience; and nothing, really, can subdue the soul, much less such a mutable thing as language.

There was a time in ancient history, during the days of Hellenism, when the Greek language was spoken far and wide and yet did not count for much in the unification of the scattered city-states of Greece. Deep in the mind of the Greek of those days was the conviction that the small city state was the last word in political convenience.

Within that city men struggled through their difficulties and lived their lives in serene indifference toward the world outside. A small population was considered the ideal scale because the fewer the people the more chance was there of understanding and of an impartial way of governing and dispensing justice.

The interest of rulers and common men alike did not transcend the borders of the city-state, except during the annual festival in honor of the god Zeus, the festival known as the Olympiad. Then it was the occasion for an outburst of literary expression, and only then did the consciousness of a common language ever dawn on the Greek mind.

Language alone could not have given that Athenian Empire of scattered states the sense of a common fate. Indeed, it required more than a mere theory to draw together the mutually indifferent Hellenic city-democracies into a sort of a league: it was a situation which furnished that unifying magic, a situation of real living danger from the advancing Persian hordes of the East.

The story of the Macedonian Alexander the Great is the story of that Persian advance and how he checked it to enable him to rule supreme over Persia, as in fact he did. Alexander, through his stupendous conquests, was able to draw the minds of men together into a common consciousness. He destroyed barriers and pushed frontiers forward. His world dominion opened the way for the Hellenization of men from Macedonia to India.

The Greek language then entered upon its full florescence. All educated men of the time spoke and wrote it. Out in Egypt the bases of the historic Alexandria had been laid—the Alexandria of Archimedes, of Eratosthenes, of Euclid; the seat of the excellent beginnings of the science of medicine, the creator of religious ceremonials, the great university of intellectual achievement.

If there was no Greek language then in the plenitude of its development, Alexandria would never have emerged into notice to attract students and scholars from all corners of the globe. Then, the language quickened human knowledge, and even the Hebrews translated their scriptures into Greek. The native tongue of Greece became the great vehicle for the dissemination of ideas. It had no frontiers as an institution for the education of mankind.

Something of the kind is happening today in the case of the English language. This is a language that really has no frontiers. In China, in Japan, in Germany, in France, and everywhere else, it is spoken and it is written as a most convenient form of transmitting ideas among men and nations. The British Empire and the United States have lost their monopoly on it: English has passed into the common inheritance of mankind.

We in the Philippines cannot fall out of step with the rest of civilization, and the English language is what will keep us in step with that civilization. Let us never dream of entering the game of nations speaking a made-to-order blend of our vernacular archaism. That is an illusion, if our aim is to move with a progressive world, rather than to fall back.

We must not be misunderstood. Our thesis is not the destruction of our native tongue. We believe that our dialects are identical at the roots, that their differences are merely lexical, rather than fundamental. And what is more, we are convinced that nothing can eventually kill the rich folklore that clusters upon these dialects, or obliterate the color and flavor of their style.

Let us cultivate these dialects, if they need cultivation and we believe they don't because they are indestructible, being of our soul. But let us face reality and admit that for speed and accuracy we have in the English language the instrument of our maximum convenience. We are seeking only our convenience in this matter of an official language. That convenience should not be confused with the tradition of our native tongue, or deliberately misrepresented as a menace to the spirit of our race—the spirit that will assert itself in any medium of expression.

Philippines Herald
September 5, 1934

* * * * *

TAGALOG AS THE NATIONAL LANGUAGE*

On the night of April 14, last, in the Philippines' Town Meeting of the Air, the task fell on me to defend the case for Tagalog as the national language of the Philippines. In serious fact, however, there is nothing more to defend, for the question of whether Tagalog should be our common tongue was settled long ago. It was settled by the first Filipinos who went to the United States in quest of learning and fortune; with a unanimity of impulse, those Filipinos took to Tagalog more quickly than they could think of it, and it has always been so with others who have followed them. The result is that Tagalog now is definitely the language of intimacy among Filipinos abroad.

Within very recent times in the Philippines we have been treated to an impressive output of Tagalog talking pictures. These pictures may not all be very good; nevertheless, they are all in Tagalog and they are accepted in every locality in the Philippines, no questions asked. This is one more proof to me that Tagalog is bound to be, if it is not yet, the language of the great mass of our people.

The conclusive last word, however, has come from the direction of the President of the Philippines himself, who, upon the unanimous recommendation of the Institute of National Language—a creation of the National Assembly of our people—has decreed the adoption of Tagalog as the national language of the Filipinos.

By common consent, the easiest to learn of the Philippine languages is Tagalog. Bicolanos, Ilocanos, and Visayans who come to Manila can speak, read, and write it in no time. (The exception to this is the Filipino who, under strange influences of philosophy or creed, has neither the will nor the interest to learn it.) Aside from the ease of it, the main stream of our national life is admittedly Tagalog. All the currents of our culture, as well as our political and commercial pursuits, converge on the capital of the Philippines, which is Tagalog; naturally enough, we have been carried by these currents and these pursuits. On the other hand, if Tagalog were spoken, not in Manila and the big progressive provinces that surround it, but out in the backwoods of Luzon, obviously there would be neither rhyme nor reason

---

* This essay is a condensation of the original, which was much longer and contained statistics and quotations from Rizal, Lope K. Santos, and Spanish scholars who wrote on Philippine languages, especially Tagalog.

in advocating its adoption. We have, in short, merely been practical and, consequently, progressive.

From whatever angle we look at it, it cannot be easier for a Filipino to learn English than Tagalog, and I would be astonished, indeed, if a countryman of mine should say that, by twisting his tongue and straining his nasal capacity, he finds English more natural to him than a language that is at least indigenous to his country. But how long, it would be asked, as it was asked of this writer during the debate, would it take us to learn Tagalog? My answer: less than forty years, the time it has taken us to realize that our President cannot even speak in the provinces without benefit of translation, all the while that we claim English and Spanish are sufficient unto our needs!

Would it be reasonable, I was asked by interrogator Mangahas, to make a great Ilocano, like the distinguished Assemblyman [Benito] Soliven, to express his sentiments in Tagalog? Substantially, my answer was, that if we placed an Ilocano in the home of a Visayan or a Tagalog, it would not be long before the Ilocano would feel perfectly at home with the other Filipino, but that in the home, say, of a Nazi, this would be impossible, no matter how fluently the Ilocano spoke the Nazi tongue. I may state, therefore, without fear of denial from my brilliant compatriot, Mr. Soliven, that as between English and a language in which he can express himself intimately to a brother of his own race, his choice as a Filipino is manifestly clear.

The core of our racial philosophy must not be anything less than sincerity. This is the central port to which we all must return after our peregrinations under the banners of a borrowed culture. That still, small voice, otherwise known as our *Conscience,* tells us that we have sinned against our own selves by neglecting a language which is our heritage from the past. Indeed, from this language, how is it possible ever to detach our sentiments? How can we think of it as we would of a banca, or a battleship for that matter, which can be moved about at our convenience, or sold down the river without doing violence to our nature?

The mirror of a people's life is their language, in which is reflected not only their style, but also their history and psychology. The language of a nation is not its mere caprice; there is something more than the wishes of mice and men in the fact that human thought has had to be expressed. It was no accident that we were cradled in a language of our own; in the plan of our existence, that language is an essential force, one of the really sublime things that have a reason to exist. For it has affected our inner lives from the very beginning, accumulating upon our soul the impressions that identify us as a people.

The language of our mothers lullabied us in our cradles. It nurtured us in infancy, diverted us in adolescence, fortified us in maturity. In it the epics of our history were made. Our forefathers spoke it in their simple justice, our heroes fought their battles under its driving force. A little touch of it, as of blessed leaven, went far to make the bread of our hopes when we lay groaning under the tyrant's feet. The Katipunan wrote its code of honor in Tagalog. Bonifacio uttered his Cry of Liberty in this language. The Prince of Tagalog poets, Francisco Baltazar, wrote verses as chaste in their beauty, and as classical in their imagery, as Spenser of the Renaissance. Emilio Jacinto, he of the lion's courage, was a Tagalog writer of no mean caliber, and so was Rizal himself, and Marcelo H. del Pilar, and Apolinario Mabini.

In the blood of these illustrious Filipinos, Tagalog lived gloriously. We can say, indeed, that they expressed what they felt, and felt what they lived, because their language was their own. In the high eminences of their thought, they communed with the sublime; those of us today who say what we have been taught to say in a borrowed language, and feel what we are dictated to feel, are fit only to depend on a society of compromise.

In the nature of a language that is alien to our psychology, how far can it serve our historic ends? Within its two dimensions such a language may indeed entertain us through a talking picture, or excite us at a baseball game, but in neither case can we say that action of any historic value is produced. Incapable of overpowering our beings, it cannot fill our lives; by the same token, it cannot fulfill our destiny. We can truthfully say that we appreciate English, but that is no more than saying that we can appreciate other languages also. The matter cannot end with appreciation. A language must take such possession of us, so to speak, as to make us feel we could die in its bosom and, therefore, also live in it.

English is so full of grace and dignity that I would not wish to be misunderstood as disparaging its worth. From Chaucer, the first great English writer, to Kipling of Victorian imperialism—a vast Sierra Madre of literature—who can travel indeed without admiration for the splendours of the English language? But we wonder at the great minds of literary England precisely because they expressed what they felt in a language of their own, because the words and phrases they employed represented the maximum of their passions and emotions—a language in which the world of today can judge the state of the English nation then, and catch the vibrations of the English spirit. A language such as theirs, answering exclusively the thoughts and images actually in their souls, cannot die. To suggest even now that those minds could have used another language than their own, would be to wish the utter loss of their splendid contributions to the literature of human thought. We can say the same of ourselves: that to wish on us the exclusive use of the English language would be, aside from presenting ourselves to the world in a radically false light, to pervert our cultural destiny.

A good number of Filipinos are masters of English, not a few of them possessing a sense of it worthy of all admiration. I must count among these Filipinos my versatile opponent in the debate, Attorney Antonio Estrada. But I would consider it a tragedy if these Filipinos were to give up serving their country better by choosing to die for a language other than that which launched them into this life. Our first loyalty is to our country, and other loyalties are but secondary. The virtue of being true to our own implies of necessity a critical eye for others. Our manifest duty is to keep within our ethnic boundaries and fulfill ourselves there as Filipinos, lest we die half-baked. I shall always maintain that this fulfillment is not possible unless we speak the language of our birth and speak it until the last breath of our lives. Obviously, this language is more than a medium for the satisfaction of our cultural curiosity or the delight of our superficial tastes.

English as the recognized language of commerce is our best bid for participation in the commerce of mankind—for our contact with other countries of the world. But let there be no illusion about English opening for us the high-roads of the earth that we may strut on them with the assurance of protection from the English-speaking segment of the universe. Our indulgence in world dreams must not supersede our interest in our own axis and our own orbit, lest we find ourselves the lamb for the sentence of the wolf. One thing we must not forget is that our private life as a people is our own exclusively, and one of the things that can guard it best is a language of our own. English was never ours and we know it. That we are fast learning it can be important to us only as far as it can enrich our store of ideas. But to propose to adopt it as our national language is to jump at a ridiculous conclusion.

We shall no doubt continue learning English, notwithstanding the assumption that our people will not be able to see the point of its vast utility, and the further assumption, perhaps, that the language of Shakespeare has neither attraction nor holding power. To those who cry prematurely over the demise of both English and Spanish, we can give our word that we shall, through the medium of these two languages, continue absorbing Western ideas as far as they are compatible with our idiosyncracies as a people. What is more, we shall bear in mind the necessity of superimposing upon those ideas the stamp of the Filipino soul, over and against this strange philosophy creeping serpent-like into our midst, which would make our access to the culture of the Occident also our bondage to it. We shall always hold that our practice of Western ideas must not mean the loss of our identity in them, for it means all the difference between conquest and surrender to allow ourselves to be absorbed.

It is written of the Spartans that it was religion to them to think that they were born, not for themselves individually, but for Sparta. Adopting this doctrine for us today, we can add that we were born for the Philippines first, and for the world second. Indeed, the clock has gone around again to the hour of national consecration. We must recapture the dramatic moments of our Revolution and live them again. We must re-express that fierce murmur of Katipunan passions which made history at Balintawak and at Tirad Pass. The last forty years have seen us wander away from the main road of our life in our effort to adopt a language which, measured in terms of our cultural integrity, has neither yesterday nor tomorrow for us. When did it begin, and where will it take us—that is the question. There has been no action in that interregnum except, perhaps, the action that leads to surrender—fitting climax to a life of commerce!

Herald Mid-Week Magazine
April 24, 1940

* * * * *

THE SPANISH LANGUAGE

There was a time in the history of the Philippines when everything was done to discourage the teaching of Spanish among our people. Men who were in power then considered it a dangerous thing to encourage the Filipinos to speak and write the language because, they said, it was one sure way of promoting filibusterism in the colony.

When it was proposed, once upon a time, to establish an Academy of the Spanish language for the youth of the land, it met with a stout opposition from all sides. This is what Rizal tells us in one of his novels. We recall the enthusiasm of the Filipino students who lived in the boarding house of Macaraig when the news arrived that the Captain General had shown no disposition to kill the project and had, instead, agreed to submit it to the *Comision Superior*. That was considered a victory for the movement.

But nothing, as one of the characters in Rizal's *El Filibusterismo*, the Reverend Father Fernandez, said, could prevent the Filipinos from expanding the range of their knowledge as they became more and more of age, and the Spanish language, whether those who ruled the Islands liked it or not, was bound to be spoken by the people. And so Spanish became an established tradition here, to the eternal glory of Spain.

When the Spanish Republic conferred upon Don Enrique Zobel, prominent resident of Manila, its insignia of merit, a fitting tribute was paid to the man whose efforts to perpetuate the Spanish language in the Philippines have no parallel in our history.

The language in which Rizal wrote his novels, the language in which he sought expression for the outraged sensibilities of his race and at the same time called attention to the capital defects of his own people, this language is in the Philippines to stay, and it will stay and flourish because the *Señor Pastas* are gone, and now we have the Zobels who find glory in making it the language of our life.

Philippines Herald
April 10, 1934

* * * * *

FREEDOM FOR OUR UNIVERSITY

More and more, the necessity of placing the University of the Philippines far from the crowd's ignoble strife is becoming apparent. Today, we read the news that President Palma will be summoned to appear before the house committee on public instruction for the purpose of explaining how he has managed the financial affairs of the institution.

There we have a situation scarcely designed to dignify the president before the student body of the university. The man who should be looked up to as a sort of a high priest of learning must go to the lower house and face a committee, essentially political, to answer for the shortcomings of his university and beg that no cuts be made in the appropriation of his office.

This is no disparagement of the honorable committee of the house of representatives. That committee is not called a political body contemptuously, but only in the sense that its members owe their positions to the vote of the people and that they are, in the nature of things, not immune to the temptation of playing to the gallery.

The president of the university, on the other hand, is not supposed to be a politician. The very nature of his delicate duties compels him not to be one. He cannot afford to be, and he should not be in the confusion of vulgar life. And politics, with its inevitable corruptions, can only degrade his office, rather than preserve its purity of purpose.

It is thus clear that while our university president need not cater to the pleasure of the crowd, the member of any committee in our legislature may have to. Because a legislator must please the people of the district that elected him, he may try to impose the desires of these people upon an institution that symbolizes complete freedom of thought. And there lies the grave danger of impairing the function of our university in the cultural life of the nation.

In the interest of academic freedom, which is the soul of university life, it is highly important that the faculty of the institution be in a position where its words and actions will not be misconstrued by the student body as in any manner or form influenced by any political considerations. The president of the university is the highest representative of faculty authority, and to demean his status as such is clearly to demoralize the life of the university under his care.

What will the students in our highest seat of learning think of their president, or even a member of their faculty, if they suspect that he addresses them with mental reservations and that he is fettered by loyalties to political gods in whose hands lies the financial destiny of their alma mater?

What would result from itemizing the budget of the university except the fostering of dissatisfaction among professors and officials who may have to resort to lobbying in the legislature for the sake of larger slices in the appropriation melon? It will not be amiss to predict that the introduction of such a plan in the university is sure to establish there what in our local politics we fondly call the "pork barrel."

The university's academic freedom must be preserved, and the only way to preserve it is to remove it completely from the control of our political leaders. The legislature must realize the function of the country's highest institution of learning to be the diffusion of the knowledge of science, natural and social, and the inculcation of a sound philosophy in the mind of our people. It must also realize that in order to perform this function smoothly and well, the university must be free to an unlimited extent. Scientific research cannot get anywhere as long as it is trammeled and so long as the researchers are not free to expound their findings and conclusions dispassionately.

This is the time to set the foundations of the University of the Philippines on solid ground. The day to elevate it to its rightful place in our national life is here. We have been recreant to our duty to higher education so long that it is time we did something to redeem ourselves. The way to redeem ourselves is to give our university its deserved free place in our life that it may guide the youth of the land along the path of wisdom with candor and without fear.

Philippines Herald
August 17, 1933

* * * * *

THE CAUSE OF OUR SCIENTISTS

Science is the foundation of human progress, the propelling force of civilization. Without it Man would live as if in a jungle, a constant prey to the superior elements and always beset with fears and doubts.

The beasts of the forests, ferocious and strong though they are, have no guarantee of security from the furies of nature. A thunderbolt may strike an elephant, a poisonous plant may inflict death on a lion, an earthquake may open up the abyss that will swallow the gigantic rhinoceros.

There is no understanding in the minds of these beasts. They have none of that questioning attitude, that spirit of inquiry, and the determination to learn and to create.

Man, on the other hand, is endowed with a reasoning power which science has aided to a point of development where it can penetrate the arcanum of nature. He knows, for instance, that it would be risky for him to remain under a tree when thunder rends the sky. He knows how to construct earthquake-proof houses upon secure ground. And he knows that there are certain plants whose sap is poison to the human body.

Scientific research has brought about facts of stupendous value. It has made man understand the world in which he lives, and understanding it, he protects himself against danger and extends the range of his happiness. Science, in short, has emancipated him from superstition and the utter drudgery of existence.

It is the dynamic power of science that has made possible the mitigation of Man's physical subserviency to circumstances. The invention of power-driven machinery has naturally eliminated the necessity of muscular exertion in the greater portions of the earth. With the steam engine railroads now traverse continents, mountains, and deserts; ships defy the waves of storm-swept oceans; automobiles promote human business and pleasure with remarkable swiftness; and aeroplanes annihilate distances that defy the imagination.

Machinery has promoted the comfort and welfare of mankind. It has made possible the acceleration of manufacture to a point where mass production now supplies the multitudes of the earth with their necessities at prices entirely within their limited means. It has given impetus to agriculture and has stimulated the activities of trade and industry.

None of the instruments of world progress would have been perfected had the world not counted with disinterested men imbued with the scientific spirit and possessed of that habit of mind of constantly searching for an explanation for the facts of life. We would not be in this stage of our human evolution if we did not have among us men devoted to the ends of pure research and scientific truth.

In a country like ours, which is still in its formative stage, we can ill afford to neglect the pursuit of science. We still have much drudgery to eliminate and many more manifestations of backwardness to overcome.

We have the material for the experiments of science, and we have the men to carry on those experiments. But we have always lacked the stimulus because we have been sluggish in trying to understand our needs.

Industrially, we are far behind our neighbors. Our agriculture is in many instances still antiquated. Our trade as yet involves an enormous waste of time and energy. Our public hygiene is still frustrated by the superstition and ignorance of our masses.

It is for these reasons that we must rush to the support of our men of science. There is now a bill pending in the legislature proposing the creation of a National Research Council, which will try to coordinate our scientific endeavors and thus make them of more permanent value to the nation.

This bill asks of the government the appropriation of the modest sum of twenty-thousand pesos whereby the council might start working.

The council proposes to devote itself disinterestedly to research in the various fields of human learning, that it might aid in harnessing our natural resources and lead the way in the work of preparing us for the responsibilities of nationhood. It seeks to promote our engineering, our medicine, our chemistry, and all other branches of science to the full measure of our mental capacity.

Here is a proposition conceived in noble aims and seeking no profit for the men behind it. Its only purpose is to replenish the stores of our knowledge and convert our laboratories into real sources of scientific wealth. Its motto will be pure research in science—the central dynamic force of our intellectual heritage.

Philippines Herald
September 30, 1933

* * * * *

IN THE MASTERS' MAGIC CIRCLE

With Johann Strauss' "The Blue Danube" as one of the features of attraction, the first popular symphony concert under the auspices of the Manila Symphony Society was given at the Metropolitan Theatre on Washington's birthday, Dr. Alexander Lippay conducting. The concert marked the beginning of what promises to be a very delightful season of music, a season which might well usher in the revival of popular interest here in the works of the Masters.

Strauss' lively and melodious waltz has always been popular, and it was a happy choice which Director Lippay made when he included it in a program designed to draw the people into the concert hall and stimulate general appreciation of good music, not the musical noise that comes to us every day in an everwidening stream to disturb our artistic conscience.

There was a time in the evolution of music when the Masters' works were the exclusive privilege of kings and princes to hear. The masses had to content themselves with their songs and hymns until the opera came into musical history and the more progressive cities were able to organize opera-houses for ordinary men.

Bach and Handel in the seventeenth century, and Mozart and Beethoven in the eighteenth, composed for a very small world which had the time and means to promote love of music in its more classical forms. But as the nineteenth century dawned, a new impetus was added to the musical activity of mankind with the development of instrumental facilities.

During this time we find Beethoven's works more widely appreciated and new names added to the Masters' list. Weber, Schubert, Mendelssohn, Debussy, Chopin, Liszt, Dvorak, and towering above them all, Richard Wagner, the dramatic composer who profoundly influenced his contemporaries—all these men maintained the purity of the world's musical sense through the power of their creative genius.

Popular interest in the works of these men had reached a very high pitch and the patronage of royalty and nobility no longer was the sole measure of musical success. Composers were looking around for new realms to explore, new moods, new colors to transmute into melody and harmony, new themes to enlarge into opera. Music which sprang from the soul of the people had returned to the people and the dispensation of the Masters became the common property of mankind.

It is a curious fact that we in the Philippines are more in a position to appreciate the works of Europe's great composers than any other people in the Orient. Our ears readily respond to the harmonies of symphony and overture, the vocal virtuosity of opera, or the exalted moods of concerto music. Our country has been called "little Italy" because here the melodies of Verdi and Donizetti linger and never die.

But our people are menaced by the sort of noisy music which is flowing into this country in increasing volume every day, music inspired by frivolous whims, aimless and without elevation, sounds and notes harsh enough to destroy our aesthetic purity. This is not entirely the people's fault. There has been so much development in the mechanical side of music and the inevitable result has been a cheapening in our common estimate of musical values. But the more unfortunate fact is the utter indifference of our government towards musical culture in general.

Manila does not even have a public concert hall and yet it is the capital of a "little Italy." It does not even have a philharmonic orchestra which it should have had long ago. These may appear like little things of no moment, and yet they should be a measure of our aesthetic culture, the evidence of our elevation as a people of artistic traditions.

It is for this reason—this official indifference toward music as an art for human uplift—that we find in the popular symphony concerts inaugurated under the direction of Dr. Alexander Lippay an opportunity for the stimulation of genuine musical activity among our people. Dr. Lippay also directs the symphony concerts of the Asociacion Musical de Filipinas during the closing months of every year.

These are efforts which readily call for encouragement, as are the efforts of the Conservatory of Music of the state university and those of the Manila Chamber Music Society in the line of grand opera by an entirely local cast of amateur singers. The pure music of the Masters is their fountain of inspiration, and that is the music that we want, music to mitigate the sordidness of present-day life in the magic circle of its ineffable beauty.

Philippines Herald
February 24, 1934

THE SHARE OF THE PRESS

We were reading today a very forceful article against the gangster menace, urging the public to lend its full cooperation to our police authorities and the courts in extirpating the lawless elements that have been the cause of so much terrorism in the last few weeks. The plea, as we have said, is forceful and should not fall on deaf ears.

The article in question points out the remarkable efficiency with which the criminal now performs his nefarious task. The old utensils employed in earlier days for doing away with human life are, it is noted, being discarded for the more deadly pistol of our modern time. Every day, in every way, the thug is becoming better and better in his work.

This, then, is clear: the menace of the gangster is here in real and living form, challenging the civic courage of our community and defying all the strength that the government can muster to maintain the public peace. But who, more than anybody else, is to blame for such a state of affairs? Is it fair to absolve the press and heap the responsibility on the shoulders of the film producer?

The unchallenged fact is that our newspapers have been guilty of this glorification of the brute of whom we hear so much these days, when the law-abiding citizen stands aghast at the bold ascendancy of criminality. Not a hold-up takes place but a graphic illustration of how it was carried out must be displayed right across the front pages of our newspapers. Not a criminal confesses to his felony but the papers must carry glaring pictures of him in the course of re-enacting his hideous deed. And every once in a while the public must be treated to a picture of a body bearing all the traces of the human perversion that snuffed the life out of its livid flesh.

Of what use, we ask, is all this emphasis we put on the ways of the transgressor of our laws? What service are we doing society by reminding it constantly of the clever methods of the underworld in its incursions into civilized life? Of what avail is all this bold relief we give to the illustration of nameless felonies unless it is to brutalize the mind and lend the Press as an instrument for the guidance of potential criminals?

Let us be frank. We are known as the Fourth Estate. We wield a tremendous power over public opinion which is ours many times to manipulate to suit our special ends. If we have not practised moderation in the pursuit of our avarice, let us practise it now. This is the time to give our share of sympathy to our poverty-ridden community, and to prove that the Press of this country is not out to make money by appealing to the base passions of man, but to carry out its aim of informing and guiding public opinion in the most decent way.

The Press of this country must be temperate, rather than wild; uplifting, rather than degrading. It must sweep public opinion not downwards to the depths of shame, but upwards to the heights of enlightened thought. Unless the Press does this, the measure of black deeds in this country will forever run high.

Philippines Herald
August 11, 1933

* * * * *

WHEN THE PRESS LOSES

Vice-President J.H. Furay of the *United Press,* addressing the Pennsylvania Press Conference recently, warned against the infringement of the freedom of the press because it "endangers the whole system of untrammeled news distribution, opening the way for other restrictions," adding that "dictatorship and censorship run hand in hand.

Mr. Furay's observation is borne out by the testimony of current facts of history. In the dictatorship of Europe the press as a force for human expression has been reduced to a phonographic apparatus merely repeating what the dictators say and never daring to contradict their voices.

In such a condition the press has lost its reason for being, as well as its personality. It is no longer the Fourth Estate, as it has always been known to be, because merged into the rigid mechanism of an all-absorbing government, it no longer has a voice in public affairs it can call its own.

A dictator's press ceases to reflect public opinion because public opinion in a dictatorship is either non-existent or false. A mailed fist crushes every sign of opposition that comes its way, and any opposition that escapes crushing naturally does not make itself heard. Nothing but praise for the dictator fills the air and that is hardly what we may call opinion.

We may say this much without any fear of successful contradiction, that when a people is ready to let its press go, it is ready also to be tyrannized. When a public is willing to relinquish its right to express its opinion freely, it can be said that its mind is ready to be enslaved. In this way human progress is held back, for when people cease to think for themselves, what are they but dumb cattle?

Mr. Furay is right. But America is in no danger of losing her freedom of the press. The news in that country will out; the danger, in fact, is that it will out not infrequently to the prejudice of the strictly personal over which, properly, the public have no claim. A muzzled press would be an anachronism in the United States, and it is when we think of the freedom of the American press that we are convinced that Democracy in America was not born for death.

Philippines Herald
July 16, 1936

* * * * *

STALWARTS OF THE FOURTH ESTATE*

It is good to think that our Press is enjoying good health. Subscription figures are soaring, the newsboys are having the time of their lives, the pages are literally bursting with advertisements. It is good to watch the bonanza, good for the newspaper owners, good for the newspapermen. It is keeping them cheerful, and cheer is tonic for this nervous world.

It is even better to know that our Press has power. Of course the newspaper that lacks financial support enjoys no power, but those that count with the subscriptions, the sales, and the merchants' patronage do. They are what we classify as stable papers, and we admit that they are with us to stay. They are what give substantial reality to the Fourth Estate of this Republic.

Health and power—these are their great assets. Health maintained by material abundance, power secured by the law of the land. The Bill of Rights guarantees the freedom of the Press, and there is where the power lies. All of us are resolved that such freedom shall not be

---

* The "stalwarts" referred to are Horacio Borromeo, Ernesto del Rosario, Armando J. Malay, Jose L. Guevara, Melchor Aquino, Teodoro F. Valencia, Teodoro Locsin, Vicente del Fierro, and Pedro Padilla.

curtailed, and because of this protection the Press assumes a position of formidable eminence.

But that same power may go to wrong use. Some newspaper owners may wield it to tyrannize, and some to suppress. As great a danger lies in the forfeiture of the power through non-use, for profit's sake. Then shorn of ideals, the newspaper is reduced to a sort of mercantilistic monstruosity.

While we are not ready to discard private ownership in the newspaper business, we should be ready to see the danger of its excesses to our fundamental liberties. Perhaps we have no Molochs in our Fourth Estate now, but that we are bound to have them if we don't watch out is a possibility that cannot be discounted. For the present, we have to admit that suppression is at least a possibility for business and other convenient reasons.

It would, therefore, profit us little to laugh off the fellow traveller's indictment of private ownership of the sources of information. His position is this: if there is so much danger, as alleged, of suppression under a system of state control, what is there to show that there is safety from suppression under private ownership? It might be well to add that, while the State may in a political sense be considered the people, private interests are never the people.

As far as possible, our men of the Press are trying to prove that their constitutional freedom is something more than a chimera. These men who, by the rules of their profession, seem fated to remain wage-earners forever, nevertheless are steeped in the ideals of their calling. For one thing, they would not stand for any form of coercion of thought.

But these same men who know with John Stuart Mill that Truth is achieved by combatants fighting under hostile banners, and that unless they know the difficulties which their truth has to encounter and conquer, they know little of the force of their truth—these men do not own their newspapers. In a number of instances in the recent past, they did essay to print their own sheets, but not much time elapsed before they were folding up.

They who have not the letter of credit to buy the linotypes, the rotaries, the newsprint, and the ink shall not inherit the kingdom of the Press. For them the pursuit of truth must be along harmless paths only. Theirs is not to question the good-will that draws the merchants, or, in a country so small as theirs, to incur for the hands that feed them the distempers of the gods.

We must find, then, that the writers of the Fourth Estate are striving towards frank expression under a severe rule of survival. The flesh weakens under the rigors of such rule, and sooner or later the writers find out to their disappointment that not only is their vaunted freedom of the stuff of Thomas More, but that the real pace that kills is in the Press, where it is quicker in the direction of want and disease.

But is there despair in the hearts of these have-nots? Nothing of the kind. One reads the columns to find a jewel of a thought here, sparkling witticism there, a calm, serious dissertation somewhere worthy of an Addison, a Lamb. One regrets the exit of a Gulliver of the implacable satire, and one wonders if he has been suppressed. Ah, where are those ironies that have made our wire-pulling statesmen squirm so much?

It is said of satire that it destroys rather than builds, but who would not want a Montesquieu or a Voltaire in this, our own era of grand monarchy? When the spirit flows off into frivolous foibles, there must be a reaction. Today, our own *Comedie Humaine* is being written with all its sordid intrigues of money-making, opportunism, and ingratitude. Goethe was quite precise when, through the mouth of Margaret, he said:

> Gold is the pole to which all point: the whole
> Big world hangs on gold. Alas, we poor!

But soon the lights will be flickering out, and what La Bruyere called the evident but artificial joys of the high places that were so much the dream of Moliere's high-brow ladies and Pere Goriot's daughters, must give way to the concealed, but real, sorrows. And now it is good to know that our own Savignys are writing their "letters"—gossipy, amusing, vivid, and with all-observant eyes for the trifles of the passing grand era.

Borromeo, del Rosario, and Malay of the *Chronicle,* Joe L. Guevara of the *Post,* Aquino of the *Evening News*, Valencia of the *Tribune,* Locsin of the *Free Press,* del Fierro and Padilla of the *Star Reporter*—long may their banners wave!

If they waver, these men who must have their own follies or they would not know wisdom, the Fourth Estate will have lost the free spirit of the Ninety-five Gripes at Wittenberg, and we will truly miss them. Or if by chance they be silenced, then we mortals will have proved ourselves possessors of the infallibility of that which Dante said "moves the sun in heaven and all the stars."

It is our conviction that these stalwarts will not leave us just for a riband to stick on their coats. Somehow we are sure their flags will remain hoisted up through hurricane or drought. At least, we may count on them to try to save the good name of the Fourth Estate when such of their masters as are so drunk with health and power should, like Luther's scorpion, think that their sins are hidden because their heads happen to lie hidden under a leaf.

The Newspaperman
November, 1947

POEMS

ODE TO A SONG SPARROW

Majestic Lyrist of the woods,
Consoler of the solitudes,
  Most welcome is your song!
Enchanter of the wand'rer's eyes,
To those blithe birds of Paradise,
  To them do you belong!

What of the dazzling gleams of gold
That brighten not your features bold?
  What of their vain control?
Away with all that proud display,
With all those fragile pomps, away,
  Those venoms of the soul!

How sweet in fresh and museful June,
You trill your wild, melodious tune,
  Till Nature all seems mute;
Methinks some cherub, mad with love,
Has left the glorious worlds above,
  And charmed some Lydian lute.

Transcendant minstrel, ever meek,
In vain my heart would learn to seek
  The secrets that you know,
O for a while to fly away,
Amid the dying pomps of day
  In twilight's purple glow!

What joy to sport with you in peace,
Amid the solitary bliss
   Of those pure hours of morn;
To skim the vales and fields so green,
To kiss the blooming flowers, serene,
   And never feel forlorn!

O where, fair creature of delight,
When slow the brooding calm of Night
   The tranquil day does close;
Where with the cool of shifting shades
Where with the day that softly fades,
   Seek you your lone repose?

Most agile bird whose simple wings
Excel the mighty hands of kings,
   The rulers of the state,
Tell me if in that spacious air,
You feel the gloomy pains of care,
   The curse of Shame or Hate!

O teach me how, you heaven-born,
To shun Temptation and to spurn,
   Most foul Hypocrisy;
And then, my friend, my heart forbid
From yielding to that vilest greed
   Of gold and luxury.

Give out some gladness from your breast,
To calm my bosom's core, oppressed
   By fruitless love and vain;
A song of sweetness and repose,
To quench my endless griefs and woes,
   And silence all my pain.

Triumphant Ruler of the air,
Permit me evermore to share
   The beauties of your life,
A life of everlasting mirth,
Despised not for its lowly birth,
   Far from the rush of strife!

With you sweet Lyrist, ever gay,
In some Elysium far away,
   Beneath some holier sky,
Where Love is Love and Right is Right,
Where Reason, Justice, conquer Might,
   O let me live and die.

THE ANNUAL
Manila High School, 1915

* * * * *

EVERING IN A GRAVE-YARD
To my Uncle in Eden

Soft fades the lingering April day
Behind the hills...fades like a scene
Of some delightful golden dream
Of Paradise; a mystic breeze,
Sweet with the dying bliss of calm,
Indistinct woodlands, stirs the trees,
And dies with lulling melodies
Of vesper lyrists...far beyond
The waving fields; the purple shades
Of twilight move like wakened ghosts
Of vanished days, and shift away
In silence...not a breath to break
The bliss of thine eternal dream...

Oh thou, who didst console the days
Of my gone childhood; from whose smiles,
I oft had drunk the bliss and love
Of homely wiles who fed my soul
With loving sentiment, aglow
With charity—for thee are past
The pains and griefs of cruel years...
There is no shifting Time to pierce
Thy blissful rest, no tyrant kings
To mar thy lone, celestial sleep;
The pangs of love and mortal shame
And hate are thine no more. How sweet

To share the calm of thy repose,
And in the solitudes of Heavens
To drink the nectared dews of life
With none to hate me then—for I
Am dead—the world must pardon me?
Oh! give me rest, some sweet relief,
From this fast-thickening gloom of cares
That dims my checkered path; some light
To guide the valor of my soul
Against the deeds and tyrant wills
Of these despotic, little kings
Of learning; let me fade away
Into the gloom of thine abode,
To suffer nevermore! My heart,
My bosom bursts! I gasp with pains
I don't deserve! I die! I fail!
Oh! save my name, my conscience's pride.
. . . .
            Night falls,
Like some ethereal cloud from Heaven
And lulls the earth to sleep. Adieu,
O sire, adieu, soon shall we meet
Again in sweet dream...away!

The Independent
Manila, July 17, 1915

* * * * *

IN THE SHADOWS

I see the daylight vanish like a dream
Beyond the meadows, summer-sweet afar...
And now the twinkle of a sunset star!
The ling'ring twilight wanes, the heavens dim
Behind the languor of the fading gleam.
I breathe the perfume of some hidden bloom,
Delusive in the calm-enamoured gloom,
And now, I dream ... How sweet my visions seem!

I cannot see the world around: the night
Seems in the calm of its ethereal sway
The closing glory of my longings vain.
And then, methinks I reel in that delight
And promised beauty of a sighed-for day....
But dreams are dreams, O cruel love! O Pain!

The Independent
October 30, 1915

* * * * *

BOOKER T. WASHINGTON

Apostle of immortal Sacrifice,
Lone Teacher and Lawgiver of a race!
For thee are past the griefs of cruel years,
For thee—the laurels of a grateful land.

Born in the quiet of a day unknown,
Beneath an humble roof where misery
And hunger lingered with the laden days
That crept,—what tender hope of distant bliss
Did guide thy silent footsteps to the realm
Of greatness and of love, where now thou stand'st
A fadeless glory to the memory?

How sweet a life was thine!—no blot, no stain,
To dim the beauty of those loving deeds!
Sublime in that simplicity of ways
Which stirs the soul to dream of better things;
That sacrifice, which steeps the heart in tears
Of human tenderness. Thine was the firm
And simple courage of a truthful man,
The stern conviction of a conscience clear
That did withstand the vile attacks of Vice,
Of Selfishness and Greed. Along the calm
Of common paths, thou did'st pursue thy way,
Casting aside the pleasures vain of men
For purifying deeds of charity
And manly love; 'twas thou who did'st proclaim

Unto the blinded world that Man is Man
According to his heart—not to his race!
And ever constant in thy faith in God
And higher Justice, thou didst stem the gales
And ranging tempests of life's stormy sea.
Nor dreams that built the Caesars didst inspire
Thee on thy way,—thy only cherished aim
Was men's equality, to lift a race
Despised before our eyes. And honors great,
Unbidden, sought thy place and crowned thy toils
With deathless glory: Thou didst stand unmoved
Before the kings and rulers of the State;
Didst utter laws to crowds of eager men,
And thou didst reap in full the laurels fresh
And praises of thy glorious countrymen.
A type of man of iron will and power—
Thou hast no equal in thy race; a firm
And humble laborer for men—thou stand'st
An honor to thy land.

   Well may we draw
From all thy life of toil and sacrifice
A precious lesson that shall ever guide
Our footsteps on the way—a loving hope—
An inspiration that shall ever dwell
And linger in our hearts.

   Thy course is done;
For thee are past the bitter pangs of life...
For thee the laurels of the world shall bloom!
And thy sweet memory shall ever live—
A deathless treasure to the human race.

The Annual
Manila High School, 1916

* * * * *

BEFORE RIZAL'S MONUMENT

> Thy soul was like a Star, and
> dwelt apart. ...
> —Wordsworth: "Milton"

Inviolate in that august monument,
Eternal emblem of our brotherhood,—
Redeemer of a race from Heaven sent,
You lie—embalmed in tears of gratitude.

The heedless feet of tempest-driven Time,
The paths you oped for us shall leave untrod;
Shall spare the doctrines of your life sublime
Imparted in the language of your blood.

Past are the days of painful tyranny,
The gloom of power no longer dims our eyes,—
Still stands the temple of your memory—
Unwithered relic of our sacrifice.

Recalling these lone memories of the past,
Your people guard you in that slumber sweet,
And reverent with gratitude they cast
The laurels of affection at your feet.

How much we owe you! In our better years,
You were the gleam that blest the desert way;
Your counsels were the glory of our tears,
Your pen—the torchlight of the gloomy day.

And like the star that led, in days of old,
The humble prophets to the Holy-Land,
You were the heavenly light, austere and bold,
That healed the suff'rings of your native strand.

The Lord forgets not:—in those cruel days,
When Justice bent before the rods of Might,
He sent the saviour of a fallen race
Whose deeds avenged the broken laws of Right.

The past is past; today the hope-star gleams,
Today against the dawn of sweeter years,
Looms that resplendent Eden of your dreams;
The heavens smile: the vast horizon clears.

Weep not within the silence of your tomb,

The land you loved from anguish now departs;
The seeds you scattered on your way have bloomed
Deep in the chambers of nine million hearts!
    Nine million hearts, undaunted in the strife,
The noble virtues of your soul proclaim.
Rizal, your death to us is glorious life,
To grim Oppression—everlasting shame!
    You fell unconquered like a Spartan brave,
But Death proclaimed your victory aloud,
And from your bosom streamed the blood that gave
The venom to the tyrants and the proud!
    Inglorious Worshipper of God, rest on!
His holy Sword defends you there apart,
And Glory, from her bright, celestial throne,
In fadeless music hails you from her heart.
    Your nation guards the silence of your sleep;
Above you are the blessings of your sky,
Before you is the grandeur of the deep,
Beneath, our gratitude that will not die.
    Drunk with ambition, kingdoms crumble down,
Great Babylons have sought the thickening dust,
Forgotten, Learning yields beneath the Crown,
But in His Hand, your monument shall last...
    And in the course of time, there it shall stand,
A sacred warning to Oppression's rod,
An everlasting glory for your land,
The Symbol and the Sentinel of God.

THE ANNUAL
Manila High School, 1916

* * * * *

ANTIPOLO

Here where the *batis* whispers sweet
    Its secrets to the air,
I find but traces of your feet
    And perfumes of your hair.

I know that where the *Virgen* treads
    Your spirit must repose,
As limpid as the dew that sheds
    Its soul upon the rose.

And when the phantom evening brings
    Its magic to the breeze,
I know you are the nymph that sings
    My prayer and my peace.

I find you in each little beam
    Of sunshine, moon, and star,
I read in skies the priceless dream
    And beauty that you are.

And more than all I know how near
    Your spirit is to mine;
You might have been the Beauty, dear,
    In Antipolo's shrine.

Tribune Magazine
May, 1925

* * * * *

THAT MAGIC DAY

Yesterday, I watched the day languish from the world,
As I watch you vanish from my sight sometimes,—
A silken vision, a joy aerial, delicate,
Exquisite. I saw the gold of the dying day
Spread over the world like wine,—

Red, bubbling wine—spilled from the Cup
Of God's eternal life, and I felt its warmth
In my veins, and quenched my avaricious soul
In all the intense magic of its splendor,
Just as I quench the immortal thirst of my spirit
In the ecstasy of your kisses.
And the violet of crepuscular hours fell on me
Just like that deep-set soul of primordial desires
That lives within your eyes.

                    I do not know
What makes me sense your presence, Dearest Heart,
In the resurrection of Nature's pure delights;
What makes me see the image of your lips
On every rose that bursts, the glory of your hair
On every cloud that floats like a dream-gem
Across the crystal skies of these sweet transient days;
Nor why, when I behold the pristine beauty of sidereal fires,
I cannot see but you.

I watched the day melt away, but could not hold
The marvel of its joy, nor make
The substance of its beauty stay,
And now, in the sweet flavor
Of its inconstant picture, I am wondering, Dear,
If you, too, Child of Fate, must disappear from me
Forevermore.... Just like that day. That magic day.

                              "Daily Chit-Chats"
                                   The Tribune
                                  July 25, 1925

* * * * *

TO THE GREAT PLEBEIAN

Inglorious Martyr Of Democracy
You whose prophetic mind foresaw the law
And present groundwork of our common life:
Blazer of fecund trails where lay the free,
God-given truths we ever longed to know,
And could not know, because the odious rod
Of sterner human powers blocked the way;
Wrecker of barriers that entrenched the fear
Of tyrants in their long, relentless sway
Of Saturnalian orgy; Pioneer
Of Filipino rights, who stirred the blood
Of brothers to the action of the strife
    And made the despots quail!
Defiant Proletaire, whose spirit rose
Undaunted from our past colonial woe;

Servant and Guardian of the native Cause.
O Bonifacio, Great Plebeian, hail!

Even against the rude assaults of Time
    Your iron will survives,
And like the phoenix that can never die,
Out of the ashes of the past sublime,
Your soul emerges to the boundless sky,
Repeating to the Fatherland that hears
    Your libertarian Cry!
Unerringly, your fighting genius steers
Our forces onward to repel the crime
    Of lawless human greed;
And if at times we are beset with fears
We know you hold the answer to our need.
We feel you: in the fiber of our thought,
The pristine force of your ideals thrives,
Compelling us to rectilinear paths,
Which your unbending conscience always sought.
We hear you, and the clash of Spartan swords
Accompanies your presence; from the dread,
Tumultuous echoes and impetuous wraths
Of consecrated battles, comes the high,
Sententious prayer of your epic words,
To reinforce our courage and to feed
Our bodies with the immaterial bread
Of higher hopes. We hear you: in the noise
Of angry cataracts, your restless soul
Utters its fearless protest, in the fall
Of mighty torrents, your imperious voice
    Resounds with liberty!
You are where mountains totter from their free,
Ethereal eminence, where eagles sweep
Down to their end, in precipices deep,
To languish there unknown, unsung—to sleep
    The sleep of wounded pride!
How much your doctrines in our midst abide,
In sanctuaries Time may not despoil,
How much we hark to your immortal call,

Genius of human toil!

And on this day, when every native home
Offers its flowers to your memory,
Hear, martyred Champion of Democracy,
Your brother toilers, contrite at your feet,
Raise their vehement prayers to the sky
   To bless your martyrdom,
And in the language of their souls repeat
   Your libertarian Cry!

The Tribune Magazine
November, 1928

* * * * *

A CHRISTMAS POEM

If you should ask me what this means—
These pealing bells that break the hush
Of early morns, these rustic scenes
Of merriment, this tireless rush
Of children's feet;
If you should ask why all this whirr
Of restless wings, these songs that rend
The air with joy, this festive stir
And laughter sweet—
If you must know what these portend—

Then feel the touch, the magic cheer
Of Christmas spreading near and far
The message of the pristine star—
The light that silenced mortal fear
And blessed with radiance, sweet and mild,
The manger of the Holy Child.

Joy is here; love has returned
To human hearts that rankled, burned,
But yesterday, with fires of greed;
Christmas has brought its tender meed
Of goodwill and the diadem
Of peace from ancient Bethlehem.

I feel the tumult in the air
The trembling riot of delights
That stirs the memory;
Far in the night the flick'ring lights
Burn in fantastic lanterns red,
To conjure up the ghosts for me—
The ghosts of loves forever dead.
Laughter of childhood free from care
Through days of frolic unconfined,
Sweet smiles of faces fair that cast
Their beauty in the starlit night;
The elder hands held out by right
Of sweet tradition for the kiss
Of veneration by the young;
Gay carols in the churches sung,
And gifts the rich and poor must share—
These joys, these haunting scenes of bliss,
These bright romances of the past
Come back to crowd the anguished mind.
To fill the heart with yearnings kind.

God's love is here; hatred has fled;
No more the pang of envy mars
The thought of mortal tongue and pen.
Under the ancient, fadeless stars
A hungering world feeds on the bread
Of common joy; the cloud of shame
Has ceased to blur the human ken
As angels from above proclaim
Peace on this earth, Goodwill to Men.

The Tribune Magazine
December 20, 1931

NOTES

Chapter I: THE POET

¹ Guillermo Tolentino became the Philippines' greatest sculptor. Justice Jose P. Laurel was the patriarch of the famous Laurel political clan. Manuel A. Roxas was the first President of the Philippine Republic after the grant of independence. He was succeeded by Elpidio Quirino. Ricardo Paras was once Justice of the Supreme Court. Nepomuceno and Barrera were also prominent justices. Pilar Hidalgo Lim, one of the nation's women leaders, was president of the Centro Escolar University for several years.

² Jose Leido was Commissioner of Internal Revenue before the Second World War.

³ Julio Nalundasan went on to become a political figure, defeating Mariano Marcos in a congressional election in Ilocos Norte. After his victory he was shot to death in his home in Batac. Ferdinand Marcos was arrested for the crime, defended himself, and was acquitted.

⁴ Salvador P. Lopez, "Does English Have a Future?" (Lecture given at a symposium held under the auspices of the U.P. English Club, February 10, 1976.)

⁵ Jose H. Hernandez, "The Periods of Our English Literature." *The Newspaperman,* January-February 1948.

⁶ N.V.M. Gonzalez, "In the World," *Weekly Nation,* March 7, 1966.

⁷ Balmaceda was a speaker at the necrological services for Mendez in 1966. It was then that he related this incident and read the poem he had kept among his papers for 48 years.

⁸ "Spurns Barbour Scholarship for Dan Cupid," *Philippines Free Press,* August 8, 1925.

Chapter II: THE RETURN OF THE NATIVE

¹ *Manila Times,* September 3, 1917.

² Carson Taylor, *History of the Philippine Press,* 1927. Fernando Maramag was editor of *The Rising Philippines* when it was a monthly publication.

³ Mauro Mendez, "Daily Chit-Chats," *Tribune,* May 17, 1925.

⁴ Narciso Ramos, a former *Bulletin* staff member and the source of this information, was present on the occasion.

⁵ Mauro Mendez, *Freedom of Press in the Philippines,* p. 5. (This paper was read at the Inter-Asian Relations Conference, New Delhi, March-April 1947.)

⁶ Professor Armando J. Malay of the U.P. Institute of Mass Communication identifies Bill the Bo'sun as William Freeman, an American oldtimer.

[7] *Freedom of Press,* p. 5.
[8] Vicente del Fierro, "Our World," January, 1947. The clipping is in Mrs. Mendez's collection, but the periodical is unknown. Prof. Malay thinks it might be the *Chinese Commercial News,* for which del Fierro used to write.
[9] Jesus Valenzuela, *History of Journalism in the Philippine Islands* (Manila, 1933), p. 147.
[10] *Ibid.,* 189-90.
[11] *Freedom of Press,* p. 3.
[12] Valenzuela, p. 147.
[13] "Daily Chit-Chats," *Tribune,* July 23, 1925.
[14] May 14, 1925.
[15] May 15, 1925.

Chapter III: THE EDITORIAL AS LITERATURE

[1] David Boguslav, "Recollections of Thirty Years of Philippine Journalism," *Fookien Times Yearbook,* 1925-1926.
[2] Related to the author by Federico Mangahas.
[3] *Freedom of Press,* p. 3.
[4] From an interview with former U.P. President Salvador P. Lopez.
[5] Arsenio N. Luz, "The Philippine Press of the Past and the Present," *Deadline,* September 1952.
[6] Valenzuela, p. 193.
[7] Isidro Retizos, "3 World Diplomats," *Weekly Graphic,* May 27, 1964.
[8] "The Share of the Press," *Philippines Herald,* August 11, 1933. (In succeeding notes *Philippines Herald* will be shortened to *Herald.*)
[9] *Tribune,* Oct. 22, 1932. This editorial was reprinted in the March 1977 issue of *The Constable,* the official organ of the Philippine Constabulary, edited by retired Col. J. Rod-Fariñas.
[10] "Christmas, 1932," *Sunday Tribune,* Dec. 25, 1932.
[11] *Tribune,* Sept. 3, 1932. A news item in the *Tribune* of Oct. 4, 1932, mentioned the *Tribune* editorials that had thus far been discussed in the House of Representatives.
[12] Sol Gwekoh, "Hall of Fame," *Manila Times,* March 11, 1968.

Chapter IV: EDUCATION AND POLITICS

[1] "In Fairness to Our People," *Tribune,* Feb. 19, 1931.
[2] Related to the author by Dr. Colayco, who is now retired.
[3] "Unjustified Fears," *Tribune,* Nov. 23, 1932.
[4] "The Language Opportunity," *Herald,* Sept. 5, 1934.
[5] "Education and the State," *Ibid.,* July 7, 1933.
[6] "The Emphasis on Externals," *Ibid.,* Oct. 4, 1933.
[7] "The People and Governor Murphy," *Tribune,* June 16, 1933.
[8] *Tribune,* June 11, 1932.
[9] Carlos Quirino, *Quezon: Paladin of Philippine Freedom* (Manila: Filipiniana Book Guild, 1971), p. 247.
[10] "Freedom for Our University," *Herald,* Aug. 17, 1933.
[11] "The Educator's Turn at the Helm," *Ibid.,* Oct. 18, 1933.
[12] "The University and the People," *Ibid.,* Dec. 17, 1934.
[13] "President Bocobo," *Ibid.,* Dec. 11, 1934.
[14] *Tribune,* Dec. 5 and 7, 1932.
[15] "In Reply," *Ibid.,* Dec. 10, 1932.
[16] "A More Representative Constituency," *Ibid.,* Dec. 14, 1932.
[17] "Your New-Found Power," *Tribune,* Dec. 16, 1932.

Chapter V: ON WITH THE DANCE!

1 Related to author by Mr. Valencia.
2 Related to author by Professor Abaya of the U.P. Institute of Mass Communication.
3 Related to author by former U.P. President S.P. Lopez.
4 See Hare-Hawes-Cutting Act of the U.S. Congress in Cornejo's *Commonwealth Directory of the Philippines,* 1939.
5 "A New Deal for the Philippine Case," *Herald,* Jan. 3, 1934.
6 *Ibid.,* July 18, 1933.
7 *Ibid.*
8 *Ibid.,* July 29, 1933.
9 *Ibid.,* July 27, 1933.
10 "Ignoring the Real Threat," *Ibid.,* Sept. 9, 1933.
11 "Gum-Shoeing for Inconsistencies," *Ibid.,* Sept. 16, 1933.
12 According to Celso Cabrera, "Andoy's Adventures in Manila" was begun by Romulo. Prof. Malay believes that Roberto Anselmo continued the series after Romulo left the *Tribune.*
13 "Juan's Soliloquy," *Herald,* Sept. 27, 1933.
14 "A Touch of Chivalry," *Ibid.,* Nov. 6, 1933.
15 See Tydings-McDuffie Act in *The Price of Philippine Independence Under the Tydings-McDuffie Act* (Manila: Barristers Book Co., Inc., 1939) by Manuel V. Gallego.
16 *Manila Tribune,* Oct. 11, 1947.
17 "Juan's Soliloquy."
18 "Who Won the 'Tanga' Game?" *Herald,* March 10, 1934.
19 Vicente Albano Pacis, *Sergio Osmeña,* Vol. II (Manila: Phoenix Press, Inc., 1971), p. 85. On page 97 of the same volume, Pacis states that the amendment eventually became meaningless because the U.S. later acquired some 21 military and naval bases under a U.S. Congressional Act, with the consent of Quezon himself.
20 "Who Won the 'Tanga' Game?"
21 *Herald,* July 12, 1933.
22 "The Right that Failed," *Monday Mail,* Aug. 28, 1933.
23 "Let the People Judge," *Herald,* Aug. 30, 1933.
24 *Herald,* Dec. 7, 1933.
25 *Ibid.*

Chapter VI: CONSTITUTION AND COALITION

1 "The Mob in History," *Herald,* April 25, 1934.
2 "Less Government Needed," *Ibid.,* Aug. 1, 1934.
3 "The Citizen in Our State," *Ibid.,* Feb. 9, 1935.
4 "Anti-War Emotionalism," *Ibid.,* Jan. 17, 1935.
5 "A Unilateral Peace Pact," *Ibid.,* Jan. 24, 1935.
6 *Tribune,* Aug. 1, 1935.
7 "The Historic Present," *Herald,* April 11, 1935.
8 "Faded Colors," *Ibid.,* Sept. 14, 1935.
9 "The Historic Present."
10 "A Point for Clarification," *Ibid.,* Aug. 22, 1935. Mendez apparently had in mind the Bonifacio monument by Guillermo Tolentino, although in that monument Bonifacio has a bolo, not a sword in hand.
11 *Ibid.,* Sept. 12, 1935.
12 "Must Terrorism Rule?" *Ibid.*
13 *Tribune,* Aug. 1, 1935.
14 "From Pulpit to Soap-Box," *Herald,* June 20, 1935.
15 *Ibid.*

16 "Two Dreamers," *Ibid.,* Sept. 14, 1935.
17 *Ibid.*
18 "The Men of the Hour," *Ibid.,* July 20, 1935.
19 "Appeal to Intelligence," *Ibid.,* Sept. 12, 1935.
20 "Statesmen of Peace," *Ibid.,* July 22, 1935.
21 "Last Call," *Ibid.,* Sept. 16, 1935.
22 "Noblesse Oblige," *Ibid.,* Sept. 19, 1935.

Chapter VII: THE COMMUNIST BEAR HUG

1 Professor Petronilo Bn. Daroy's critique, "The English Language and the Philippine Short Story," delivered on Feb. 9, 1976, at the launching of *Philippine Short Stories, 1925-1940,* notes the writers' failure "to come to grips with the more dynamic processes of society." Only two of the 66 stories compiled by Dean Leopoldo Y. Yabes deal with the peasant problem. The others revolve around romantic or idyllic situations.
2 A.B. Saulo, *Communism in the Philippines* (Manila: Ateneo Publications Office, 1969), p. 15.
3 "Scarecrows," *Tribune,* Oct. 7, 1932.
4 "The Red Menace," *Herald,* Sept. 9, 1933.
5 "Examining Ourselves," *Tribune,* Aug. 21, 1932.
6 "Recognizing Soviet Russia," *Herald,* Sept. 23, 1933.
7 *Ibid.*
8 *Herald,* Nov. 20, 1933. Some of Mendez's contemporaries recall having seen "Hands Across the Sea" (as well as other editorials of his) reprinted in American newspapers. Isidro Retizos mentions it in his article, "3 World Diplomats" (*Graphic,* May 27, 1964). However, the editorial he remembers deals with Philippine-American relations.
9 "The Fetish of Rank and Glitter," *Herald,* Feb. 28, 1934.
10 "Keeping Faith with the Public," *Ibid.,* Nov. 11, 1933.
11 "Symbols and Reality," *Ibid.,* Feb. 26, 1934.
12 "Our Red Agitators," *Ibid.,* April 12, 1934.
13 "Where Vigilance is Necessary," *Ibid.,* April 14, 1934.
14 "Eliminate the Reds," *Ibid.,* Aug. 18, 1934.
15 "Insidious Propaganda," *Ibid.,* Sept. 19, 1934.
16 Saulo, p. 16.
17 "A New Deal from Labor," *Monday Mail,* Nov. 13, 1933.
18 *Tribune,* Sept. 18, 1934.
19 "Inflaming the Ignorant," *Herald,* Sept. 19, 1934.
20 *Ibid.,* Oct. 6, 1934.
21 "Ensuring Our Peace," *Ibid.,* Sept. 22, 1934.
22 "Just a Warning," *Ibid.,* Dec. 19, 1934.
23 "Enlightened Capitalism," *Ibid.,* Nov. 15, 1934.
24 "What Prophecy Is This?" *Ibid.,* Nov. 10, 1934.
25 "What the Bolsheviks Forgot," *Ibid.,* Dec. 1, 1934.
26 "The Red Terror," *Ibid.,* Dec. 8, 1934.
27 "Our Recalcitrant Cains," *Ibid.,* May 23, 1935.
28 "The Slums Again," *Ibid.,* July 2, 1935.
29 "Looking Ahead," *Ibid.,* Jan. 5, 1935.
30 "The Little Man's Cause," *Ibid.,* Aug. 25, 1934.
31 "The Forgotten Farmer," *Ibid.,* Nov. 10, 1934.
32 "The Other Side of the Picture," *Ibid.,* April 6, 1935.

Chapter VIII: SAKDALISM AND SOCIAL JUSTICE

1 "Let It Be Known," *Herald,* Jan. 2, 1936. Jesus Vargas later became Secretary of National Defense, Chief of Staff, and Secretary General of the SEATO.
2 "The Point of It," *Ibid.,* Jan. 3, 1936.
3 *Ibid.,* Jan. 18, 1935.
4 Mauro Mendez, "A Monument Against the Government," *National Review,* Feb. 14, 1936.
5 "Our High Officialdom," *Herald,* May 6, 1935.
6 "Where Would He Head Us?" *Ibid.,* March 8, 1935. (The word "Head" should probably be "Lead.")
7 Renato Constantino, *The Philippines: A Past Revisited* (Q.C.: Tala Publishing Services, 1975), p. 370.
8 "Four Horsemen of Darkness," *Herald,* June 12, 1935.
9 *Ibid.,* April 27, 1935.
10 "Our Parties and the Masses," *Ibid.,* May 4, 1935.
11 "The Government's Side of the Case," *Ibid.,* May 15, 1935.
12 "Our Parties and the Masses."
13 *Ibid.*
14 "The Forgotten Village," *Ibid.,* July 25, 1935.
15 "Light, Not Vengeance," *Ibid.,* Aug. 19, 1935.
16 "Discrediting Us," *Ibid.,* Oct. 29, 1935.
17 *Ibid.,* Aug. 5, 1939.
18 Mauro Mendez, "Problem for Narcissus," *National Review,* Jan. 17, 1936.
19 "Fighting Poverty," *Herald,* Oct. 16, 1935.
20 Manuel L. Quezon, *The Good Fight* (New York: D. Appleton Century Co., Inc., 1946), p. 166.
21 "P.I. Justice—Will It Come from the Law or from the Heart?" *Herald,* Aug. 22, 1936.
22 Quezon, p. 171.
23 "When the Mob Howls," *Herald,* Sept. 6, 1935.
24 "Words of Warning," *Ibid.,* Nov. 16, 1936.
25 "A Test Case," *Ibid.,* March 2, 1935.
26 *Ibid.*
27 "On Our Merry Way," *Ibid.,* April 25, 1935.
28 *Ibid.*
29 "The Poor People Pay," *Ibid.,* Feb. 1, 1936.
30 *Ibid.*
31 "On Our Merry Way."

Chapter IX: THE COMMON TOUCH

1 Mendez, "A Monument Against the Government."
2 From the funeral oration delivered by Foreign Secretary Ramos during the necrological services for Mauro Mendez on Jan. 5, 1966.
3 Leon Ma. Guerrero, Jr., "Apostle of Malacañang," *Philippines Free Press,* Sept. 18, 1937.
4 Jose Luna Castro, "The Radio and the Masses," *Herald Mid-Week Magazine,* Nov. 17, 1937. Castro became one of the editors of the postwar *Manila Times.*
5 *Herald,* July 13, 1937.
6 "Tagalog Should Be Our National Language," *Herald Mid-Week Magazine,* April 24, 1940. (See anthology in this volume. The title has been shortened to "Tagalog as the National Language.")
7 *Pahayagang Ca-la-lag,* April 1940.

8 "Manila Court Uses Assessors for First Time in 20 Years," *Philippines Free Press*, Aug. 12, 1939.
9 *Ibid.*
10 *El Debate*, Dec. 5, 1941.
11 "Mendez, Dissenting Assessor, Gives Reasons for Decision," *Herald*, Oct. 31 and Nov. 1, 1939.
12 Gallego was to become Secretary of Education and later, ambassador.
13 *El Debate*, Nov. 4, 1939.
14 *Ibid.*, Nov. 5, 1939.
15 *Ibid.*, Dec. 5, 1941. Josefino Cenizal went on to become a success in show business.
16 *Herald*, March 30, 1940.
17 Related to author by Professor Abaya.

Chapter X: ON THE WARPATH

1 "Dictators Dragging the World to War," *Herald*, Sept. 12, 1936.
2 "Japan's Man-Power," *Ibid.*, July 25, 1936.
3 "The Writing on the Wall," *Ibid.*, Sept. 14, 1933.
4 "Japan's Man-Power."
5 "A Fundamental Commonplace," *Ibid.*, Nov. 14, 1934.
6 *Ibid.*, Jan. 25, 1935.
7 "An Old Prescription," *Ibid.*, Jan. 26, 1935.
8 "The Davao Betrayal," *Herald*, Sept. 24, 1934.
9 "The Surrender of a Heritage," *Herald*, Oct. 25, 1933.
10 "The Hayun Maru Incident," *Ibid.*, Sept. 25, 1934.
11 *Herald*, Dec. 9, 1935.
12 "Our Military Defense," *Ibid.*, Nov. 2, 1935.
13 "A People Speaks," *Ibid.*, Nov. 26, 1935.
14 *Freedom of Press*, p. 7.
15 *Tribune*, Jan. 1, 1943.
16 *Ibid.*, Oct. 12, 1943.
17 As related to author by Armando Malay.
18 *Tribune*, Jan. 7, 1943.
19 *Ibid.*, Oct. 11, 1944.
20 Mrs. Perez became Secretary of Social Welfare during the administration of President Osmeña.

Chapter XI: LET FREEDOM RING

1 Manglapus became prominent in public life; he was elected senator in the '60s. Buencamino, married to Zeneida Quezon, was killed in 1948 in a Huk ambush, together with Mrs. Aurora Quezon and her daughter, Baby.
2 *This Week*, Aug. 19, 1945.
3 "Open Secrets," *Philippine Press*, Oct. 25, 1945.
4 *Star Reporter*, Oct. 20, 1945.
5 *This Week*, Aug. 19, 1945.
6 *Ibid.*, Sept. 25, 1945.
7 "Open Secrets," Oct. 14, 1945.
8 *The Newspaperman*, Nov., 1947.
9 *Express*, Sept. 5, 1945.
10 *Philippine Press*, Sept. 8, 1945.
11 *This Week*, July 22, 1945.
12 *Courier*, Sept. 5, 1945.
13 *Ang Bayan*, Sept. 5, 1945.
14 *Manila Post*, Sept. 5, 1945.

15 *This Week*, Sept. 25, 1945.
16 "Open Secrets," 1945 (Exact date unknown, but clipping is extant.)
17 Teodoro Agoncillo and Milagros Guerrero, *History of the Filipino People* (Q.C.: R.P. Garcia Publishing Co., 1970), p. 492.
18 Pacis, *Sergio Osmeña*, Vol. II, pp. 329-30.
19 *Philippines Free Press*, April 20, 1946.
20 Pedro Padilla, "Issues and Men," *Star Reporter*. (Date unknown; probably shortly before April 1946.)
21 E.P.H., "The Jaywalker," *The Daily News*, 1946. (Complete date unknown, although clipping is extant. Armando Malay believes that the initials stand for the first names of certain newsmen who took turns writing the same column.)
22 "A Little Mix-Up in Concepts," *Morning Sun*, May 22, 1946. (All quotations from the *Sun* are dated 1946.)
23 Ernesto del Rosario, "Off the Beat," *Manila Chronicle*, May 23, 1946.
24 As related to author by Ernesto Rodriguez, Jr.
25 "What of Filipino Business?" *Morning Sun*, May 25.
26 "We Must Draw the Line," *Ibid.*, Aug. 7.
27 "Jose Abad Santos," *Ibid.*, Aug. 21.
28 *Ibid.*, Aug. 2.
29 Feleo was kidnapped and killed by government agents in 1946. See Agoncillo and Guerrero, p. 528.
30 "Peace and Arms," *Morning Sun*, May 24.
31 "A Price to Pay," *Ibid.*, June 20.
32 *Ibid.*, Aug. 18.
33 Norberto de Ramos, "Mendez's Exemplary Career," *Sunday Chronicle Magazine*, Jan. 15, 1966.
34 *Freedom of Press*, p. 11.
35 *Ibid.*, pp. 11-12.
36 "A Wrong Start," *Herald*, Sept. 26, 1935.
37 "A Satisfactory Solution," *Ibid.*, Sept. 27, 1935.
38 *The Newspaperman*, November 1947.
39 *Freedom of Press*, p. 6.
40 Jose L. Guevara, "Post No Ill," *Manila Post*, June 25, 1947.

Chapter XII: HANDS ACROSS THE SEA

1 "Mendez, Philippine Diplomat, Wears New SDX Pin with Pride," *The Quill*, Aug. 1965.
2 From an interview with Dr. Salvador P. Lopez.
3 "Asia Unfurls Her Colors," *Manila Times*, May 1, 1947.
4 *Ibid.*
5 "Interview with Nehru," *Ibid.*, April 13, 1947.
6 "Are the Philippines Free—India Asks," *Ibid.*, April 19, 1947.
7 *Ibid.*
8 "Renaissance in India," *Ibid.*, May 19, 1947.
9 *Ibid.*
10 "A Giant May Rise," *Ibid.*, May 23, 1947.
11 Vicente del Fierro, "Notes and Footnotes," *Star Reporter*, Aug. 30, 1948.
12 *Manila Times*, Nov. 21, 1949.
13 "Forced Labor," *The Philippines in the United Nations*, Vol. II, 1954, p. 759.
14 "Free Exchange of Information," *Ibid.*, p. 721.
15 "Self-Determination of Peoples," *Ibid.*, pp. 756-57.
16 "Hacks Donate Relics to PI," *Manila Times*, March 26, 1960.
17 "Rizal Centenary in Germany," *Journal of History*, March 1962.

256 MAURO MENDEZ: FROM JOURNALISM TO DIPLOMACY

[18] "Our Diplomats Serve Beyond Call of Duty," *Manila Times*, March 23, 1960.
[19] Alejandro R. Roces, "Dedicated Men in Foreign Service," *Ibid.*, March 28, 1960.
[20] Paraluman Aspillera, "Tunay na Kinatawan," *Ibid.*, March 23, 1960.
[21] "Japan's Power," *Herald*, April 29, 1935.
[22] "Banzai," *Ibid.*, April 29, 1936.

Chapter XIII: THE PREMIER POST

[1] *Manila Times*, April 28, 1964.
[2] *Daily Mirror*, April 29, 1964.
[3] *Herald*, April 30, 1964.
[4] From an interview with Mr. Valencia.
[5] Alfonso Policarpio, "Advantage of Age," *Herald*, May 23, 1964.
[6] *Manila Daily Bulletin*, May 7, 1964.
[7] *Herald*, May 7, 1964.
[8] Nestor Mata, "Mr. Mendez Is in Town," *Herald*, May 7, 1964. Mata's regular column was entitled "Men and Events."
[9] Alfonso Policarpio, *Herald*, May 2, 1964.
[10] *Herald*, May 9, 1964.
[11] *Ibid.*
[12] Amando Doronila, "Check and Balance," *Daily Mirror*, June 22, 1964.
[13] *Straits Times*, June 20, 1964.
[14] *Sunday Chronicle*, June 28, 1964.
[15] Maximo Soliven, "By the Way," *Manila Times*, June 19, 1964.
[16] *Sunday Times*, July 4, 1964.
[17] *Sunday Chronicle*, July 5, 1964.
[18] J.V. Cruz, "Here and There," *Manila Times*, July 8, 1964.
[19] Apolonio Batalla, "Second Thoughts," *Bulletin*, July 4, 1964.
[20] Cruz, *Manila Times*, July 8, 1964.
[21] Mata, "Mr. Mendez Thinks Aloud," *Herald*, July 5, 1964.
[22] Oscar Villadolid, "Padre Faura's New Chief," *Bulletin*, July 20, 1964. Villadolid's daily column was "The Listening Post."
[23] Villadolid, "The Contribution of Mendez," *Ibid.*, Dec. 22, 1965.
[24] Cruz, *Times*, Aug. 8, 1965.
[25] *Ibid.*, June 6, 1965.
[26] Jose Ma. Hernandez, "The Philippines and Vietnam," *Manila Chronicle*, Aug. 10, 1964.
[27] Luis D. Beltran, "Straight from the Shoulder," *Evening News*, Sept. 28, 1964.
[28] Beltran, "Mendez was proudest of fact that he was a newspaperman," *Evening News*, Jan. 3, 1966. "Straight from the Shoulder" was the title of Beltran's daily column and of his weekly television program.
[29] Soliven, *Manila Times*, Sept. 5, 1964.
[30] *Manila Times*, Sept. 4, 1964.
[31] Soliven, Feb. 9, 1965.
[32] *Ibid.*, March 28, 1965.
[33] From a speech delivered by Mendez before the Philippine Society of International Law and the Philippine Commission of Jurists, July 26, 1965.
[34] *Manila Chronicle*, July 5, 1964.
[35] *Bulletin*, July 11, 1964.
[36] "Self-Determination of Peoples," *The Philippines in the United Nations*, Vol. II, pp. 757-58.
[37] *Chronicle*, Sept. 18, 1965.
[38] Filemon V. Tutay, "The Indonesian Problem," *Philippines Free Press*, Feb. 27, 1965.

NOTES

39 *Bulletin*, July 11, 1964.
40 *Herald*, Aug. 29, 1964.
41 Saulo, pp. 13-15.
42 *Chronicle*, Aug. 5, 1965.
43 *Herald*, Feb. 28, 1965.
44 Quijano de Manila, "The Other Court-Martial," *Philippines Free Press*, March 13, 1965.
45 Quijano de Manila, "Judgment at Clark," *Ibid.*, March 6, 1965.
46 Napoleon G. Rama, "Of Bullets and Bombs," *Ibid.*, Jan. 2, 1965.
47 *Manila Times*, Jan. 5, 1965.
48 Teodoro M. Locsin, "Was This Necessary?" *Free Press*, Feb. 13, 1965.
49 "The Questionable Elements in the Picture," *Weekly Graphic*, Feb. 3, 1965.
50 "The Storm Over Blair, Mendez," *Ibid.*, Feb. 17, 1965.
51 *Manila Times*, Feb. 3, 1965.
52 Villadolid, "Mendez and the N.P.s," *Bulletin*, Feb. 5, 1965.
53 "Storm Over Blair, Mendez."
54 *Herald*, Feb. 8, 1965.
55 "The Questionable Elements in the Picture."
56 *Bulletin*, Feb. 5, 1965.
57 Rama, "Of Bullets and Bombs."
58 Villadolid, "The Contribution of Mendez."
59 Doronila, *Daily Mirror*, Jan. 8, 1965.
60 Cruz, Jan. 12, 1965.
61 Doronila, May 20, 1965.
62 Beltran, May 20, 1965.
63 Jose C. Balein, "Another One," *Chronicle*, March 25, 1965.
64 Felixberto Serrano, "Guiding Principles for Bases Parley," *Herald*, Feb. 2, 1965.
65 Press release of Department of Foreign Affairs, Aug. 10, 1965, explaining provisions of Article XIII as amended.
66 From the official correspondence between Secretary Mendez and Ambassador Blair.
67 Beltran, Aug. 21, 1965.
68 Beltran, June 1, 1965.
69 Doronila, Dec. 9, 1965.
70 Beltran, July 28, 1965.
71 *Herald*, June 10, 1965.
72 Cruz, June 6 and 9, 1965.
73 Claude A. Buss, "Mission to What?" *Free Press*, June 26, 1965.
74 *Daily Mirror*, Nov. 5, 1965.
75 Beltran, Aug. 6, 1965.
76 Press Questionnaire with Secretary Mendez on Sept. 17, 1965, released by the Department of Foreign Affairs and published in the newspapers the following day.
77 *Herald*, Dec. 22, 1965.
78 Mata, "To Mendez, Au Revoir!" Dec 24, 1965.
79 *Ibid.*
80 Beltran, "Mendez was proudest of fact that he was a newspaperman."

Chapter XIV: THE LAST DEADLINE

1 *Herald*, Jan. 2, 1966.
2 Valencia, "Over a Cup of Coffee," *Manila Times*, Jan. 6, 1966.
3 "The Late Mr. Mendez," *Daily Mirror*, Jan. 5, 1966.

POSTMORTEM ON THE MENDEZ-BLAIR AGREEMENT

1 *Manila Times,* July 15, 1969.
2 All the Manila papers carried the news on October 12, 1969.
3 *Manila Times,* Oct. 12, 1969.
4 *Bulletin,* Oct. 9, 1969.
5 *Herald,* Oct. 17, 1969.
6 *Manila Times,* Oct. 21, 1969.
7 Quoted by Apolonio Batalla in the *Bulletin,* Oct. 9, 1969.
8 *Manila Chronicle,* March 12 and 29, 1970.
9 *Ibid.,* March 25, 1970.
10 For recent cases, see the following: "Base pact violations protested," *Bulletin Today,* March 25, 1977; "DFA asked to protest Clark ploy," *Times Journal,* April 1, 1977; "5 GIs in assault get duty papers," *TJ,* Sept. 6, 1977; "US Airmen's 'official duty' claim rejected," *Bulletin Today,* Oct. 10, 1977.
11 Judge Milagros German, "Will the Real Owner of These Bases Please Stand Up?" *Philippine Panorama,* Jan. 23, 1977.
12 "Romulo Upholds Collantes Stand on Holman Imbroglio," *Herald,* Nov. 12, 1970.
13 "Justice Dept. asks DFA to protest Clark snub," *TJ,* July 12, 1977.
14 Reacting to persistent publicity about duty certificates and servicemen who reportedly leave the country pending the conclusion of cases against them, Lt. Col. Jerry A. Butler of the U.S. Air Force, who served for five years as legal adviser to the U.S. embassy, wrote an article which was published in the *Bulletin Today* on July 13, 1977. In the article he stated that "in an average year, approximately 900 U.S. servicemen are charged with various offenses by Philippine authorities. Most of these charges are very minor in nature." In only 25 cases per year do the military authorities grant duty certificates to the offenders; Philippine courts and fiscals assume jurisdiction over the other 875 cases.
Butler says:

> No US serviceman charged in any of these cases has left the Philippines until the cases were resolved. In one case, a serviceman has been kept here at considerable personal inconvenience for almost eight years awaiting the final resolution of his case.
> All the misleading press stories about American servicemen departing the Philippines while charges against them are pending seem to involve the very small number of "official duty cases." Even in these few cases, the servicemen are kept in the Philippines until full consultations are held between US and Philippine authorities.

Butler also points out that in civil cases the individual US serviceman is treated like any other foreigner or Filipino citizen before local courts. There are no provisions under the Military Bases Agreement or under Philippine law to restrict the movements of a person charged in a civil case. "Thus, in a few rare cases a serviceman may be required by government orders to report to a new assignment before civil proceedings are concluded."
[Unlike those charged in civil cases, American servicemen accused of criminal offenses are placed under legal or international hold. They may not leave the country until cleared of the charges. U.S. officials are required to present the accused before Philippine authorities for investigation, trial, and judgment.]

INDEX

A.D.B., *see* Asian Development Bank
Abad Santos, Jose, 103, 185-87
Abad Santos, Pedro, 72
Abad Santos, Vicente, 162
Abaya, Hernando J., 34, 75, 76, 84
Abelardo, Nicanor, 211
Academic freedom, 29-30, 224
　Preservation of, 225
Academy of the Spanish language, 223
Ackerman, Dean, 114
Ad Hoc Political Committee of the General Assembly, 116
Addis, John Mansfield, 155-56
Adult education, 70
Afro-Asian Conference in Algiers, 150
Agence France Presse, 135
Aglipay, Gregorio, 36, 49, 52-53, 55
Agrarian unrest, 104
Aguinaldo, Emilio, 36, 49, 50-51, 55, 71, 87, 114
Air Corps Tactical School, 183
Akihito, Crown Prince, 126
Aklat ng Mamayanan (Citizen's Handbook), 76
Alagar, Vicente G., 21
Alexander the Great, 181, 204-05, 216
Alexander II, Tsar of Russia, 195
Alexandria, 216
The Alhambra, 26
America, diplomatic relations with Russia, 192-94
American Chamber of Commerce Journal, 20
Amnesty, 103
Amor, Glicerio, 158
Amorsolo, Pablo, 19
Angeles City, 141-43
Annapolis, 182
Annual of the Manila High School, 2, 4
Anselmo, Roberto, 12

Anti-Communist crusade, 72
Antiplebiscite campaign, 67
Antipolo, 7-8, 15, 26, 243-44
"Anti-war emotionalism", 47
Apostol, Cecilio, 2
　A Rizal, 5
Aquino, Jr., Benigno, 150,
Aquino Sr., Benigno, 36
Aquino, Melchor, 232, 234
Araneta, Salvador, 37
Archimedes, 216
Aristocracy, 58, 193, 200
Arizabal, Antonio V., 34
Artistic conscience, 228
Asedillo, Teodoro, 65, 66
Asian Development Bank, 151
Asociacion Musical de Filipinas, 229
Aspillera, Paraluman, 123
Associated Press, 121
"Association of the Sons of the Country", *see* Katipunan
Astilla, Francisco, 12
Atienza, Hermenegildo, 34
Aunario, Pedro, 80-81, 82-83

Bach, 228
Bakri, Iljas, 139
Balagtas, Francisco, *see* Baltazar, Francisco (Balagtas)
Balagtas, Rogelio, 140
Balintawak, 169-70, 222
Mga Balitang Pangbayan, 76-77
Balmaceda, Cornelio, 6, 151, 156
Baltazar, Francisco (Balagtas), 21, 170-73, 220
Barrera, Jesus, 3
Bases treaty, 141-42, *see also* Military Bases Agreement
Batalla, Apolonio, 133
Bautista, Jose P., 11, 12
Ang Bayan, 97

Beethoven, 228
Before Rizal's Monument, 5-6, 242-43
Bell, Edward Price, 13
Bell, Jasper, 102
Bell Trade Relations Act, 102-03
Bella, Ben Ahmed, 151
Beltran, Luis D., 134-35, 148, 151, 153
Benavides, Anacleto, 12, 34
Benitez, Conrado, 11
Benitez, Paz Marquez de, 4
Bill of Rights, 47, 232
Bill the Bo'Sun, 12
Bisnar, Gauttier, 142
Blair Jr., William McCormick, 140, 142, 144, 147, 155
Blumentritt, Ferdinand, 172
Bocobo, Jorge, 27, 30, 36, 37
Boguslav, David, 17
Bohlen, Charles, 142, 160
Bolshevism, 57
Bolshevist Party, 72
Bolshevist revolution, 62, 196-97
Bonifacio, Andres, 1, 6, 165, 169, 220
Booker T. Washington, 3, 240-41
Booth, Mildred G., 3
"Bootleg item 85", 31-32
Border-crossing agreement, 140
Borja, Jacinto, 128
Borromeo, Horacio, 232, 234
Boxer Rebellion, 213
Brisbane, Arthur, 19, 34
Bud, Panamao, 21
Buencamino III, Philip, 94
Bulletin, see Manila Daily Bulletin
Butler, Jerry A., 258
Byroade, Henry, 159

C.E.A., *see* Civilian Emergency Administration
Cablenews American, 11
Cabrera, Celso, 12
Cabrera, Gene, 122
Cambodian Mission to U.N., 124
Camp Stotsenburg (Pampanga), 41
La Campana Restaurant, 11
Capadocia, Guillermo, 72
Capitalism, 62, 193
 Social system of, 180
Capitalist system, 63, 179
"Capitan Kulas", *see* Encallado, Nicolas
Carpio, Victorio D., 114
Carter, Anna H., 3
Cases, Manuel T., 144
Castrence, Pura Santillan, 122
Castro, Jose Luna, 78, 122
Castro, Pacifico, 160
Cayco, Librado D., 129, 136, 142

Cedula tax, 195
Cenizal, Josefino, 80
Censorship, 196
Centro Escolar University, 89
Charlemagne, 181
Charles I, 191
Chaucer, 220
Chekhov, 58
Chiang Kai-shek, 126
Chicago Daily News, 13
"Children of hate", 37
Chopin, 228
A Christmas Poem, 7, 247-48
Cid, Cipriano, 12
Cigar importations, curtailment of, 60
Cisneros, Luis Fernan, 115-16
Citizenship training, 183
Civilian Emergency Administration, 84
Clark Air Base, Pampanga, 140, 141, 158
Cocheros, 19, 45-46
Code of Civil Procedure, 81
Colayco, Clemencia Joven, 26
Cole, Larry, 140-41, 145
Collantes, Manuel, 162
Comedie Humaine, 234
Commerce, Bureau of, 9
Commission on Appointments, 96-97
Commission on Human Rights, 116
Commitee on the Freedom of Information, 116
Commonwealth, 50
 Government, 49, 75, 94
 Inauguration of, 71
 Period, 36
Communism, 41, 56-57, 104-05, 129, 193
 Crusade against, 62-63
Communist Party of the Philippines, 143
Communistic system, 179
Coniconde, P.V., 38
Conservatory of Music, 229
Constantino, Renato, 68, 114
Constitutional Assembly, 47
Corregidor Island, 149
Craig, Austin, 37
Criminal jurisdiction, 142, 146
Cristobal, Epifanio de los Santos, 171, 172
Crow Valley, death in, 140-41
Cruz, J.V., 133, 134, 146, 150
Cryptia Debating Club, 3
Cuenco, Mariano Jesus, 96
Cultural cooperation, 112
Cultural identity, 221
Cultural integrity, 222
Culture

Aesthetic, 224
  Filipino, 25, 172
  Human, ethics of, 211
  Musical, 229

Dacanay, Jose Q., 76
"Daily Chit-Chats", 14-16
Daily Mirror, 128, 131, 156
Daily News, 100
Dante, 235
Davao, 138
  Japanization of, 87
  A "miniature Nippon", 86
"Davaokuo", 86, 138
David, Rafael, 37
Davis, Governor-General, 25
De la Cruz, Jose, 34
De la Rosa, Recaredo, 12
De los Reyes, Cornelio, 12
De Ramos, Norberto, 106
De Vera, Teodoro P., 37
De Veyra, Sofia, 43
El Debate, 33, 82
Debussy, 228
Declaration of the Rights of Man (France), 48
Defense program, national, 87-88
Del Barrio, Concepcion, 2
Del Fierro, Vicente, 12, 17, 113, 234
Del Mundo, Fe, 49
Del Pilar, Marcelo H., 220
Del Rosario, Ernesto, 102, 234
Delgado, Francisco, 86
Demagoguery, fiascos of, 67
Democracy, 45-47, 198, 201, 204
Dictatorship, modern, 198
Diplomatic service, 110
Discontent, hotbeds of, 63-64
Donizetti, 229
Doronila, Amando E., 131, 149, 152-53
Duran, Pio, 93
Duty certificate, 161-62
Dvorak, 228

E.C.A., *see* Emergency Control Administration
Economic and Social Council, 116
"The Educator's Turn at the Helm", 30
Edelstein, Julius Caesar, 103
Edwards, Jose A., 141
Eight-hour labor law, 58, 178-80
Elegy Written in a Country Churchyard, 103
Elizalde, Joaquin, 33
Emergency Control Administration, 95
Empire State Building, 114
Encallado, Nicolas (Capitan Kulas), 65-66

English language, 27, 78-79, 214-17, 220-22
  As the language of commerce, 221
  As the language of instruction, 28
  As the official language of the Philippines, 27
  Compared with Greek language, 27
English Parliament, 188
Enrile, Juan Ponce, 158
Escoda, Antonio, 11, 93
Escoda, Josefa Llanes, 43
Escuela Municipal de Manila, *see* Manila High School
Estrada, Antonio, 79, 221
Euclid, 216
Evangeline, 26
Evangelista, Crisanto, 72
Evening in a Grave-Yard, 5, 238-39
Evening News, 134, 234
Executive Commission, Chairman of, 89

Family values, Filipino, 57
Farolan, Modesto, 34, 110
Federation of Malaysia, 130
Feleo, Juan, 104
Fernandez, Estanislao, 37, 144
Fernandez, Rev. Fr., 223
El Filibusterismo, 119, 165-69, 223
Filipinization, 11
Filipino
  Culture, 25, 172
  Family values, 57
  Flag, 6
  Immigrants, 36
  Labor movements, 180
  Literature in English, 14, 56
    Evolution of, 4
  Music, 211
  Newsmen, 33
  Poetry in English, 1
  Press, 11
  Soul, 211, 222
  Women, 43-44
    Suffrage, 41
  Young men, 182
Filipino-Japanese friendship, 130
"Filipino-type treaty", 147
Fitzgerald, F. Scott, 10
Florante at Laura, 171-73
Forced labor, 116
Foreign Affairs
  Department, 124, 158-59, 160
  Secretary, 110
Foreign-office system, 213
Foreign subjugation, revolt against, 169
Fort McKinley, 41
Fort Santiago, 41, 93

Fourth Estate, 230, 231
  Stalwarts of, 232-35
  See also Press
Free education, 28
Free press, 90-91, 95, 231-33
  Absence of, 116
Freedom of information, 116
French Revolution, 202
Friar estates, 76
Fulbright, William, 127
Furay, J.H., 231, 232

Gaines, Joseph, 162
"Galilean Gospel of Peace and Goodwill", 63
Gallego, Manuel V., 82
Gancayco, Emilio, 141
Gandhi, Mahatma, 111-13
Garcia, Adriano, 114
Garcia, Bernardo, 11
Garcia, Carlos P., 13
Garcia, Leon T., 139
George V, King of England, 212-14
Girls' Literary Society (1914), 3
Glasgow Evening Citizen, 114
Goethe, 234
Golden age of journalism, 20
Gonzales, Rogelio, 158
Gonzalez, Crispin, 12
Gonzalez, N.V.M., 4
Gray, Thomas, 103
Greek
  Aristocracy, 200
  Language, 27, 216-17
Guerrilleros, 94
Guerrero Jr., Leon Ma., 77-80, 132
Guevara, Jose L., 101, 108, 232, 234
Guevara, Pedro, 36
Gwekoh, Sol, 24

H-H-C Law, *see* Hare-Hawes Cutting Law
Hack, Fritz, 120-21
Hack, Hans, 120-21
Hack family, 121
Handel, 228
Hare-Hawes Cutting Act, 35-37
Hare-Hawes Cutting Law, 29, 42
  League for the Acceptance of, 36-38
Harrison, Francis Burton, 11
Hayden, Ralston, 197-98
Hayun Maru, 87
Heidelberg, 119, 120
Hellenic city-democracies, 216
Hellenism, 216
Henry, Patrick, 50
Herald, see Philippines Herald
Hernandez, Amado, 34, 38

Hernandez, Jose H., 4
Hernandez, Jose Ma., 134
Hidalgo, Felix Resurreccion, 119
Hirohito, Emperor, 125
Hiroshima, 126
History of Journalism in the Philippine Islands, 14, 20
Hodobu, 92
Hohenzollerns, 213
House Foreign Affairs Committee, 144
House of Representatives, 23, 31
Hukbalahap guerrillas, 104-06

Illiteracy, 70
  Campaign against, 27
  Provincial, 68
Ilocano(s), 218, 219
Imamura, Enrique, 89
Immigration laws, Philippine, 138
Imperial Army of Dai Nippon, 85, 86, 91
Imperialism, 213
Imperialistic drama, 213
Independence, campaign for, 41, 71
The Independent, 2, 4
India-Pakistan dispute, 137
Indian Serenade, 5
Indonesian(s), 112
  Embassy, 138
  Immigrants, 138
Indonesian-Malaysian skirmish, 138
Indonesian-Philippine relations, 138
Information, Department of, 92, 96
Ingles, Jose D., 114, 160
Inheritance law, 72
Institute of National Language, 218
Institute of Pacific Relations, 110
"Intelligentsia", 68
Intengan, Jesus M. "Fatso", 34
Inter-Asian Relations Conference, 110;
  Accomplishments of, 112, 210
Interior, Department of, 75
International Court of Justice, 130
Internationale of Moscow, Third, 62-63
Irving, Washington, 26

Jacinto, Emilio, 165, 169, 220
Jakarta
  Political situation in, 138
  Relations with the Philippines, 139
Japan, 125-26, 217
  Militarism in, 86
Jazz Age, 10
Jesus Christ, 7
Joaquin, Nick, 141
Johnson, Lyndon, 144
Jose Abad Santos, 185-87
Jose Rizal Memorial Museum, 121

INDEX

Journalism, 34, 110
  As a profession, 211
  Philippine, 12
    Golden age of, 20
Jueteng capitalist, 74
Jurado, Emil, 159

K.M., see Kabataang Makabayan
KZRM Radio Manila, 78
Kabataang Makabayan, 143
Kalaw, Maximo, 36, 37
Kalaw, Pura Villanueva, 43
Katipunan, 1, 169, 220
Katipunan ng mga Anak Pawis, 65
Katipuneros, 1
"Kartilla", 169
Kellogg Pact of 1928, 47
Kempei-Tai, 91, 93
Kerensky, 193, 194
Kipling, Rudyard, 212-13, 220
Klinefelter, Mary, 3
Kulaks, 73
Kundiman, 211

La Bruyere, 234
Labor, 178-80
  And capital, 62
  And management, reconciliation of, 61
Labor Compensation Act, 58
Laboring classes, 68
Lacson, Arsenio, 94, 95, 99
"Laissez faire", 74
La Minerva Cigar Factory strike, 60
Land reform program, 76
Langwell Hotel, 113-14
Lansang, Jose A., 34
Laos, 123-24
Laurel, Jose P., 3, 36, 89, 92
Laurel, Salvador H., 160
Laviña, Nelson, 160
Law of exclusion, 204
Ledesma, Oscar, 144
Leftist intellectuals, 72
Legarda, Trinidad Fernandez, 11
Legaspi, Miguel Lopez de, 189, 190
Leido, Jose, 3
Lenin, 196
Liberal Party, 108
Liberal Wing, 98
Libertinism, 45
Liberty, 188
  Cry of, 220
  Roman concept, 200
Lichauco, Marcial P., 132
Lim, Peter, 138
Lim, Pilar Hidalgo, 3, 42, 43
Limet, Monsieur, 119

Lippay, Alexander, 228, 229
Liszt, 228
Literary expression, 216
Literary renaissance, 171
"Little Brown Americans", 133
"Little Bung Karnos", 133, 140
Locsin, Teodoro M., 143, 232, 234
Longfellow, 26
Lopez, Salvador P., 3, 19, 34-35, 110, 114, 116, 119, 128, 129, 130, 133, 139
Lopez-Rizal, Leoncio, 121
Luna, Juan, 119
Luther, Martin, 235
Luz, Arsenio N., 12, 23, 90-91

Mabini, Apolinario, 165, 220
Mabini Literary Society, 3
Mabuhay, 38
Macapagal, Diosdado, 18, 107, 125, 129, 131, 132, 137, 138, 141-42, 143, 151, 152, 155, 159
MacArthur, Douglas, 93, 99, 100, 183
McDuffie, John, 39
Machado, President of Cuba, 180
Machiavelli, 213
Mactan Island, 189
Madrigal, Vicente, 12, 40
Magellan, Ferdinand, 189, 190
Magna Charta (England), 48, 187-88
Magsaysay, Ramon, 99
Makapili, 93
Malacañang Palace, 70
Malaka, Tan, 139
Malaria Control Field Laboratory, 67
Malay, Armando, 91, 234
Male chauvinism, 41
Malik, Jacob, 115
Mangahas, Federico, 17, 34, 79
Manglapus, Raul, 94
Manila Chamber Music Society, 229
Manila Chronicle, 12, 95, 234
Manila Daily Bulletin, 9, 20, 145, 159
Manila High School, 1, 2-4
Manila Post, 97, 108, 234
Manila Symphony Society, 228
Manila Times, 9, 11, 12, 110, 120, 122, 132, 159
Manila Tobacco Association, 60
Manila Tribune, 11-14, 18-24, 27, 29, 49, 61, 91, 92, 234
Mao Tse-tung, 126-27
Maphilindo Summit, 130-32
Marabut, Mike, 152
Maramag, Fernando, 4, 11, 12
Marcos, Ferdinand E., 152, 154, 160
Marin, Luis Muñoz, 116
Mariño, Salvador, 142

Marking, Agustin, 90
Marking, Yay, 90
Marking's guerrillas, 89
Marquez, Nati, 15
Martial law, Japanese occupation, 92
Martinez, Josefa Jara, 43
Martini, Carlo, 156, 157
Marx, Karl, 63, 179, 199
Marxist socialism, 138
Mata, Nestor, 133
Matsunaga, Mr., 91
Mehan Gardens, 32, 61
Melencio, Carmen A., 49
Mendelssohn, 228
Mendez, Esteban, 2
Mendez, Mauro
    "Apostle of Malacañang", 77
    The "Arthur Brisbane of the Philippines", 24
    Birth, 1-2
    Death of, 154-57
    "The prototype of the professional journalist", 19
    Role in the United Nations, 115-17
Mendez, Paz Policarpio (Pacita T. Policarpio), 8, 14, 43, 113
Mendez-Blair agreement, 145-49
    Postmortem on, 158-62
Metropolitan Theatre, 228
Michiko, Crown Princess, 126
Militarism, 182
    Doctrine of, 181
    In Japan, 86
Militarist, 199
Military Bases Agreement (1947), 140
    Abrogation of, 143
    Revision of, 146-47
Military Bases (U.S.), 115, 140
    Lease of, 160
    Personnel, 147
Military Police Command, 104
Military preparedness, 182-83
Military training, 183
Mill, John Stuart, 233
Miller, Marilyn, 10
Mindanao, 22, 138
La Minerva Cigar Factory, 59
    Strike at, 60-61
Minimum wage, 72
"The Mob in History", 45
Mob rule, 46-47
"Mohammedanism", 112
Monarchy, 213-14
Moncado, Hilario, 94
Monday Mail, 38, 42
Montejo, Ceferino, 12
Montinola, Ruperto, 36
Moomey, Michael, 158-59

Morality, laws of, 206
More, Thomas, 234
Morley, Christopher, 156
Morning Sun, 100-03, 107
Moscow, 56, 60, 63, 76
Mozart, 228
Murphy, Frank, 29, 42, 43, 59, 70, 200, 201
Muslim Pakistan, 112

NATO countries, 147
NATO-type agreement, 147
N.I.B., *see* National Information Board
Nacionalista Party, 36, 96, 98
Nagasaki, 126
Nalundasan, Julio, 3
Napoleon, 181
"Nasaan Ka Irog?", 211
National Assembly, 72, 87, 92, 218
National defense, 180-84
    Bureau, 183-84
    House Committee on, 138
National Federation of Women's Clubs, 42
National Information Board, 75-76, 78, 83
National Research Council, 227
National Review, 66, 71
National Socialist Party, 72
Nationalism, 183
    Clash with proletarian internationalism, 62
Navarro, Vicente, 12
Navy Court-Martial, 158
Nazario, Montano, 34
Nazi movement, 24
Nehru, Jawaharlal, 111, 207-11
Nepomuceno, Ricardo, 3
Neutralism, futility of, 136-37
News for the Nation, *see Mga Balitang Pangbayan*
The Newspaperman, 96
New York Journal, 19
Ninety-five gripes at Wittenberg, 235
Noli Me Tangere, 120, 165-69, 172
"*Noli* village", 122
"Non-Aligned Newsmen's Association", 134
Northwestern University, 34
Nuguid, Fernando, 162
Nuguid, Zacarias, 101

Ocampo, Galo, 114
Ocampo, Pedro, 60-62
Ochs, Adolph S., 211
Ode to a Song Sparrow, 4, 235-37
Official duty, 148-49, 161
Official Gazette, 84

INDEX

Office of War Information, 96
Ohira, Masayoshi, 130
Oligarchy, 204
Olympiad, 216
One World, 113
Orata, Pedro T., 102
Order of the Rising Sun, First Class, 130
Osias, Camilo, 13, 25, 36, 37, 39
Osmeña, Sergio, 3, 35, 39, 49, 53-54, 95-96, 97-98, 99
Os-Rox mission, 35-36
"Our Balete-Strangled Government", 19-20
Our Government—What it is Doing For You, 76

P.K.I., *see* Partai Kommunis Indonesia
Pacis, Vicente Albano, 12, 34, 41, 110
Padilla, Ambrosio, 37
Padilla, Pedro, 100
Palma, Rafael, 29, 36-37, 224
Pamontjak, Nazir, 139
Paras, Ricardo, 3
Paredes, Quintin, 36-37
Paris, 118
Parkway Village, Jamaica, Long Island, 114
Partai Kommunis Indonesia, 138-39
Partido Filipinista, 49
Partido Nacionalista Democrata, 49
Partido Nacionalista Democrata Pro-Independencia, 49
Pathet Lao Communist forces, 123
Pearl Harbor, 84
Peking, 135-36
Pelaez, Emmanuel, 34, 150
Pennsylvania Press Conference, 231
Pensacola School of Naval Flying, 183
People's Hour, 78
People's Republic of China, 126, 136
Perez, Asuncion, 43, 89, 93
Perez, Cirilo, 93
Perfecto, Gregorio, 36
Philippine Army, 88
Philippine-Chinese Advocate, 9
Philippine cigar industry, 60
Philippine Commercial Agency, 9
Philippine Commonwealth
 Elections of, 203
 Inauguration of, 55
Philippine Constabulary, 59, 65, 68
Philippine Constitution, 36
Philippine High School Readers, 25-26
Philippine independence, 101
Philippine-Indonesian relations, 209
Philippine journalism, 1, 12
Philippine Law School, 80

Philippine Mission to the U.N., 94, 114-17
Philippine National Bank, 70
Philippine Newspaper Guild, 106
"Philippine plutocracy", 68
Philippine Press, 94
Philippine press, 4, 20, 129
 Professionalism in, 17
Philippine Primary Geography, 26
Philippine Prose and Poetry, 26
Philippine Readers, 25
Philippine Review, 9
Philippine security, 128
The Philippines, 76
The Philippines: A Past Revisited, 68
Philippines Free Press, 8, 9, 77, 80, 141, 143, 234
Philippines Herald, 10-11, 12, 33, 34, 38, 39, 42, 66
Philippines' Town Meeting of the Air, 218
Phnom Penh, 124
Phouma, Souvanna, 123
Pimentel Jr., Narciso, 37
Plaza Hotel, 37
Policarpio, Alfonso, 129
Policarpio, Paz T., *see* Mendez, Pacita Policarpio
Political rights, 199
Political struggle, 54
Political thought, 59
Politicalization, 68, 70
"Politics of despair", 51-52
Pond, Horace B., 197
"Pork barrel", 225
Post-Bagumbayan period, 5
Potts, Merrill S., 26
Press, 230-32
 A force for human expression, 231
 American, freedom of, 232
 Freedom of, 231, 232-33
 Irresponsible, 61
 Puppet, 90-93
 See also Fourth Estate
"The Prince of Tagalog Letters", 21, 169-72
Proletarian internationalism, clash with nationalism, 62
Proletarian workers, 196
Proletariat, 193, 199
Proletarius, 23
Provincial communities, 76
Public Information
 Department, 75, 95
 Director, 62
 Office, 62
Public opinion, 20, 230, 231
 In a dictatorship, 231

Public school(s), 25
  System, 28-29
  Teacher, 28
Puerto Rican problem, 116
Pugad-Lawin, 170
Pulitzer School of Journalism, Columbia University, 9-10, 13
Purana Qila, New Delhi, 111
Puyat, Gil, 154
Pyramids of Egypt, 201

Quezon, Aurora, 43, 49
Quezon City Bar Association, 142
Quezon, Manuel L., 10, 11, 29, 35, 36, 37, 38, 39, 40, 49, 53, 65, 71-73, 75, 79, 99
  Image of, 38
Quezon-Osmeña alliance, 53, 67, 68
Quijano de Manila, see Joaquin, Nick
The Quill, 110
Quimson, Sofronio, 37
Quirino, Alicia, 49
Quirino, Carlos, 34
Quirino, Eliseo, 9
Quirino, Elpidio, 3, 13, 36, 37, 76, 78, 83, 99

"The Radio and the Masses", 78
Rahman, Tunku Abdul, 131
Ramos, Benigno, 68, 71, 93
Ramos, Godofredo, 144-45
Ramos, Narciso, 11, 75, 110, 152, 156, 160
Rasjid, Karim, 140
Razak, Tun Abdul, 130, 131
Recto, Aurora, 49
Recto, Claro M., 36, 184-85
"Red Menace", 58-59
Reibold, Adam, 121
Reign of Terror, 192
Reischauer, Edwin O., 127
Repression, policy of, 194
Republican Party, 52
Resistance movement, 93
Retizos, Isidro, 20-21
"Revolution of May 1935", 67
Reyes, Jose S., 3
Reyes, Narciso G., 114, 117, 138
Ricarte, Artemio, 68
"Riot-and-run Communist", 61
The Rising Philippines, 9
Rivera, Godofredo, 11, 34
Rizal, Jose, 5, 6, 67, 118-22, 165-68, 172, 220, 223
  A la Juventud Filipina, 26
  A Rizal, 5
Rizal Centennial Commission, 119
Rizal Debating Club, 3

Rizal-Ullmer relationship, 121
Robb, Walter J., 20
Roces Jr., Alejandro, 12, 91
Roces Sr., Alejandro, 12, 13-14
Roces, Joaquin, 144
Roces, Ramon, 12
Rodin, Auguste, 119
Rodriguez Jr., Ernesto, 101
Rodriguez, Maximo, 65-66
Romero, Jose E., 145
Romulo, Carlos P., 1, 3, 10, 12, 17, 33, 34, 35, 95, 110, 111, 156, 187, 209
Romulo-Quezon relationship, 12
Roosevelt, Franklin D., 35, 55, 185
Rotary Club, 200
Rotary Club of Quezon City, 128
Roxas, Manuel A., 3, 15, 35, 37, 94, 96-97, 98-100, 101, 103-04, 108-09, 188, 189, 209
Royal Theatre, 3
Runnymede, 188
Rusk, Dean, 160
Russia, diplomatic relations with America, 192-94

SEATO, see Southeast Asia Treaty Organization
SOFA, see Status-of-Forces Agreements
Sabah claim, 130
Sabido, Pedro, 36
Saigon, 137
Sakdalan, Benito, 12
Sakdalistas, 66-69
  Moral lesson for, 77
  Problem, approach to, 70
"The Salariat", 23
Salonga, Jovito, 144, 160
Samson, Marcelo, 104
San Francisco, 113
San Isidro, Nueva Ecija, 88, 93, 94, 104
Sangley Point, Cavite, 158
Santos, Lope K., 37, 97
Sanvictores, Jose G., 12
Schubert, 228
Scientific research, 225-27
Self-censorship, 91
Self-defense, 181
Self-government, 54
Sensationalism, 21
Serfdom in Russia, 195
Sergio Osmeña—Highlights of a Leadership Unequalled by That of Any Living Filipino, 98
Serrano, Felixberto, 124, 142, 143, 145, 146, 160
Shelley, Percy Bysshe
  Indian Serenade, 5

Skylark, 4
Sicatuna, 189
Sigma Delta Chi, 10, 110
Sihanouk, Norodom, 137
Sison, Jose Ma., 143
Slums, the "hotbeds of discontent", 64
Smith, Kenneth, 158
Social discipline, 183
Social evils, 64
Social extravaganzas, 64
Social justice program, 72
Social reform, 202
Social unrest, 68
Society of compromise, 220
Socio-economic unrest, 71
Sohrab and Rustum, 26
Soliven, Benito, 219
Soliven, Maximo, 132, 135, 136
Song of Hiawatha, 26
South Vietnam, 134
　Philippine aid to, 137
Southeast Asia Treaty Organization, 137
Sovereignty, 41, 188, 192, 200
Soviet-American agreement, 59
Soviet Revolution, 209
Soviet Russia, 179
Soviet system, abuses of, 63
Soviet Union, 56, 117
　Diplomatic relations with U.S., 57
Sovietism, 57
Spanish
　Language, 222
　Misrule in the Philippines, 189
　Republic, 223
　Volunteers, 1
Spartans, 222
Spenser of the Renaissance, 220
Stalinism, 72
Stalin, Josef, 63
"Stalwarts of the Fourth Estate", 108, 232-35
Star Reporter, 113, 234
Status-of-Forces Agreements, 160
Stechow, Johann Karl von, 122
Stonehill, Harry, 138
Straits Times, 131
Subandrio, Indonesian Foreign Minister, 131
Subic Bay Naval Base, 141, 158
Subido, Abelardo, 97
Suffrage, 41-44
Sugamo Prison, 185
Sukarno, President, 130, 131, 132, 138, 150
Sulu, 138
Sumulong, Juan, 68
Sumulong, Lorenzo, 36

"Sun Beams", 102-03
Sunday Times, 133
Sunday Tribune Magazine, 6, 8, 38
Svobodny, 76
Sweden, 198
Switzerland, 198
Symbolism, power of, 215

Taft Avenue, Pasay, 88
Tagalog
　Language, 79, 218
　Literature, 170, 171-73
　Press, 97
　Writers, 170
Taliba, 12, 61
Tariff, 22
Tatad, Francisco, 135
Taxation, 191-92
Taylor, Carson, 9
Teehankee, Claudio, 158, 160
"Territorial integrity", 40
Textbooks, Filipinization of, 25
Thailand, 137
That Magic Day, 8, 244-45
Third Internationale of Moscow, see Internationale of Moscow, Third
Thomas, James B., 141
"A Thousand and One Nights", 13
Times of India, 208
Tirad Pass, 222
"To the Filipino Flag", 156
To the Filipino Youth, 26
To the Great Plebeian, 6, 245-47
Tokyo, 126-27
Tolentino, Arturo, 37
Tolentino, Guillermo, 2-3
Tolerance, policy of, 194
Tolstoy, Leo, 58
Tom's Dixie Kitchen, 17
Tonogbanua, Francisco, 12
"Torch of Liberty", 187-89
Torres, Ramon, 34, 60
Town Meeting of the Air, 79
Tribune, see Manila Tribune
Tribune Magazine, 13
Tydings, Millard, 39
Tydings-McDuffie Law, 39-41, 50, 68

U.P. Alumni Association, 37
U.P. Woman's Club, 8
USAFFE guerrillas, 104
Ullmer, Pastor Karl, 120, 121
"Unilateral Peace Pact", 47-49
United Nations, 94, 137
　Committee for Drafting a Convention on Freedom of Information, 116
　General Assembly, 123

Philippine Mission to, 114-17
United Press, 231
United States, 9, 36, 40, 76, 92, 198, 217
   Armed Forces, 147
   Army, 68, 185
   Diplomatic relations with Soviet Union, 57
   Embassy, 158
   Military bases in the Philippines, 115, 140
     Lease of, 160
     Personnel, 147
University of Ghent, 119
University of Heidelberg, 118
University of Michigan, 8
University of Santo Tomas, 26, 34
   School of Journalism, 106
University of the Philippines, 6, 8, 29-32, 224-25
   Financial fate of, 29
   President of, 224-25
     Mendez's definition of, 30
   Student Council, 32
   Students, 31
University of Toilers of the East, Moscow, 56
Urdaneta, Father, 189, 190
Usury, 64

Valdes, Basilio, 12, 61
Valencia, Abelardo, 12
Valencia, Teodoro F., 34, 100-01, 129, 156, 234
Valenzuela, Jesus, 65
   History of Journalism in the Philippine Islands, 14, 20
La Vanguardia, 12, 81, 83
Vargas, Jorge B., 43, 89
Ventura, Maria Valdez, 26

Verdi, 229
Vernacular archaism, 217
Veteranos de la Revolucion, 49
Vietnam
   Policy, 132
   War, 132
Viewing the World of Letters, Volume II (1966), 26
Villa, Jose Garcia, 7, 118
Villadolid, Oscar, 133-34, 146
Villanueva, Pete, 34
Villareal, Cornelio, 96
Villa-Real, Manuel, 12
Villedo, Gonzalo, 141
Villedo, Ricardo, 141
Villegas, Antonio, 142
Vinzons, Wenceslao, 31-32, 37
Vishinsky, Andrei, 114

Wagner, Richard, 228
War, 182
   Renunciation of, 47-48
Wealth, unequal distribution of, 68
Weber, Pfarrer (Pastor) Gottlob, 120, 121, 228
Wecker, Louis de, 119
Weekly Graphic, 143
West Point, 182
Who Are the Usurers?, 7, 64
Wilhelmsfeld, 119-21
Woman suffrage, 41-44
Women's First National Popularity Contest, 49
Wood, Leonard, 11

Ymson, Eliseo, 80
Youth, education of, 70
Yulo, Jose, 3

Zobel, Enrique, 223
Zulueta, Jose, 105-06